*The Great
Southern Babylon*

The Great Southern Babylon

SEX, RACE, AND RESPECTABILITY IN
NEW ORLEANS
1865–1920

ALECIA P. LONG

LOUISIANA STATE UNIVERSITY PRESS   BATON ROUGE

Published by Louisiana State University Press
Copyright © 2004 by Louisiana State University Press
All rights reserved
Manufactured in the United States of America

Louisiana Paperback Edition, 2005

Designer: Barbara Neely Bourgoyne
Typeface: Adobe Minion
Typesetter: Coghill Composition, Inc.

LIBRARY OF CONGRESS CATALOGING-IN-PUBLICATION DATA

Long, Alecia P., 1966–
    The great Southern Babylon : sex, race, and respectability in New
Orleans, 1865–1920 / Alecia P. Long.
        p. cm.
Includes bibliographical references and index.
    ISBN 0-8071-2932-1 (cloth)
    1. Prostitution—Louisiana—New Orleans—History. 2. Sex-oriented businesses—
Louisiana—New Orleans—History. 3. Sex customs—Louisiana—New Orleans—History.
4. Women—Louisiana—New Orleans—Social conditions. 5. African Americans—
Louisiana—New Orleans—Social conditions. 6. New Orleans (La.)—Race relations.
7. Miscegenation—Louisiana—New Orleans—History. 8. New Orleans (La.)—Social life
and customs. 9. New Orleans (La.)—Social conditions. 10. Social status—Louisiana—
New Orleans—History.   I. Title.
HQ146.N6L66 2004
306'.09763'35—DC22
                                                                            2003017757
    ISBN-13: 978-0-8071-3112-1 (pbk.)

The paper in this book meets the guidelines for permanence and durability of the Committee
on Production Guidelines for Book Longevity of the Council on Library Resources. ⊗

For my parents,
Andy and Karen,
and for Sam

If I had to live in a city I think I would prefer New Orleans to any other—both Southern and Catholic and with indications that the Devil's existence is freely recognized. I can somehow see you installed in that city very well.

—FLANNERY O'CONNOR

Contents

Illustrations

MAPS

Preface

The statue on the dust jacket of this book was placed atop a newel post in a fancy New Orleans brothel shortly after 1900 and remained in that spot until at least 1917. The statue has a name—*Brise Légère*—probably in reference to the light breeze that appears to be lifting the hem of the woman's diaphanous gown. It is currently owned by a descendant of Tom Anderson, the entrepreneur and impresario who was known by many as "the Mayor of Storyville." Storyville, of course, is the name now commonly applied to the notorious vice district that existed in New Orleans between 1897 and 1917.[1]

I began this book with two objectives: first, to understand the history of Storyville, and second, to explain how it came into existence in the first place. I also wanted to learn about the lives of the women who lived and worked in the district. Perhaps that is why the statue *Brise Légère* spoke to me so eloquently. A silent witness to much that went on in the district, the statue served as a metaphor for so many women who worked there. Their history has too often been either overlooked or portrayed in a manner that, when not actually insulting, has been stilted, stereotypical, and woefully incomplete. The final two chapters of this book will cover, in detail, the lives of two of those women. But the history of the city's prostitution districts and its broader culture of commercial sexuality is much longer, richer, and infinitely more significant than has commonly been understood. The first three chapters will explain the variety of roles men and women of all classes, colors, and convictions played in the historical events leading up to Storyville's creation in 1897. In their variety, the historical episodes that serve as narrative devices for each of the chapters that follow are also testament to the treasure trove of historical themes that remain to be explored by others. In this work, I hope simply to revise the discussion and deepen the dialogue about sex, race, and respectability in one of the American South's most important but least understood locales.

Although writing is a solitary activity, no book is written without a great deal of help and guidance from others. Peter Kolchin, the Henry Clay Reed Professor of History at the University of Delaware, was the director of the dissertation that, over time and with his help, became this book. He was a wise and generous adviser and guide who managed to keep me on track while letting me go my own way. Anne Boylan, Catherine Clinton, and Jim Curtis served on my dissertation committee and, through careful reading and candid commentary, contributed immeasurably to the work that follows. So did Larry Powell, who read the entire manuscript twice and offered astute advice both times. Other historians read parts of this book along the way, shared sources, or simply offered invaluable encouragement and advice at critical points; they include Peter Bardaglio, Jim Bennett, Adrienne Berney, Katy Coyle, Jane Dailey, Gaines Foster, Christine Heyerman, Emily Landau, Gary Mary, Ted Ownby, Gary Ralph, Rixey Ruffin, LeeAnn Whites, and James D. Wilson.

In Delaware and in New Orleans, a number of persons offered me cheerful assistance and good counsel as I researched and wrote. Although they are too numerous to list individually, I extend special thanks to Pamela Arceneaux, Wayne Everard, John Kelly, Florence Jumonville, John Magill, Patricia Orendorf, Irene Wainwright, and the extraordinary Marie Windell, my guide to the rich records of the Louisiana Supreme Court. I also thank Eric Brock, The Historic New Orleans Collection, the New Orleans Public Library, the University of New Orleans, and the Louisiana State Museum for permission to reproduce images from their collections.

At the Louisiana State Museum, Jim Sefcik and Tamra Carboni were and are generous and beneficent supervisors. Without their assistance and understanding, at one critical juncture in particular, this book might never have been completed. Other museum colleagues and New Orleans friends who deserve thanks include Maxine Blum, Cathy Rogers Franklin, Shannon Glasheen, Nathanael Heller, Jeff Rubin, and Sam Rykels; all provided critical assistance and support at different times. Thanks also to Sylvia Frank Rodrigue and George Roupe at LSU Press, who showed great enthusiasm for the project and helped bring it to fruition. Ruth Laney was a wise and patient copy editor who improved the text significantly.

Finally, I would like to thank my parents, Karen and Andy Long, and my siblings, Anwhitney, Aundria, and Andy, for their support and encouragement. Thanks to them and to Kenny, Kendahl, Juliakate, and Stuart for sitting in the rain at graduation even though I did not. You can always count on family. I want to reiterate my thanks to Sam Rykels, who is more than just my colleague at the Louisiana State Museum. Sam has helped me with this book in ways too numerous to list. I think it is enough to say that I learned from him to love the chaos of living with dogs and to keep moving forward no matter what gets in your way—in the words of his ancestors to *"thole and think on."* Hail Tumbledown!

*The Great
Southern Babylon*

Introduction

People believe two things about New Orleans. The first is that it is different from the rest of the United States. According to most observers, the city was and is a place apart—stubbornly unlike the rest of the rapidly homogenizing nation and region. The second, related belief is that the city is decadent, and that its cultural distinctiveness is related to its reputation for tolerating, even encouraging, indulgence of all varieties. There is ample historical evidence to support both of these popular beliefs.

While the city has always had a reputation for difference and decadence, between 1865 and 1920 New Orleans began to exploit that reputation in order to profit from it and draw people to the city. As the states of the former Confederacy struggled to come to terms with Emancipation and a new, postslavery economic order, New Orleans underwent a profound transformation. The city ceased to be the nation's largest slave market and most permissive port. Instead, it became a tourist destination that encouraged and facilitated indulgence, especially in prostitution and sex across the color line.[1]

The city was eighty-five years old when it became a part of the United States; by that time, it had already established a reputation for choosing sensuality over seriousness. Although New Orleans was a Catholic city by dint of its French and Spanish colonial heritage, it was not known for its piety. In fact, just a few years after the Louisiana Purchase a visitor remarked that the city's Catholicism provided "for the salvation of the soul" but did "not interfere with the more important pleasure of the body." This theme was repeated by many other nineteenth-century observers who suggested that the residents of New Orleans worshiped at the altar of good times and performed rites of pleasure that ultimately became the city's trademark.[2]

James Davidson was a young Virginia lawyer when he toured the Deep South in 1836. The first line he wrote upon arriving in New Orleans was, "I am now in this great Southern Babylon—the mighty receptacle of wealth, depravity and misery." Although he spent only four days in the city, his recorded impressions emphasized the features and characteristics of life in antebellum New Orleans that no doubt underlay his idea of the Crescent City as the "Great Southern Babylon." Davidson was not the first—nor would he be the last—visitor who was much more impressed by the city's vices than its virtues. Fifteen years earlier, Rachel Jackson had expressed strikingly similar sentiments while visiting the city with her husband Andrew. In a letter to a friend she wrote, "Great Babylon is come up before me. . . . Oh the wickedness, the idolatry of the place! Unspeakable the riches and splendor." Both Davidson's and Jackson's descriptions captured the contradictory nature of the city's appalling appeal. Both visitors believed the city to be wicked, yet both were fascinated by it, simultaneously charmed and scandalized by its aura of disorder and its culture of sexual permissiveness and sensual excess.[3]

On the morning of his first full day in the city, Davidson recorded his impressions of Chartres Street, which was in his estimation "the *'Broadway'* of New Orleans and the resort of the fashionable of the city for shopping and promenading." As he wrote about the life of the street, Davidson gave the bulk of his attention to three topics: the beautiful quadroon women he saw "at almost every step"; the "fashionable prostitute[s]" who flaunted their "gaudy trappings"; and, finally, the slave auction he observed at Hewlett's Exchange. In describing the Exchange and the activities that took place within it, Davidson wrote, "It seems to be the Soul of New Orleans." In fact, Davidson, like many other antebellum visitors, wrote as if slavery, prostitution, and sex across the color line were the most characteristic elements of life in the city in the first half of the nineteenth century.[4]

New Orleans's standing as the South's Babylon sprang from its reputation as a center of tolerated prostitution and its position as the region's largest slave market. And, as many antislavery writers were eager to point out, those two functions sometimes overlapped in the city's notorious marketing of "fancy girls," the slang term for light-skinned female slaves who were sold for implicitly sexual purposes. The city's reputation as a bastion of commercial sexuality and sex across the color line survived the Civil War and Emancipation and, in the years that followed, generated enormous economic dividends and considerable controversy.[5]

Although New Orleans had established an enduring reputation as a sinful, sensual, and sybaritic place before the Civil War, between 1865 and 1920 that reputation played an even more critical role in the city's culture, economics, and politics. As cross-country travel became easier and tourism became common, the city's reputation as a place of pleasurable pilgrimage became more entangled with and dependent upon its reputation for promoting prostitution and tolerating sex across the color line. In 1897, city leaders made a fateful decision that sealed this aspect of the city's reputation and seared it into the national consciousness in perpetuity. That year they established two sets of vice-district boundaries, one of which became known as Storyville, a district that developed a national reputation and a broad regional appeal. In fact, one reformer claimed that owing largely to the vice district's existence, the city had become a nationally recognized "notorious attraction" by the early twentieth century. Yet, in one of the little-known ironies of Storyville's history, this area and its lesser-known counterpart were the city's last and smallest tolerated prostitution districts.[6]

As early as 1857, in fact, the city adopted its first comprehensive antiprostitution ordinance, known as the Lorette Ordinance. Reflecting the city's colonial heritage, the ordinance took its name from a French slang term for prostitutes who solicited customers near the Church of Notre Dame de Lorette in Paris. The Lorette Ordinance required that prostitutes vacate single-story buildings, and the ground floors of those with multiple stories, to make the practice of prostitution less visible. It also forbade street-level solicitation, indecent dress, and the creation of scandal or disturbance by individual prostitutes, under the threat of penalties as high as a twenty-five-dollar fine or thirty days' imprisonment. Finally, it established licensing fees for both prostitutes and their landlords. Its aim was to regulate rather than to suppress prostitution. Ironically, the delineation of four large geographic areas within which prostitution would be tolerated enabled the practice to thrive throughout the city.[7]

Local and state appellate courts declared the licensing aspects of the ordinance unconstitutional. But in July 1865, only three months after the formal end of the Civil War, city leaders passed another ordinance designed to regulate the city's still robust population of prostitutes. That ordinance, No. 6302 O.S., retained the same broad geographic boundaries set down eight years earlier in Lorette and established similar behavioral requirements for "public prostitutes and women notoriously abandoned to lewdness." Over the next thirty-two years, city leaders passed numerous additional and revised ordinances, each ostensibly designed to get a better handle on the city's continuing problem with prostitution. But whatever their multiple and evolving motives, city leaders failed to diminish the city's reputation as the Great Southern Babylon. On the contrary, by the early twentieth century, reformers from across the nation focused on New Orleans as an example of a city with a troubling history of and propensity for protecting its prostitution districts, tolerating sex across the color line within their boundaries, and profiting from its reputation for licentiousness.

Not all of the city's residents were complacent about these criticisms. Although the influence of antiprostitution reformers was slight, their efforts and arguments reveal a larger tension at play in the city in the years between the Civil War and 1920. Many Americans sought to achieve some semblance of respectability in the conduct of their private lives during this period, and New Orleanians were not immune to such aspirations. Thus many native-born Americans who aspired to middle-class status, and first- or second-generation immigrants on the rise, sought to model their public deportment on behavioral norms that stressed sobriety, sincerity, and personal restraint. But in a city so well known for and dependent on its reputation for extravagance and immoderation, the quest for respectability was always fraught with conflict. Thus the quest for respectability, and the difficulty or contingency of achieving it in the "Great Southern Babylon," is one of the themes that emerges in the chapters that follow.[8]

In the years between Reconstruction and 1920, the city's sexual culture, like most other aspects of life in the region, underwent dramatic shifts and transformations in response to the struggles and controversies that emerged from defeat in the Civil War and the abolition of slavery. Yet, despite the city's reputation for difference, the evolution of sexual culture in New Orleans exhibits many of the same trends that historians John D'Emilio and Estelle B. Freedman identify as national in scope. One of those changes was a shift "toward consumption, gratification, and pleasure" in the lives of average Americans. "One result was that the commercialization of sex, previously an underground, illicit phenomenon, moved somewhat into the open, as entrepreneurs created institutions that encouraged erotic encounters." The results of that process in New Orleans are chronicled in the pages that follow and help to explain how and why the city chose to create a tightly defined prostitution district in 1897.[9]

Yet, as much as New Orleans was like the rest of the nation, the commercialization of sex in New Orleans also had distinctive characteristics and outcomes. The city's location in an otherwise overwhelmingly rural and religiously conservative region, its complex racial history—especially the prevalence of sex across the color line and repeated attempts by municipal authorities to control yet profit from prostitution—all set it apart from the rest of the country. So did the size, duration, and nationwide reputation of Storyville.

In fact, it is the recognition of the city's complex combination of similarity and difference that sets this book apart from most other historical studies of New Orleans. The city's culture of commercial sexuality was notable partly because it was typical of what was happening in other American cities. But it was also notable because some of the decisions city leaders made in these years were unique; they provided a model that other cities imitated; and they had unforeseen and extremely long-lasting results. Until now, most historians have chosen to exclude New Orleans from comparative studies of sexuality. Yet the following chapters conclusively demonstrate the city's importance and reveal that its experiences with commercial sexuality between 1865 and 1920 were both typical and atypical. In the process, this book provides a long-overdue narrative account of the city's experiences with prostitution and the commercialization of sex at the turn of the century. Unlike many other studies of New Orleans, it also places those experiences in a national context.[10]

Countering conventional wisdom on another front, this study also insists that New Orleans, although distinctive, was very much a part of the South and must be considered in that context in order to appreciate its function within and its importance to the region. Historian Nancy Hewitt has observed that geographically southern cities like New Orleans, Tampa, Miami, and El Paso have been defined "as in, but not of the South" precisely because of their diversity and complexity. Leaving them out of southern historiography has created a false picture of southern homogeneity that is just beginning to be corrected. Hewitt insists that in order to appreciate the complexity of the region "we have to recognize that [these cities are] the South, however uncomfortable [their] fit with dominant conceptualizations." New Orleans is southern, although it is many other things as well.[11]

The following chapters explain the role New Orleans played in the region, acting as a geographic and metaphoric safety valve—a place where southerners came to escape, if only temporarily, from the racial, religious, and behavioral strictures that dominated their home communities. Ironically, in fact, it was the city's reputation as a place apart that drew so many southerners and other Americans to it, making it the South served up, paradoxically, in a form that was simultaneously diluted and concentrated. In New Orleans, southern pieties and pretensions became more obvious in the glaring contrast between the city and its rural surroundings. New Orleans was the South redux, tarted up and trotted out for visitors to see, experience, and enjoy. It was and remains a permissive playground for the masses from the immediate region and beyond.

Race is another category that complicates the study of sexuality in general. In New Orleans, those complications are enhanced by the city's own intricate racial history and, in the nineteenth century, the astounding array of racial descriptions for people of color. In her landmark book *White Women, Black Men: Illicit Sex in the Nineteenth-Century South*, Martha Hodes comments that, in the nineteenth century, New Orleanians "more formally recognized an intermediate class between 'black' and white thereby adding another and quite different dimension to the issue of sex across the color line." This study elucidates what some of those dimensions were and suggests that the city's regulation and toleration of prostitution and its fluid color line are positively linked in demonstrable ways. In fact, city leaders created a vice district in 1897 that would become one of the most racially integrated sites in the South. Because it took place at a time when the benefits and necessities of racial segregation permeated the thinking of so-called "progressive" reformers, the creation of Storyville was a physical manifestation of how evolving ideas about race, prostitution, and the power of segregation were linked. This book will explain how and why.[12]

In the chapters that follow, I rely on phrases that may be unfamiliar to readers. Some may already wonder why I often use the phrase "sex across the color line" rather than the more familiar term "interracial sex" when writing about sex between people with different skin colors. The answer lies in the fact that the whole idea of race—of who was "white" and who was "black" and why it mattered—was under construction in the period about which I write. The racial categories of "black" and "white" that dominated life in the South for much of the twentieth century were not foregone conclusions in the late nineteenth century, and using precise terminology can help us recall that uncertainty. Martha Hodes writes that the term interracial "implies fixed categories of race and therefore [gives] an overly natural quality to those categories." I concur, and I use the expression "sex across the color line" to remind readers that in late-nineteenth-century New Orleans race was being constructed in even the most intimate details of people's lives.[13]

I also use the terms "commercialized sex" and "commercial sexual culture" to refer to the broad range of situations and sites where New Orleanians and visitors to the city exchanged money for sexual titillation, spectacle, or physical satisfaction. Although many historians have pointed out the connections between prostitution and the growth of sexual behaviors like petting and casual sex that emerged in courtship rituals in these years, the focus of this study is squarely on the exchange of money or its equivalent for sexual activity or spectacle. Prostitution was the backbone of the city's culture of commercial sexuality, but it did not exist in a vacuum. Thus readers will be introduced to alternate kinds of sexual arrangements that had important economic aspects, particularly the practice of concubinage, the condition of living together in a long-term, committed relationship without benefit of marriage. Readers may also be unfamiliar with the word *plaçage*. Although it was largely an antebellum phenomenon, plaçage referred to formal and sometimes even contractual arrangements between white men and women of color in New Orleans, which spelled out the financial terms of the relationships; such arrangements were often made by the mothers of women of color. Like concubinage, the word plaçage described a relationship that resembled marriage in significant respects but did not have the legal sanction of the state.

This book has been influenced by the work of many other historians, particularly those who bring a feminist perspective to studies of sexuality. They include Catherine Clinton, Barbara Meil Hobson, Ruth Rosen, Judith Walkowitz, and others whose analyses of prostitution shifted the focus of such studies away from strictly legal issues toward questions about women's lives. Deploying a feminist perspective, these authors argue that resorting to prostitution in the nineteenth century was the result of severely constrained economic choices and opportunities for women, especially those who were members of immigrant groups, despised racial groups (African Americans in particular), or the working class. Limited economic options were compounded by widespread acceptance of a sexual double standard that assumed women's inherent lack of libido and contrasted it to uncontrollable male sexuality that had to be indulged by prostitutes to protect respectable women from male lust.[14]

This study is also inspired and informed by several histories that focus on the development of sexual culture in other locations. George Chauncey,

Tim Gilfoyle, Kathy Peiss, and Christine Stansell have all produced histories of sexuality in New York City. Each of them analyzes prostitution and other leisure activities of a sexual nature to show how they affected and were, in turn, affected by that city's changing demographic, economic, political, and social realities. These authors are particularly sensitive to the ways in which gender, race, social class, and ethnicity acted in concert with economic development to shape sexual culture and erotic life. I have tried to follow their example.[15]

The five chapters that follow explore significant aspects of the city's culture of commercial sexuality between 1865 and 1920. Each is drawn from and inspired by a legal case that made its way to the Louisiana Supreme Court. Testimony in these cases includes frank, first-person commentary about aspects of sexuality in late-nineteenth- and early-twentieth-century New Orleans. Although the chapters rely on sworn testimony in lower-court cases, the contextual materials embedded in them, and their attendant appeals, this is not a judicial or legal history per se. Instead, I use the legal cases to open windows onto the city's sexual past. Those windows, both of process and of outcome, provide fascinating and compelling narratives that reconstruct individual stories and complex events, suggest their relevance to the city's evolving culture of commercial sexuality, and put singular events and individual stories into a broader social, political, and economic context.[16]

The historical episodes reconstructed and chronicled here have meaning beyond the particular. There is no question that the fascinating people you are about to encounter are, for the most part, obscure. In the words of one attorney, the following chapters are full of "unusual situations and remarkable people." But their stories, when combined with broader contextual information, provide a new and long-overdue explanation for how and why New Orleans chose to segregate all of its commercial sexual enterprises and prostitutes into a single neighborhood in 1897. They also revise our understanding of the South and of New Orleans's place in it.

This book was written with the conviction that sexual practices and the politics that surround them provide an important barometer for measuring and understanding other things that are going on in a society at the same time. The laws that governments pass and people accept, the ways individual communities reward or punish sexual expression, and the ways people behave in defiance of those restraints can tell us a great deal about the character, politics, and culture of a particular time and place. They can also tell us a great deal about the people who called that place home in the past. Ultimately, through the reconstruction of a related group of historical narratives, readers will learn more about New Orleans. In exploring the history and significance of the Crescent City's culture of commercial sexuality between 1865 and 1920, I hope to provide new insights into the city's history and to question long-held notions about its place in the nation, the region, and the national imagination.

1

"It's Because You Are a Colored Woman"

SEX, RACE, AND CONCUBINAGE
AFTER THE CIVIL WAR

The sexual status quo in antebellum New Orleans made all enslaved women vulnerable to their owners' sexual whims, while those sold as fancy girls were implicitly marketed as sexual slaves. Long-term affairs between white men and free women of color in New Orleans were also virtually institutionalized in the form of plaçage. Emancipation ended some of these practices and posed a challenge to others, but sex across the color line continued in the city, even if it took new forms. In fact, there was a range of historical situations and contexts in which sex across the color line occurred in New Orleans between 1865 and 1920. For the city's women of color, those situations could include unwanted sexual advances or violent rape, exchanging sex for money or other favors on an intermittent or ongoing basis, being a mistress to one or a series of men, marrying across the color line, which was legal in Louisiana from 1870 until 1894, or living with a man in a committed relationship without benefit of marriage. No matter what the race of the participants, the latter relationship was called concubinage.[1]

Although concubinage is not normally considered an aspect of commercial sexuality, such relationships in New Orleans historically had important economic dimensions, including but not limited to formalized agreements that spelled out the financial terms between white men and their concubines of color. Although concubinage was considered illicit per se, its longevity and exclusivity generally distinguished it from prostitution. The public or private character of these relationships varied with the desires and domestic situations of individual participants, but economic issues often brought concubinage to broader public attention and imprinted it on the historical record. In fact, we know about many cases of cross-racial concubinage only because of the court cases and legal settlements that sprang from them.

In writing about the antebellum period, historian Judith Schafer points out that Louisiana's laws on concubinage were "identical for all involved in these liaisons, male and female, Negro, mulatto and white." She concludes that, "in this instance Louisiana law was oblivious to gender and color." While the wording of the statutes supports Schafer's argument, in the post-bellum period the adjudication and outcome of concubinage cases often hinged on the color, gender, or social class of the parties involved. This was certainly the case when Adeline Stringer filed suit against Louis Mathis, her deceased lover's brother, in 1887. Because Stringer was "a colored woman" who had been involved with a white man, the courts considered her claim in ways that made clear their acceptance of an ideology that defined light-skinned, mixed-race women primarily in sexual terms. And while nearly all women involved in similar suits were at a disadvantage because of their gender and their participation in illicit sex, white women often received the benefit of the doubt when it came to questions about their virtue, respectability, or culpability in becoming concubines in the first place.[2]

Although concubinage in Louisiana's state statutes was not defined in race- or gender-specific terms, New Orleans's long history of concubinage between white men and women of color contributed significantly to the stereotypical eroticization of light-skinned, mixed-race women. Certainly the ubiquity and virtual institutionalization of such relationships in the fancy-girl sales, quadroon balls, and plaçage of the antebellum period played some role in the blasé toleration of such relationships in New Orleans immediately after the Civil War. Their persistence is also explained in no small part by the double standard that many white men applied to themselves when it came to crossing the color line sexually.[3]

While interracial sex evoked discomfort and increasing social disapprobation as the nineteenth century wore on, prostitution across the color line remained a lucrative and much touted feature of the city's culture of commercial sexuality for decades after Emancipation. But white men and women of color who engaged in committed relationships found themselves subject to rising social disapproval and the passage of laws that sought specifically to end the existence of concubinage across the color line as the nineteenth century came to an end.

The well-documented relationship between Joseph Mathis and Adeline Stringer illustrates how this process occurred. Joe and Adeline initially be-

came involved while both were relatively young and while she was still enslaved. The details of their life together are compelling but, beyond the
particulars, the evolution of their long-term, committed love affair mirrors
changes in race relations in New Orleans and throughout the South following the Civil War. It also illustrates important aspects of the city's evolving
culture of commercial sexuality. Joe and Adeline's relationship endured, but
it changed significantly in response to the profoundly altered social, political, and economic conditions that prevailed in the city following Emancipation. Although sexual relationships between white men and women of color
play a central role in the city's romanticized erotic mythology, there is very
little extant first-person documentation of such relationships. Joe's letters to
Adeline provide the narrative device for this chapter. They are also rare and
important historical documents that provide insight into the complexities of
a single relationship and guide us toward an understanding of its larger historical significance.

Their story is singular, but its unusually well-documented history offers
a unique opportunity to explore a relationship across the color line in great
detail. The issues at stake in *Stringer v. Mathis* also enable us to explore the
economic dimensions of concubinage. Because state laws severely limited
the amounts concubines could bequeath to one another, Adeline's ability to
share in Joe's estate was always circumscribed. For other plaintiffs in similar
cases, gender, skin color, social class, and assumptions about white female
respectability contributed to more successful outcomes and financial settlements.[4]

One caveat should be offered. Because this chapter is about a relationship
between a white man and a woman of color, the reactions of the parties
involved were certainly a great deal less vehement than if the relationship
had been between a white woman and a man of color. In fact, Martha Hodes
has argued persuasively that it was only after Emancipation that sex between
white women and black men began "to provoke a near-inevitable alarm, one
that culminated in the tremendous white violence of the 1890s and after."
Even in New Orleans, a city long known for its lax sexual mores and forays
across the color line, white women began to receive warnings in local newspapers about the potential dangers of engaging in sex with men of color.
Marriage between white brides and "dusky grooms" also evoked harsh journalistic commentary.[5]

The historical toleration, if not acceptance, of relationships between
white men and women of color in New Orleans certainly contributed to the

lack of alarm with which most people involved in the court case viewed Joe and Adeline's relationship. Some witnesses—Joe's brother Louis in particular—expressed distaste and disbelief at the idea of a white man's being involved in a long-term, committed relationship with a woman of color. But no one ever suggested that physical violence should have been used to separate Joe and Adeline, or that the relationship was particularly dangerous to the emerging social or political order. When it came to sex across the color line, for white men at least, such admonitions would be the exception rather than the rule for several more decades in New Orleans.

"I Remain Yours Faithfully until Death"

Joseph Mathis died in the early morning hours of April 1, 1887, in a boardinghouse at 466 Magazine Street. He left behind two residences, two families, and the remnants of two very different lives. Dr. Samuel Olliphant, a close friend and a prominent physician from whom Joe had rented a room for several years, owned the house on Magazine Street. At 14 Dryades Street, less than two miles but in many respects a world away, Adeline Stringer, Joe's companion of more than thirty years, must have received word of his death second-hand. Adeline had not been allowed to see Joe since Dr. Olliphant had escorted him from her home two weeks earlier. Perhaps she even had to learn the specific details of Joe's death from the April 3 issue of the *Daily Picayune,* in which his brief obituary stated "on Friday April 1 at 3:35 o'clock a.m., [died] Joseph Mathis aged 54 years and 8 months, a native of this city."[6]

Although Mathis's obituary was modest, his estate was substantial, and the battle waged between Adeline Stringer and Louis Mathis over that estate ensured that the story of Joe and Adeline's thirty-year romance would become a permanent part of state and local court records. Those records tell the story of an enduring romantic relationship between Joe, the son of immigrant parents, and Adeline, a mixed-race woman who had been a slave before the Civil War. Joe once ended a letter to Adeline with the words, "I remain yours faithfully until death," but the state of race relations in New Orleans at the time of his death, and laws designed to limit the inheritance of concubines, meant that Joe's relationship with Adeline became most controversial after he passed away.

During her lifetime, Adeline experienced both slavery and freedom. In her post-Emancipation incarnation she was a boardinghouse keeper. Yet, during the trial over Joe's estate, Louis Mathis, his lawyers, and other defense witnesses described her most often as Joe's concubine, and they discounted her role and her economic success as a domestic entrepreneur. Although she ran a small business, remained in a monogamous relationship, and lived out her life as a free woman in a domestic environment, she could never have been considered a southern lady. Her skin color, if nothing else, ensured that. Slave and free, boardinghouse proprietor and concubine, described as both griffe and mulatto, Adeline presents us with an intriguing example of life "in-between" for light-skinned women of color in postbellum New Orleans.[7]

Joe too was a liminal figure, albeit in strikingly different ways from Adeline. He was the oldest surviving son of prosperous immigrant parents, and, thanks to a generous inheritance, could have become a prominent, respected, and wealthy businessman like his younger brother Louis. Instead, Joe lived in relative obscurity, especially after the Civil War, first in a series of boardinghouses with Adeline and later moving between two separate residences to continue his clandestine relationship with her. It is not exaggerating to say that, by the end of his life, Joe was living both a white life and a life across the color line. Very likely, in fact, it was the combination of his relationship with a woman of color and his severe though intermittent physical disabilities that guaranteed his liminality. Unlike Adeline, whose marginality and inferiority were assumed in a racist culture, Joe chose, at least on some level, to become a marginal figure by continuing his committed relationship with a woman of color in a time and place in which such connections were increasingly problematic.

The lives of individuals, although they defy strict historical categorization, simultaneously reflect and illuminate important aspects of the times in which they lived. Peering into the particulars of Joe and Adeline's story gives the historian an opportunity to cut through the myths about interracial relationships in New Orleans and to look at the evolution of at least one enduring love across the color line. Charting the turbulent yet touching course of Joe and Adeline's life together gives us a glimpse of how the day-to-day aspects of their romance ebbed and flowed in response to the vicissitudes of larger social and political processes at work in late-nineteenth-century New Orleans.

Because of the illicit or legally informal nature of most enduring affairs and other interracial sexual connections, there has been little historical evidence to date that directly chronicles the thoughts and experiences of the participants. Although painstaking genealogical research and forays into the

city's rich notarial archives can yield impressive data about such relationships, the discovery of a cache of love letters from Joe to Adeline offers us a
unique window into the intimate details of their relationship. The letters
also illuminate evolving ideas about sex and race in New Orleans after the
Civil War.[8]

"Your Sincere and True Lover, Joe"

Mobile
June 11, 1877
My Dearest and Only Addie,
Your kind letter of the 7th inst. only reached me this minute and I immediately hasten to respond. You have no idea how glad I was to hear from you, as
it is the first letter that I have received from you in many, many years, it carried me back to twenty years ago, when we met, [and used] to write love letters to each other and I never hailed a letter then from you with more pleasure
than I do yours now. . . .

I shall remain in Mobile a few days longer ("to see and to be seen") perhaps until next Sunday as I can save 4 or 5 dollars in fare. I have not seen any
of Miss Hettie['s] friends yet but the Capt. has introduced me to half of Mobile already. I suppose it will surprise you when I inform you that I have not
spoken to a female except Miss Hettie since I left home, but such nevertheless
is a veritable fact and now give me credit for being better than you thought I
was. Mr. Cruzat has just arrived and wishes me to remember him very kindly
to you and all.

Miss Hettie says you are putting in a dam sight of frills by not writing to
her although she owes you one. Buddie says he is going to New Orleans with
me but will take Mobile night shirt with him this time, he like New Orleans,
loves his auntie (and especially Marie) but objects to New Orleans night shirts.

Little Hettie feels very much hurt that Marie did not send her remem-
brance to her. Miss Hettie, the Capt. and Mr. Gus all wish to be remembered
to you. Kiss Marie for me and receive a thousand for yourself. . . .

I will write again, dream of me and only me and may they be pleasant ones.
Answer this and oblige your sincere and true lover,
Joe[9]

The first preserved letter from Joe to Adeline was written the same year
the Compromise of 1877 resulted in the removal of Union troops from New
Orleans. The letter above and the thirteen that accompany it make it clear
that their relationship endured beyond the demise of political Reconstruc-

tion. Joe was in his mid-forties and on a sojourn in Mobile when he wrote this affectionate, playful letter to Adeline. The letter reveals the length of their affair, the complex web of family, friends, and acquaintances they had in common, and the abiding affection Joe felt for Adeline more than twenty years after they had originally become involved.

The letters became a part of the court record when they were taken from Adeline and introduced as evidence after she sued Louis for a portion of Joe's estate. The case first went to trial in the spring of 1888. Many witnesses repeated what Joe's letter to Adeline confirmed—that their affair had begun sometime in the last half of the 1850s. Louis asserted that Adeline "had been his brother's girl" before the war. Godfried Gaisser, who had "grown up with Joe," also confirmed that the relationship had begun when Joe was a young man. According to Fanny Brickell, who had been a slave in the Mathis household, Joe "could have been 22 somewheres along there," when the relationship began. That would put the beginning of the affair in 1855.[10]

Brickell also confirmed that Adeline Stringer was called "Addie before the war and that she was a slave girl." On the stand Louis, who was four years younger than Joe, recalled that before the war "my brother as a general thing boarded or staid [*sic*] out—he was very seldom at home." It is unclear whether Joe's relationship with Adeline was the reason for his separation from the family household, but Louis's testimony does suggest that Adeline's visits to the Mathis home caused some tension. He recalled, "she used to come there often and inquire about my brother Joe until I ordered her away."[11]

Louis's testimony on this matter suggests two things about slave life in late antebellum New Orleans. First, as many scholars have suggested, urban slave life often included a freedom of movement that life on isolated rural plantations did not. Especially in a city like New Orleans, slaves, even young female slaves like Adeline, had enough freedom of movement to go to the Mathis household many times and inquire about Joe. Her visits to the Mathis home also suggest a boldness on her part that one does not often associate with women, let alone slave women, in the pre-war South. The act of calling on Joe upset both the established etiquette of color deference and gender expectations in the antebellum South. But Louis's ability to "order her away" also suggests that there were limits to Adeline's efficacy, no matter how bold she was. Enslaved persons may have been able occasionally to subvert the patriarchal and gender systems that defined life in the antebellum

South, but very rarely could they do so directly without being censured in some way.[12]

We know from his obituary that Joe was born in New Orleans in August or September of 1832. His parents were Joseph Mathis and Susan Lind Mathis. His father immigrated to New Orleans from Obernai, a small German-speaking town in the Rhine River Valley, in 1828. Joe's mother, a native of Hungary, gave birth to two more sons in the four years following Joe's birth. Martin was born in 1834 and Louis in 1836. By the late 1830s Joe's father was the keeper of a coffeehouse and tavern at the corner of Market and Tchoupitoulas Streets. One imagines that young Joe's experiences in a tavern near the Mississippi River must have been lively and marked by exposure to a great diversity of people and languages. Situated near the docks, the tavern would have been frequented by a local population dominated first by German and later by Irish immigrants as well as those associated with the river trades. The Mathis family lived near, perhaps even on the same premises as, the tavern until they moved a short distance to St. John the Baptist Street in the early 1850s and then to St. Thomas Street in 1859. The area in which the family settled would come to be known as the Irish Channel, and some blamed its unsavory reputation in the late antebellum period on its majority immigrant population. According to the *Daily Picayune*, St. Thomas Street was "lined on both sides with groggeries, and groceries which sold more whiskey than food," and, in 1861, the *True Delta* had this to say:

> St. Thomas Street is keeping up its ancient reputation. . . . The inhabitants.
> . . . appear for the most part to be an intemperate and bloodthirsty set, who
> are never contented unless engaged in broils, foreign or domestic, such as the
> breaking of a stranger's pate or the blacking of a loving spouse's eye. . . . Honest people, doubtless, live on St. Thomas Street, but they must have a hard
> time of it if they manage to keep their skulls uncracked and their reputations
> unstained.[13]

Despite the rough-and-ready reputation of the neighborhood in which they lived, the Mathis family prospered. Joseph Sr. kept running the coffeehouse through the mid-1850s, but he also began acquiring rental properties. By 1859, he was describing himself as a "clerk," rather than a tavern keeper. Joseph Jr., known by those close to him as Joe, first appears in a separate city directory listing in 1854. At the time he would have been twenty-one, near the age at which witnesses remembered that he began the affair with Adeline. Throughout his twenties, he held several different jobs and changed residences nearly every year. He always lived within a mile or two of his parents' house on St. Thomas Street but far enough away to limit intimate observation and knowledge of his day-to-day activities.[14]

Joe's whereabouts become very sketchy during the early 1860s and throughout the Civil War. Court testimony confirms that he went to California some time during the early part of the decade, but does not give a specific date or reveal the reason why. Although Joe may have gone to California to seek his fortune, to end his attachment with Adeline, or to avoid service in the Civil War, it is also possible that his poor health was a contributing factor in his decision to go West. Joe suffered from chronic "rheumatism." Based on the symptoms described in court testimony and in his letters, he probably had severe but intermittent arthritis. Although his bouts were periodic, he was variously described as having his arm in a sling, being confined to bed, or having to be carried by other persons from place to place. He also spent time at two natural springs in the 1880s seeking relief from his symptoms. Whatever his reasons for leaving, Joe returned to New Orleans from California some time in 1867. On his return, Louis recalled, Joe "was so helpless that he had to be almost carried into my father's house."[15]

If Joe did not fare well physically in California, his family also suffered during the Civil War, primarily through the loss of their middle son Martin. Both Martin and Louis had been volunteers in the Fifth Company of the prestigious, all-volunteer Washington Artillery. The Fifth Company was notable for its large membership of clerks and other young New Orleans men on the rise. The brothers volunteered on July 10, 1861, two months before compulsory conscription began, and they served side by side once their company was deployed to the Army of Tennessee. They participated in several major engagements including those at Shiloh, Vicksburg, and Chickamauga, where Martin was injured and hospitalized but recovered.[16]

On May 28, 1864, Martin was injured again and lost an arm in combat near Dalias, Georgia, in what would come to be known as the Battle of New Hope Church. A description from a soldier who was there noted that "[n]early all those wounded were hit by cannon balls and most were badly mangled." Martin clung to life for five days but finally succumbed on July 2, reportedly dying "in the arms of his brother" Louis, who was four months shy of his thirtieth birthday. Surely Louis was affected profoundly, not only by his extensive battlefield experiences in the Confederate Army but by the ordeal of watching his older brother suffer terribly before dying of a gruesome wound. Their parents must have suffered extreme grief as well. They did not schedule a memorial service until October 7, 1865, more than a year after Martin's death, very likely in recognition of what would have been his thirty-first birthday. Family, friends, and members of the Fifth Company were invited to attend the service.[17]

Although the war brought separation, death, and dislocation to the Mathis family, they continued to prosper materially. By 1867, Joseph Sr. was describing himself as a "capitalist" in the city directory. When he died later that year, he bequeathed nineteen properties, most of them commercial and residential rentals, to his wife and two remaining sons. Susan Mathis continued to live in the house on St. Thomas Street, and Louis, always the dutiful son, remained there with her until her death in August 1871. Upon their mother's death, Joe and Louis divided their inheritance equally. They split the nineteen properties equitably and assigned 50 percent interest in the properties to each other, inextricably linking their financial affairs until Joe's death in 1887.[18]

Based on the ages she gave in later census rolls, Adeline Elizabeth Stringer, as she was identified most often in official documents after the Civil War, was born sometime between 1833 and 1837. In the census of 1870 she listed her state of birth as Louisiana. A search of Catholic baptismal records for New Orleans has yielded several female children born to slave women in the 1830s named Adeline or Elizabeth, but none of them recorded their owner as "Stringer" at the time of their christening. Given the dislocations and uncertainties of life for most slaves, it would not have been unusual for Adeline to have changed hands, and perhaps even names, several times between the 1830s and Emancipation. An additional mystery about the origins of her last name emerges because Adeline alternately identified herself as married and single following the war. Did Adeline marry someone named Stringer during Joe's sojourn in California, or was the Mrs. an affectation? Most indications are that it was, but there are also suggestions that Adeline gave birth to at least one child prior to Joe's return to the city in 1867. If there had been a marriage that accompanied that event, it did not last far beyond Joe's return to the city.[19]

Given the fact that she was enslaved until her early thirties, it is not surprising that we know less about Adeline's early life than we do about the Mathis family. Still, the genesis of her relationship with Joe in the 1850s confirms that New Orleans had been her home for some time before the war, and that she decided to continue living there afterward even though Joe was still absent from the city. Joe's letters reveal that Adeline spent several con-

secutive weeks in Mobile and Biloxi on at least two occasions after the war
for health reasons, and that she had friends and family in Alabama in the
1870s and 1880s. Her persistence in New Orleans, even after Joe's death in
1888, and her lack of enthusiasm for his oft-repeated suggestion that they
consider moving away, make it clear that Adeline considered New Orleans
her home.[20]

She first appeared in postwar city directories in 1867 as "Stringer, Adeline," with no courtesy title of any kind. Listed as a keeper of furnished
rooms at 183 Customhouse Street, she continued there in 1868 but disappeared from city directories from 1869 through 1871. Joe was also missing in
1869 and 1870 but reappeared in 1871, described as a 'bookkeeper' living at
97 Gasquet Street. The 1870 census confirms that Joe was indeed living at 97
Gasquet, and, separated by one space from Joe's name on the enumeration
sheet, is an "Adeline Mathis." She may have been identifying herself as Joe's
wife in this period, or the census taker may have assumed they were married.
Marriage across the color line became legal in Louisiana in 1870, so it was
possible for Joe and Adeline to marry if they chose to. However, other documents and circumstances of the case make it clear that Joe and Adeline never
took advantage of this liberalization of postwar sexual culture in Louisiana.
Adeline never identified herself as Joe's wife during the court proceedings in
Stringer v. Mathis. If she had been his widow, and could demonstrate that
fact, no trial would have been necessary. She would have been a forced heir
and, as his wife, entitled to at least a third of his estate. Perhaps the two
lovers were simply testing the waters in June 1870 when the census taker
came around.[21]

Substantial numbers of other people took advantage of the newly established right to marry across the color line in the decade that followed. John
Blassingame located 205 such marriages in his check of the 1880 census. One
hundred seventy-six of those marriages were between white men and
women of color and only twenty-nine were between white women and men
of color. The numbers are significant enough to suggest that it was socially
possible, as well as legal, for people like Joe and Adeline to seal their interracial unions with legal matrimony. All indications are, however, that they
never actually took this step. Although marriage would have solved some
problems for the couple, particularly for Adeline, it would have created
many others. Louis, in particular, was disgusted by Joe's liaison. At one
point he refused to visit Joe as long as he lived with Adeline. Joe's letters also
suggest that Louis threatened to call in loans Joe owed him if he did not

break off his relationship with Adeline. The 1870 census aside, no other records indicate that the two ever married. In 1872 Adeline reappeared in the city directory as "Stringer, AE Mrs."[22]

Why then did Adeline give the surname Mathis to the census taker in 1870? The 1880 census provides an intriguing possibility. In that year Adeline Stringer was the head of a household of seven boarders, one cook, a fourteen-year-old "niece" named Anaise, and a ten-year-old "daughter" named Marie. Henry Dart, Louis's attorney, asserted in court that Anaise Hutchinson, who Adeline claimed was her niece in the 1880 census and who testified on Stringer's behalf, was not, in fact, a blood relative of Adeline's. Given that Stringer was acting in the capacity of Hutchinson's aunt, it is reasonable to wonder whether Marie was actually Adeline's biological daughter. If she was, it seems almost undeniable that Joe was Marie's father—or, at the very least, that he was taking responsibility for the pregnancy in 1870 by acting the part of Adeline's husband. The two had been living together and identifying themselves as husband and wife at the exact time Adeline would have been pregnant with Marie. A visible pregnancy would certainly help to explain why Adeline had identified herself as Joe's wife to a census taker and might also explain the relatively short duration of that masquerade.[23]

Other intriguing facts about Adeline's life after the Civil War can be gleaned from the 1870 census. For instance, Adeline listed the value of her personal property at five hundred dollars and her occupation as "keeping house." Although the 1870 census did list many noncompensated housewives under the designation "keeping house," for Adeline it was a paying profession. The five hundred dollars' worth of personal property she claimed likely consisted of the furniture and other household goods she needed as a boardinghouse keeper. Drawing on the skills she had acquired while enslaved, Adeline had established herself as a domestic businesswoman in her first few years of freedom.[24]

During Joe and Adeline's lifetime, it was common for women to run boardinghouses in New Orleans, particularly mixed-race women, according to contemporary sources. Some kept house commercially only as a sideline, taking in an occasional boarder or two to help a family make ends meet. But for others, like Adeline, "keeping house" was a full-time occupation and a profession in which they took great pride. Joe's correspondence clearly demonstrates that Adeline considered herself a businesswoman. Certainly she considered her boarders to be more than conduits to cash, but it is clear that she also saw such relationships in business terms. She even considered expanding her business to two locations in 1884, revealing the entrepreneurial spirit with which she approached her work.[25]

Her occupation as a boardinghouse keeper is yet another place where Adeline exists on a threshold. Because her business was providing a home to boarders, and because it was conducted within the confines of a domestic space, it is easy to overlook the economic aspects of work that was simultaneously domestic and commercial. Because domestic work was assumed to be women's work—and, in the postbellum South, black women's work in particular—women like Adeline had an advantage in this occupation. With a small amount of start-up capital, they were able to translate the domestic skills they had acquired as house slaves into an immediate postwar profession. Further, the identification of domestic work as women's work meant that men, no matter what their race, did not want to compete with women of color in this profession—although, as the court record showed, some white women did.[26]

One final insight can be gleaned from Joe and Adeline's address in the 1870 census and the other addresses they occupied before and after that date. Between 1867 and 1879, Joe and Adeline lived together in at least four locations: 183 Customhouse, 97 Gasquet, 218 Common, and 57 Dauphine. With the exception of the Common Street address, all of the houses were in neighborhoods that were identified either with prostitution, promiscuous racial mixing, or both. For example, the house on Gasquet was near the corner of Basin Street. In the years after the Civil War, Basin Street began to evolve into a street that would, by the early twentieth century, boast the largest and most garish concentration of brothels anywhere in America. Likewise, Customhouse (now Iberville) and Dauphine, both in the French Quarter, had reputations for being thick with houses of assignation and prostitution. Herbert Asbury wrote that "[i]n the Dauphine and Burgundy Street vice areas white women and Negresses crowded together indiscriminately and were patronized by men of all races and colors, a situation which persisted for many years before and after the Civil War." Other court cases from the 1880s and 1890s also commonly identify Customhouse as a street lined with brothels and assignation houses.[27]

There is no suggestion in any of the records of this case that Adeline herself engaged in prostitution or kept an assignation house. There is no indication of any such activity in Joe's correspondence with her, nor did any of the witnesses for the defense suggest that Adeline's business was anything other than respectable and above board. If she had been involved in keeping such a house, the defense would certainly have made an attempt to draw out such facts in order to defame her. But Adeline and Joe were living in or adjacent to neighborhoods with marginal reputations. In 1870, when they lived on Gasquet Street, there were 117 persons enumerated in their immediate neighborhood. Eighty-two were white, twenty-eight were listed as mulatto (including Adeline), and seven were black. White women were the largest group overall, followed by white men and then by mulatto women. Many of the women in the neighborhood were listed as having "no occupation" or rather cryptically as being "in a house of." The Gasquet Street neighborhood was one of many in New Orleans where reputations for commercial sexuality and racial integration intersected. This combination, which existed in most of the neighborhoods Joe and Adeline inhabited up to 1880, would eventually characterize those areas the municipality singled out and formally designated as vice districts.[28]

After the 1870 census, Adeline never again described herself in official documents as "Adeline Mathis." But even if they did not share a name, Joe and Adeline lived together openly during most of the 1870s, albeit in neighborhoods with marginal reputations. Throughout the decade Joe appears in city directories independent of Adeline and describes himself as a clerk. Adeline is also listed independently as "Mrs. A E Stringer" or "Addie Stringer," and always with the notation "furnished rooms," but they both use the same address. Whether they shared a bedroom or kept their affair secret from other boarders remains a mystery, but this period of relatively open cohabitation mirrors other openings in the city's emerging postwar culture.

Joe Gray Taylor and others remind us that many whites engaged in violence against African Americans in Louisiana in the years immediately after the war. While acts of murder and violence against African Americans in the Louisiana countryside were numerous and often publicized in the northern press, the outrageous acts of violence that took place in New Orleans, particularly the 1866 Mechanics Institute Riot, were the ones that captured national attention and helped to usher in the reestablishment of Federal authority in the city and state later that year.[29]

With the beginning of Military Reconstruction in 1867, political possibilities and social opportunities began to expand for the city's population of former slaves. According to Eric Arnesen, the constitutional convention that convened in November 1867, although much contested and controversial, "adopted much of the black delegates' agenda for civil equality." The constitution of 1868 opened public schools to black and white children on an equal basis, barred segregation in state institutions of higher education, and, in Article 3 of the state's first Bill of Rights, guaranteed "equal rights and privileges to every citizen—black and white—on public transportation and in licensed businesses and public resorts."[30]

While those constitutional precepts were often ignored in practice, the presence of Federal troops and the exertion of their leaders' authority meant that at least some of those constitutional provisions were grudgingly initiated in the decade that followed. By putting Joe and Adeline's open cohabitation during this period in context, one sees that changes resulting from the adoption of the new Constitution in 1868 may have eased their way. The exigencies of reinvigorated Federal authority provided at least one of the circumstances that allowed Joe and Adeline to have an open relationship in this period, without overt harassment from members of the general public or from Louis Mathis. By 1874, however, the White League had formed in the city and, for the next three years, the political and social integration of African Americans was challenged in the streets by armed men rather than debated in constitutional conventions. Sex across the color line became just one activity among many that was openly and sometimes violently contested by members of the White League and their supporters.[31]

In fact, much of the action in the so-called Battle of Liberty Place played out just a few blocks from where Joe and Adeline were living in 1874. During the trial Louis offered into evidence a lease signed by Adeline on October 1, 1871, for a house at 218 Common Street. Joe served as guarantor on this and on subsequent leases that Adeline signed for the house up to September 30, 1877. Louis also offered into evidence check stubs and a group of mortgage notes made out to Duncan Sinclair, the owner of the house, that together totaled in excess of eight thousand dollars, which he asserted went to pay Adeline's rent and other household expenses. Louis provided details of other expenses and accounts that Joe had paid for Adeline in the 1870s and 1880s, including bills from a grocery and dry goods store and a millinery shop.[32]

Based on his letters and on the financial documents Louis entered into evidence at the trial, Joe appears to have been a man of great punctiliousness in his financial affairs. He made a decision in 1876, however, that made his subsequent financial dealings much more difficult to trace. The last check stub that Louis presented in court was dated May 26, 1876. Louis testified that, to his knowledge, Joe "never kept any account in any bank after this." Instead, he recalled, Joe began keeping "a private account of moneys received and moneys paid out." Louis found detailed account books among

Joe's effects at Dr. Olliphant's house. Although the account books were not preserved among the records of the court case, Louis's attorney offered into evidence three account books dating from 1874 through 1887 in which Joe kept detailed notes of his financial affairs. According to Louis's testimony, the accounts included substantial and continuous expenditures for Adeline's rent and other household expenses.[33]

Why did Joe decide to stop keeping bank accounts in mid-1876? He was a substantial property owner, held stock in at least one local company, and would have had large sums of cash coming to him in rents from his properties. We have no definitive knowledge of why Joe made such a decision, but the financial instability in New Orleans and the rest of the country in these years suggests one possibility.

In fact, the Bank of Lafayette, with which Joe had his checking account up to 1876, failed the following year. Perhaps Joe made more conservative financial decisions in response to the depression that followed the panic of 1873. But it also seems likely that he did not want anyone, particularly Louis, to have intimate knowledge of his financial dealings. Given Louis's disapproval of Joe's relationship with Adeline, and detailed financial disclosures Joe made to her in his letters, it seems likely that his decision to stop keeping detailed banking records was motivated, at least in part, by his desire to prevent Louis from monitoring or controlling his financial affairs.[34]

Louis had certainly become a financial force to reckon with in the years following the Civil War. In addition to the income-generating properties he and Joe shared, Louis was one of the founders of the Lafayette Fire Insurance Company, a concern established in 1869 by a group of prominent, German-descended businessmen to provide fire insurance to local residential-property owners. One of twenty-five "prominent businessmen" named to the original board, and the company's first secretary, Louis became its third president in 1877 with an annual salary of fifteen hundred dollars. The most famous member of the original board was Michael Hahn.[35]

Hahn was elected to an abortive term in the U.S. Senate from Louisiana in 1863, was elected governor of the state in the military-sponsored election of 1864, and was again elected to the Senate in 1865. He survived an attack by a white mob during the riot at the Mechanic's Institute in 1866, and he edited the *Republican*, a newspaper that advocated black male suffrage. Such a heavy slate of duties suggests that Hahn probably attended few board meetings of the Lafayette Fire Insurance Company. But he and Louis were surely acquainted; both were part of an emerging group of successful New

Orleans businessmen who had immigrated to New Orleans as youngsters
or who, like Louis, were the children of immigrants who had established
themselves before the Civil War.[36]

Even though Hahn's racial views were uncharacteristically liberal for the
time, he once said in reference to Negroes that although he favored the abolition of slavery and the education of blacks, he was "opposed to their political and social equality with the white race." Louis's court testimony indicates
that he agreed with Hahn on the latter point and was extremely perturbed
by Joe's ongoing connection with a woman of color. During the course of
Stringer v. Mathis, he was forced to admit the relationship's existence and
duration. On the one hand, he attempted to show that his brother's relations
with Adeline had been sexual in nature, thus meeting the legal definition
of concubinage or intimate cohabitation, minus only the legal sanction of
marriage. But because of his mortification that Adeline was a woman of
color, he also attempted to minimize the length and significance of his
brother's association with her. When asked if he knew where his brother
boarded prior to 1878, his first response was "I don't recollect. I don't know
that I ever knew."[37]

As questioning continued, however, Louis was forced to admit that he
had visited several homes where Joe had lived with Adeline throughout the
1870s, sometimes as often as "two or three times a week" when Joe was sick.
Louis admitted that Adeline had acted in the capacity of a nurse in these
instances, but he also continued to insist that the relationship was primarily
sexual in nature. Although he testified that "he had never seen them together
in bed," his petition to the court read:

> That the plaintiff was for more than twenty years, the mistress or concubine
> of the late Joseph Mathis, and said Mathis paid the house rent and expended
> other and large sums of money in her behalf and for her account, and said
> concubinage was the sole motive and course of the said Mathis living with said
> Stringer.[38]

In Louis's estimation, the sexual nature of Joe's relationship with Adeline
lay at its core. Thus the rent and "other large sums of money" he spent on
her amounted, in principle, to no more than payments for sexual relations
with her. The implications of such an assertion were obvious. Concubinage
in this case was distilled down to sexual relations only. Thus Joe's financial
contributions to Adeline amounted to payments for sex. The accusation of
prostitution was never made explicit, but Adeline's racial identity and the

fact that her relationship crossed the color line, made her particularly vulnerable to charges of sexual impropriety.

Louis's testimony suggests that he avoided intimate knowledge of his brother's relationship with Stringer by limiting his visits to Joe's residences in the 1870s. He also minimized the level of his acquaintance with Adeline herself, often referring to her as "she" or as "that woman." In fact, Louis claimed that he did not even know Adeline in the earliest years of her relationship with Joe and recalled that their first meeting took place on Carondelet Street "right after the war." He explained that "she was walking ahead of me. I didn't know who she was, when I accidentally stepped on her dress. She recognized me and she asked me where my brother Joe was. I didn't know her before that." But elsewhere in his testimony, Louis equivocated about whether Adeline's visits to the Mathis home had begun, like the relationship itself, before the Civil War.[39]

Although Louis had attempted to ignore the situation during Reconstruction, in 1878 he had an opportunity to take an active role in terminating Joe and Adeline's relationship. While Joe had closed his bank accounts in 1876 to limit Louis's knowledge of his financial affairs, in 1878 he moved to separate himself financially from Adeline, and he asked Louis to help him do it. On October 26, 1878, a notarized agreement that included the following stipulations was signed by Adeline and witnessed by Louis:

> Know ye, That I, Adeline Elizabeth Stringer, unmarried of New Orleans, Louisiana, for and in consideration of the sum of one thousand dollars . . . paid by Joseph Mathis . . . have remised, released, and forever discharge the said Joseph Mathis, his heirs, executors, and administrators of and from any and all manner of action[,] . . . accounts, bonds, bills[,] . . . securities[,] . . . and demands whatsoever in law or in equity which against said Joseph Mathis I have ever had, now have, or which I or my heirs, executors, or administrators, hereafter, can, shall, or may have for, upon, or by reason of any matter cause or thing whatsoever from the beginning of the world to the date of these presents and especially for and by reason of boarding, lodging, washing and attendance and any and all services rewarded to the said Joseph Mathis, up to the date hereof.[40]

Although the document codifies the formal end of Joe and Adeline's relationship, Joe's signature does not appear on the agreement. His lack of official participation suggests that Louis had a very active hand in administering the agreement. It also provides an interesting foreshadowing of events that would follow.

In addition to the thousand dollars Joe agreed to pay Adeline, six hundred of which he had borrowed from Louis, he turned over to her two pieces of property. The legal agreement excerpted above agrees with descriptions given by nineteenth-century observers of the kinds of "contracts" that were negotiated between Creole gentlemen and their quadroon mistresses in antebellum New Orleans. If agreements of the kind signed by Adeline were typical in the antebellum period, such "legal" exchanges of property between white men and their "colored" concubines help to explain how free women of color acquired such significant property holdings in the city in the antebellum period. These agreements also situate those relationships within the boundaries of the city's culture of commercial sexuality. Nothing in Joe's letter to Adeline dated June 11, 1877, indicated that such a break was on the horizon. He closed that letter by reminding Adeline that he was her "sincere and true lover." If that sentiment was genuine, the agreement of 1878 is hard to explain. But if Joe was a "sincere and true lover" to Adeline, perhaps he was less than candid with Louis in 1878. Joe and Adeline were living in extraordinarily volatile times, times when anything was possible. The agreement of 1878 might even have been an elaborate ruse concocted by Joe so he could borrow money from Louis and legally transfer money and property to Adeline.[41]

For Louis, however, there was only one possible explanation for why Joe had initiated the agreement of 1878. In testimony he stated that it was "because he wished to rid himself of his concubinage, the relationship that existed between him and this woman. . . . [H]e told me he wanted to get rid of her. I couldn't imagine anything else in the world." Louis may have been lacking in imagination where Joe and Adeline's relationship was concerned, but if he had a hand in creating the document of separation, he was certainly a thorough and exacting businessman. The agreement was exhaustive in its demands that Adeline release Joe from all future financial claims—up to and including claims dating to "the beginning of the world." The end of Joe and Adeline's relationship seemed to have been spelled out in black and white in the agreement of October 26, 1878. Yet their relationship continued for another nine years.[42]

If their affair was interrupted as a result of the agreement, the break was short lived. According to Louis's testimony, "immediately after" the agreement was signed Joe "sought board elsewhere." He lived for a brief time at the Upper City Hotel and, shortly thereafter, moved into a house with Dr. Olliphant. According to accounts by other witnesses and his own correspondence, however, Joe also continued living with Adeline. Whether or not the 1878 agreement was a ruse, Joe was about to pull off an even more astounding feat. In the next decade, with Adeline's complicity—or, at the very least, her toleration—he would begin to lead two separate lives.[43]

"Our Future and Money Prospects Are Not as Bright as They Should Be"

If Joe did intend to break with Adeline in 1878, his resolution had failed in less than a year. In addition to the letter from 1877, thirteen others were submitted into evidence, all written after the agreement of 1878, dating between July 1879, and July 1886. The first of these read, in part:

> 57 Dauphine St., Tuesday, July 29, 1879
> 12 1/2 o'clock P.M.
> My dearest Addie,
> I shipped your tin trunk today by the Southern Express. . . . I intended to wait until tomorrow but as the yellow fever has broken out in this City, I could delay no longer as I was afraid of Mobile quarantining New Orleans before morning and then it would be too late to send [the] trunk. . . .
>   I marked the trunk Mrs. A. E. Stringer care Capt. Willis and Barmon, Corner St. Joseph and Anthony Streets, Mobile, Ala. It will be sent around to the house so you need not go around to the Express Office. In your last you stated that you were unwell and confined to your bed but I am in hopes this may find you in improved health. How about that Florida trip? I would like very much if you could manage to see the place, if you only stayed there two days and then we would know what to do. I am getting alright again, no rheumatism of any consequence. Aunt Jane is managing the house finely don't let that worry you. Everything is O.K. . . . Again hope that you are not seriously ill I remain more than ever your sincere old man.
>   Remember me to all,
> Joe[44]

Joe wrote at least five letters to Adeline during her sojourn in Mobile. Two of those we know about only because he mentioned them in the letter of July 29. The others, dated August 5 and 13, are preserved in the court record. Based on those letters, Joe seems to have had four major concerns in the summer of 1879. The progress of the yellow-fever outbreak—as Joe put it, a "more or less" regular occurrence in the city in those years—was the first. Second, he expressed concern about both his and Adeline's health. A third concern was household matters and day-to-day events. Finally, Joe was eager for Adeline to "see the place" in Florida so they "would know what to do."

In his letter of July 29, he enclosed a copy of that day's newspaper. Like Joe, the *Daily Picayune* downplayed the importance of two cases of yellow fever that had been discovered in the city in the previous two days. The real yellow-fever epidemic that summer was in Memphis. By the end of the season nearly two hundred people had died of a total population of sixteen thousand. Such numbers pale in comparison to the ten thousand lives lost in New Orleans in 1832 and 1833 and the astounding ten thousand deaths that occurred between July and November of 1853. Joe had seen yellow fever come and go nearly every year of his life, which probably accounts for his blasé tone and his ultimately correct conviction that yellow fever would not reach epidemic proportions in New Orleans in 1879.[45]

He was also right, however, that Mobile and other cities would quarantine New Orleans as a precaution. Mobile's quarantine, raised on August 15, was short lived. Acting Governor Louis Wiltz advised other cities to follow Mobile's example. In a proclamation dated August 17, Wiltz reiterated that there had "been no case of yellow fever in the city . . . [o]r its vicinity since the 29th day of July, 1879, and that the general health of the city is now as good and its sanitary condition as favorable as ever before known here in summer." Wiltz went on to describe the remaining quarantines as "damaging, annoying and wholly useless obstruction[s] to travel and commerce." Joe shared his irritation regarding quarantines and panic related to the fever. But in his next letter, dated August 5, he reported on the health of various friends and relatives including "Tillie" who, he wrote, was "getting a little better. Louis will move her from Oshatown to Pontchatoula tomorrow. A bad move I am afraid."[46]

Tillie was Louis's wife, the former Mary Matilda Kopp, whom he had married on May 13, 1873. During the summer of 1879, Tillie was in the early stages of her fourth pregnancy. Perhaps she was being kept out of town during the hot summer months as a precaution, but Joe's comment that she was "getting a little better" suggests that she may already have been ill before she left. In any case, Joe's premonition that moving her was a bad idea proved prescient. Tillie carried her pregnancy to term and in mid-December gave birth to a boy who was named Joseph Benedict, presumably in honor of his grandfather or his uncle Joe; but she died on December 19, shortly after the child's birth. The infant lived only four days, succumbing on December 22. Once again, death had struck close to home for Louis and Joe. Within a fifteen-year span, they had lost a brother and both parents, and now Louis had lost his wife and infant child. Somehow, he remained resilient, single-minded, and increasingly successful through it all. His business life was bur-geoning, and two family members came to his aid in the domestic sphere. An aunt and a female cousin moved into the house on St. Thomas Street where they helped Louis raise his three older children.[47]

Joe credited the rain with inhibiting the yellow fever in the summer of 1879, writing on August 5 that "it rained pitchforks downward for about two hours this morning flooding the streets and sidewalks rendering navigation impossible without the aid of skiffs. . . . It is next to folly for Yellow Jack to attempt to raise his hydra head again this summer." Even though the yellow fever was mild in 1879, both Joe and Adeline had other health concerns. Al-though Joe's rheumatism does not seem to have plagued him that summer, he fretted about its return. Adeline's trip to Mobile had been undertaken in an attempt to improve her health. Although the exact nature of her ailment was never specified, Joe wrote on August 5, "I am exceedingly sorry and grieved to hear that you are still unwell, but I trust God will smile on you and give you good health when this reaches you." By August 13, her health seems to have improved; Joe closed his letter of that date with the salutation, "[r]emember me kindly to the captain, to Mrs. Hettie, to Buddie, to little Het, to Maria, to Annie and to all. A thousand and one kisses for you old woman, and trusting that your long stay has improved your health so much that you will never, no never be sick again. I remain yours faithfully until doom's day, Joe."[48]

While Adeline was in Mobile in the summer of 1879, she stayed with the same people Joe had mentioned in his letter from Mobile in 1877. The letters of August 5 and 13 reveal that Joe and Adeline had a large and complex circle of shared acquaintances in both Mobile and New Orleans. Joe sent regards from many people in New Orleans, including their mutual friend Jake Ringer, probably a local grocer or tavern keeper, who asked Joe to tell Ade-line, "if you are not home shortly there will be no beer left for you." The salutation above also confirms that there was constancy in the relationship and that, even if they were not formally married, they had connections with a variety of people in Mobile that exhibited some of the qualities of kin-ship.[49]

In addition to emphasizing the rich web of friends and acquaintances they had in common, the letters reveal how deeply Joe was enmeshed in the day-to-day affairs of Adeline's household. On August 5, for example, he relayed information to her from a letter she had received at 57 Dauphine Street. He wrote, "I took the liberty of opening it as you do mine." The fact that they opened each other's mail demonstrates the level of intimacy between them and also suggests that Joe received his mail at Adeline's house. In the same letter he informed her that "The Water Works . . . cut off *our* hydrant yesterday" (emphasis added). Such excerpts make it clear that they shared their lives and a home on a day-to-day basis. Even though Joe was living with Dr. Olliphant at the time, it is clear that he also continued to make his home with Adeline and that, because he usually saw her daily, he felt her absence keenly, as he noted in his letter of August 13: "It is 3 weeks and 4 days since you left me and that short time seems to me an age and you have no idea how I miss you."[50]

But while Joe expressed loneliness in his letter of August 13, he also revealed some irritation that Adeline had not yet made a trip to Florida as he had urged her to do in his letter of July 29. He wrote, "I have not written you in the last 3 days, as I expected to receive a letter from you dated Jacksonville, Fla., as in your last you stated you would leave Mobile last Sunday for Florida." Joe said that he wanted Adeline to "look at the place." Did this mean he had (or hoped to acquire) some property there, or was he referring to the city at large? Whatever the circumstance, Joe's choice of Jacksonville was probably not random. According to historian Robert A. Taylor, "Jacksonville had a reputation of being a 'good town' for blacks generally" after the war. The population of the city and surrounding county was only about a tenth of that of New Orleans in the 1880s, but it boasted a lively river trade and increasing tourism. In the second half of the 1880s tourism "attracted some 75,000 guests a year to Jacksonville's 40 hotels and 80 boarding houses."[51]

Jacksonville's population was evenly divided racially. Blacks outnumbered whites in Duval County in the 1880 census, 10,850 to 8,580, and in Jacksonville proper, the racial breakdown "was 3,991 whites to 3,658 blacks." According to Taylor, Jacksonville's racial composition "made it a biracial political entity and not a white-controlled fiefdom. Despite Democratic 'redemption' in 1876, blacks still enjoyed political influence."[52]

Perhaps Joe felt that in a town so evenly divided by race he and Adeline could live together openly and stop the masquerade they had been forced to adopt in New Orleans. Or maybe he wanted a place far from Louis's watchful, disgusted surveillance. Adeline, however, did not go to Jacksonville that summer as Joe had urged. She did make the trip two years later but did not care for the city. Joe's two lives in New Orleans would have to continue for the foreseeable future.

In 1880 Joe gave his address in the city directory as 388 Magazine Street. This was the house he was sharing with Dr. Olliphant, but his correspondence confirms that he was splitting his time between the Magazine Street address and Adeline's house at 57 Dauphine. The strain of maintaining two places of residence began to show, both in his letters to Adeline and in his personal finances.[53]

The court record contains two letters that Joe wrote to Adeline in the summer of 1881. The first of those began with the warm and affectionate German word for butterfly at once revealing his German heritage, and his love for his long-term companion:

> New Orleans, July 20, 1881
> My dearest Schmetterling,
> Your kind favor of 18th inst, came duly to hand, should have answered it yesterday, but as Nell and Marie had both written I thought it would not do to smother you with letters in this hot weather. We are all well, I have a slight touch of my old complaint in my right elbow hope it is only a passing pain to remind me that I am human. Well the agony is over, Daisie had her ears clipped yesterday and she don't seem to mind in the least, it has improved her looks 100 per cent. I am taking medicine, it has made me very nervous so that I can hardly write. Mr. Mutchler and Minvo paid Annie. I told her to keep it with the fifteen dollars which I have given her already she ought to keep the house a going until your return without any further expense to me. I told her to write you fully in regard to household matters and leave it entirely to her. As to renting any rooms during your absence, do not make any calculations on it, as there has not been a single application. Marie from what I can see is behaving herself well. She is ready at all times to do my bidding. . . . Everything is lovely and the goose hangs high. Splendid nights for sleeping and fine breezes during the day, it has been cooler here than in Mobile all summer according to the daily (newspaper) weather report. . . .
> Mr. Black leaves her[e] about the 1st of next month for Galveston to be gone 2 or 3 weeks. I would like to go with him, but have not the money to do it, but do not regret it, if you only will regain your health and enjoy yourself but you will never do it in Mobile. If God spares me next year perhaps I might take a trip. The health of the City never was better. Remember me to all, good bye, old woman, I miss you very much. May God guide you, keep you from harm, give you good health, and a safe return is the sincere prayer of yours until death separates us.
> Joe
> Annie, Marie, Aunt Jane wishes me to remember them kindly to you.[54]

Although "the health of the city never was better" according to Joe's letter of July 20, both his and Adeline's health continued to be a central concern in 1881. Concern about their finances was also prominent in the letters from this year. The letter above reconfirms Joe's intimate knowledge of the day-to-day affairs of Adeline's household. For example, when two boarders paid their rent, Joe told Anaise to keep the money along with a contribution from him "in order to keep the house a going." He also advised Adeline not to count on having new boarders when she returned, because there had been no applications during her absence. His note that Marie was behaving herself and ready to do his bidding raises an interesting possibility. Although Joe never explicitly confirmed it in writing, Adeline's decision to leave Marie in his care during her absence suggests that Marie was his daughter. This letter also tells us that Joe and Adeline shared at least one pet, presumably a dog—Daisie, whose ear clipping had "improved her looks 100 per cent."[55]

The letter also confirms, as Louis contended in court, that Joe was making financial contributions to the household. Such contributions clearly played a role in his inability to go to Galveston that summer, but Joe assured Adeline he did not "regret" his inability to afford the trip, especially if the trip improved her health. But tension over money matters seems to have been mounting. In his next letter, written just eight days later, Joe expressed exasperation with Adeline over her request for more money. In fact, his inability to offer her the sums she requested would become a recurrent theme in his correspondence to her. From the context of Joe's letters, we can tell that Adeline not only asked Joe for money from time to time, but that she also sought his advice in conducting her boardinghouse business. He always tried to give her judicious advice, but giving her money was becoming more and more problematic. The letter of July 28, 1881, read, in part:

> Dear Addie,
> You know if I had the means I would have given you more than I did but God knows I could not do better and I am surprised that you are writing for more money, it is with regret that I must inform you that [I] cannot send you any more without a great sacrifice. I have not yet paid Mr. Black that $20 I borrowed from him. I hope Mrs. Hettie did not charge you anything for the time you were with her. My advice to you is if your money is all spent to come home immediately you will be better off here than without means. Enclosed please find memorandum what it has cost me or will before the month is out. If you had gone to Jacksonville, I would have sacrificed myself further, if it

took the last piece of property that I have left, but I cannot do it for Mobile
or Biloxi.[56]

The statements in this letter are the first and clearest indication we have
that Joe was beginning to feel a financial strain from Adeline's requests for
money. Although the "memorandum" he sent along with the letter was not
included with the preserved correspondence, its inclusion in the original letter gives us another glimpse at Joe's financial meticulousness. His calcula-
tions of how much something would cost him a month in advance, and his
worry over a twenty-dollar loan he had yet to repay, confirm his financial
conservatism. In the letter of July 20, Joe had assured Adeline that he did not
begrudge her the cost of her trip, but on July 28 he expressed his continuing
resentment over her refusal to visit Jacksonville, stating that "if you had
gone to Jacksonville, I would have sacrificed myself further." By the end of
the letter, however, his tone again grew warm, reminding her that a second
pet named Dickie "runs in anticipation of meeting you" at the door "every
time the bells ring." The mix of warmth and irritation is an indication that
Joe and Adeline's relationship was subject to the vagaries of all long-term
romantic relationships. Although frustrated with Adeline, Joe issued no
threats or ultimatums. He wanted her to return home, and he told her in no
uncertain terms that he had no more money to spare. Still, he closed the
letter "goodbye dearest" reminding her, and us, that the two of them remained very much attached, even when they disagreed.[57]

Joe had a comfortable annual income from his properties. In court testimony Louis estimated that it "was something over $2,000 per year," and
that Joe's annual expenses were significantly less than $1,000. He went on
to say that Joe lived modestly. When his lawyer asked him if Joe had "any
extravagant habits," Louis responded, "None, except in regard to this
woman. He furnished her groceries and paid her rent." While most of the
expenses Louis documented were modest—a few hundred dollars for groceries, bonnets, and millinery supplies—the sums Joe spent for Adeline's
rent were substantial, amounting to several hundred dollars per year. Apparently, he was beginning to feel the pinch from the expense of maintaining
two places of residence, one of them surreptitiously, during the 1880s.[58]

By 1880 Adeline had moved to 14 Dryades Street, an area known in this
period for its heavily Jewish and immigrant populations. Joe continued to
list his address in the city directory as 388 Magazine Street and to give his
occupation as "clerk." The letters from 1881 and all but two of the others

that follow were written on stationery from Louis's company, the Lafayette Fire Insurance Company. According to testimony from a variety of witnesses in the case, Joe walked from his house on Magazine Street to the offices of the insurance company a few blocks away, and he spent most of his mornings there. Statements from several witnesses suggest that Joe worked as a clerk in the company and that he also collected rents on properties that he and Louis owned. Witnesses also agreed that Joe's workdays ended by 1:00 or 2:00 in the afternoon. What did he do with the balance of his days?[59]

If he spent them at Adeline's, he could have come and gone without eliciting much notice in the largely male household. In the 1880 census, Adeline was listed as the head of the household at 14 Dryades. She, Anaise, Marie, and a fifteen-year-old cook shared the house with seven male boarders. All of them were classified as white, all were between the ages of twenty-five and forty, and only three of the seven were native to Louisiana. Two of the boarders were from Germany, and the other two were from England and Scotland. The diversity in Adeline's household reflected the diversity of the neighborhood in which she lived. And, in a household of so many single men, Joe's comings and goings were not apt to have attracted a great deal of attention in the household itself or in the surrounding neighborhood. In a sense, Joe was hiding his relationship with Adeline right out in the open.[60]

One of Adeline's former boarders, a Dr. George W. Lewis, who had lived and kept an office in Adeline's house, recalled seeing Joe in the house at 14 Dryades often and assuming that he lived there. While Lewis was on the stand, Henry Dart tried to force him to testify that Joe and Adeline had been intimately involved, but Lewis resisted. The exchange between the two men continued in this way:

> DART: It is charged in this case that Mathis' primary object in being in that house was to carry on illicit relations with that woman who had been his mistress since the war—do you know anything about it?
> LEWIS: Nothing at all.
> DART: Nothing that lends color to that?
> LEWIS: Never saw a thing.
> DART: Did this woman ever give you her story of her relations with Mr. Mathis?
> LEWIS: Never.
> DART: You never heard it either from her lips or his lips?
> LEWIS: No Sir. She told me once that she was very much attached and devoted to Mr. Mathis and was very solicitous of having anything happen to him and

asked me to do the best I could to save him, if there was anything possible to cure him to do so.

DART: I ask you candidly to say whether or not the position she occupied toward him left on your mind an impression that there was an intimacy existing between them?

LEWIS: That you can't say. You can suspect a great many things—unless you see it you sometimes make mistakes.

DART: Was it sufficient to create a suspicion in your mind?

LEWIS: That perhaps she was friendly with him, and still I don't know anything about it.[61]

Dr. Lewis's reluctance to corroborate Dart's insinuations of intimacy is intriguing; it suggests that even members of the household who came into close contact with Joe and Adeline could not, or perhaps simply were not willing to, say for certain whether they had been intimately involved. The letters, however, were the most revealing evidence in this regard. Six of the fourteen preserved letters were written in the summer of 1884, while New Orleans was preparing to host the eagerly anticipated Cotton Centennial and Industrial Exposition. The Exposition, which marked the centennial anniversary of "the first exportation of American cotton to England," was also intended to showcase the South's progress and modernization after the Civil War. While the Exposition's promoters worked hard to present an image of progress and New South prosperity to its visitors, at least some of those observers took particular note of the city's still very visible legacy of sex across the color line. On January 3, 1885, Lafcadio Hearn began a continuing series about the Exposition and life in New Orleans for *Harper's Weekly*. Although Hearn's focus was squarely on the fair in his first installment, the full-page illustration that accompanied it focused on more than its alleged subject, "the approach to Horticultural Hall." The building itself was barely visible behind trees, but, in the foreground of the picture, Exposition visitors seem preoccupied with a woman of color wearing a *tignon* and holding an umbrella. The woman is accompanied by a younger, lighter-skinned girl of color with whom she is walking arm-in-arm. Their physical intimacy suggests a close relationship, perhaps mother and daughter. The *tignon* (an elaborately tied head scarf associated with free women of color in the city as early as the colonial period), the umbrella to protect the darker woman's skin from the sun, and the girl's long, lustrous black hair—all are features that antebellum travelers typically remarked on when they described quadroons and octoroons. From the viewers' perspective, this mixed-race duo was presented as a prominent and characteristic, though curious, feature of New Orleans, like the Spanish moss in the live oak trees behind them.[62]

Hearn returned to the same theme in his next story, "The Creole Patois." Trying to account for its appeal, he wrote that "the creole patois is the off-spring of linguistic miscegenation, an offspring which exhibits but a very faint shade of African color, and nevertheless possesses a strangely supple comeliness by virtue of the very intercrossing which created it, like a beautiful octoroon." Although Hearn's was but one voice, it reached a national audience. Even locally produced promotional materials did not shy away from exploiting the city's mixed-race women and their reputation for what might politely be called hospitality. One guidebook went so far as to recommend the houses of quadroon and octoroon women to single men. Referring to "the Creole portion" of the city, the guidebook writers claimed that "one can secure from the landlady (who is certain to prove either a very stout Creole, or, more likely a quadroon or octoroon) a furnished room, always kept in the neatest of order." To further drive home the point, the guidebook claimed that "This system will be found extremely agreeable to bachelors."[63]

While observers and promoters of the fair used the stereotypical, eroticized appeal of mixed-race women to commercial advantage, Joe and Adeline's situation during the same period belied the erotic ideal. But during the same period in which the quadroon image was promoted to attract or entertain northern industrialists and visitors and to accommodate visiting "bachelors," Adeline and Joe's relationship was becoming increasingly difficult, precisely because of its interracial character. In 1884, Joe told Adeline that he could no longer live with her openly in New Orleans.

The two preserved letters from 1884 were written in May and June. The first, dated May 3, reveals that Adeline had finally made the much-delayed trip to Jacksonville. In her letter to Joe she had apparently expressed disappointment with the city and described the physical discomfort of the long journey. In his reply Joe, as usual, seemed even-tempered and circumspect. He wrote, "I am sorry that you are so stoved up from your recent trip and that your first impressions of Jacksonville are rather unfavorable, both, will wear off in time." He closed the letter by reassuring her that "you will never find in all your travels a spot that you will like so well as home, sweet home and the longer you remain from home the better you will like it."[64]

Joe encouraged Adeline to stay away for a month or six weeks to recover her health, assuring her that Anaise's health was good and that she was run-

In this *Harper's Weekly* illustration (Jan. 3, 1885) of the New Orleans Exposition, the mixed-race woman and girl in the left foreground are the focus of Exposition visitors' attention.
Courtesy Louisiana State Museum

ning the house splendidly. He reported that "every room is as clean as a pin, and you can bet she manages everything economically nothing is wasted and just buys enough to go around, she can run the establishment cheaper than you can. I am satisfied that you will be more than pleased with her management."[65]

The letters are filled with reports about the weather, the house, and Joe's daily activities, including the news that he was stopping and eating at Louis's house since Louis had recently returned from Mobile. In his next letter, dated June 4, Joe encouraged Adeline to continue her sojourn, but seems to have relented somewhat on his preference for Jacksonville. "I desire you to remain away until your former good health is restored to you, if it takes all summer to do it," he wrote. "If you get tired of Jacksonville go somewheres else I want you to enjoy yourself while you can for when you get old you can't."[66]

By the middle of July, however, Adeline had returned to New Orleans. In the matter of their health, the tables had turned once again. Joe had taken ill and had gone to Bladon Springs, Alabama, to try to recover. His letter of August 1 (the first preserved in the court record from this Alabama sojourn but the fifth he had written to Adeline since he left New Orleans) reveals the extent of his health problems and the steps he was taking to cure them. It also confirms Louis's opposition to their affair and the financial influence he exercised in Joe's life. Joe began the letter "My Dearest Addie," and, after some general news about the state of his health, wrote, "it is so strange how affectionate we are when apart and always quarrelling when together, it is owing no doubt to our being sickly which makes us peevish, besides our future and money matters are not as bright as they should be. I feel as if I could not exist without you."[67]

Later in the same letter Joe offered Adeline advice about whether she should expand her business during the Exposition by renting "Mr. Herman's house on Rampart St." He wrote:

> Of course I am not in a position here to judge correctly in the first place, I don't know the condition of this house, how many stories, and rooms, etc. . . . My advice is to hold on to 14 Dryades St. at all hazards for another year even if the rent is raised to $150 per month and [if] it will cost you nothing to refit, refurnish or extra furniture, take it by all means. The coming year will crowd the City for 6 months more than she ever has been and you will have to make a year's rents in 6 months. If it was not for the Exposition I would under no

consideration advise to take it. If you and Anaise were in the enjoyment of good health I know that you can make money with the 2 houses but I am afraid Anaise will overwork herself. Don't be too hasty study over the matter, your judgment is better than mine.[68]

Adeline's ambition and the entrepreneurial nature of her boardinghouse business are apparent in this letter, as is Joe's respect for her business acumen. Although Adeline was a mixed-race woman, she was no rarefied quadroon or octoroon courtesan. Nor was she merely a victim of postwar chaos and politics, swept to and fro by the events of the times. Adeline knew that the Exposition offered an important opportunity to increase her profits and expand her business, and she sought ways to do just that.

She and Anaise worked hard keeping the house neat and clean for her boarders. In fact, Joe worried that they might overwork themselves. And his concerns about their health, particularly Anaise's, proved correct. In a letter dated August 6, he wrote: "I am sorry to hear that Anaise has the rheumatism in her right wrist. I hope it has left her before this reaches you. She has suffered too much already from other diseases." Even for young, strong women like Anaise, who was seventeen at the time, disease and poor health were an all too common part of life in late-nineteenth-century New Orleans.[69]

In a letter written the day before, Joe had described his own symptoms in detail to Adeline: "I am still confined to my room, very weak, and thin, rheumatism still in right foot, knee [and] hip swollen and right hand much inflamed and swollen." But by the end of the summer, he once again felt well enough to return to New Orleans; he planned to arrive by the first of September. As the Exposition was due to open then, he worried about finding a place to stay. In his letter of August 6 he wrote:

If I knew that you could get a room for me in Mobile I would not have worried myself so much as I could not get a room in N.O. (outside your house) I had to get one in the Hotel Dieu. Your intentions God knows are good when you say you would take care of me without money (if Louis desired) but my dear we would starve, you can hardly get along by yourself. I will live with you as long as I am well, but must make some arrangement to be when I am sick so that Louis can visit me. It would please him too much to give him that hold on me now. This is the Exposition year I wish you to earn all the money you can, if we have to live together it must be outside of New Orleans. I am determined to that effect. If I am to starve it shall not be at home.[70]

In the letter dated August 1, Joe had written to Adeline that he did not feel he "could exist without" her, but the letter of August 6 reveals that he did not necessarily mean they could live together either, at least not openly in New Orleans. Perhaps this is what he meant when he wrote "our future and money matters are not as bright as they should be." The preceding passages suggest that Louis had issued some sort of ultimatum. It is not clear whether Louis knew the level of intimacy that still existed between his brother and Adeline, but Joe's comment about refusing to "starve at home" suggests that Louis might have issued a threat with financial ramifications. He had clearly told Joe he would no longer visit him in a house he shared with Adeline. The passage also suggests that Louis had enough control over Joe's financial affairs to withhold part or all of the property receipts from him. Why else would Joe write that it "would give him too much pleasure to have that hold on me now?" When Joe died, he owed Louis $3,550. Perhaps Louis had threatened to call in that note. If he had, there would have been no way for Joe to pay immediately since his annual income was only in the neighborhood of $2,000. For whatever reasons, financial and otherwise, Joe had determined that a second place he could call home was absolutely necessary, especially in the event that he became ill.[71]

For Adeline, leaving New Orleans at this moment in time would have been unthinkable. It is understandable that a boardinghouse keeper, especially one as energetic and ambitious as she, would wish to remain in the city when business was so brisk. Joe had often expressed his own affection for New Orleans, and his correspondence makes clear that Adeline felt it too. But Joe's unwillingness to live openly with Adeline during this period not only suggests disagreements between Joe and Louis but also speaks to changes in the city's long history of toleration for such relationships. In a city so well known for concubinage between white men and women of color, acceptance of such arrangements was fading, at least in some circles. Even though marriage across the color line would remain legal until 1894, Joe's conundrum suggests that the informal demands and decisions made by individuals struggling to shape the city's postbellum sexual culture laid the foundation for the legal sanctions against such relationships that would follow. The Mathis family was neither Creole nor strictly American. They were assimilated and very successful immigrants. As such, their position between the most often posited extremes of postwar New Orleans society, upright American and decadent Creole, suggests that affairs across the color line were not the exclusive domain of Creole gentlemen. Joe and Adeline's affair also helps us to plot the de facto attitudes and opinions that preceded legal sanctions against such relationships.

One final letter from Bladon Springs, dated August 18, is preserved in the court record. In it, Joe wrote, "[t]his is the 10 letter that I have written you since my arrival here and I hardly know what to write." He mentioned the weather, and the surprising lack of insects, and closed with information about other visitors from New Orleans. "You would think that Bedlam had broke loose when those 13 fat butchers from the Poydras Market get excited they all talk at the same time and don't speak the same language [to] me 3 minutes at a time." For such a lighthearted letter, the closing was unusually frank. "I must close by wishing you good health, wealth, and prosperity and the same bed."[72]

In 1884, New Orleans was a city that could still boast multilingual butchers who spoke simultaneously in different languages, and the city retained a cosmopolitan patina, but the polyglot character that had defined it was becoming less acceptable when the line of demarcation was race. Cross-racial concubinage, though once an acknowledged privilege for white men, was becoming less respectable over time. Joe's wishes for Adeline seem simple, the kind of wishes we all have for those we love. Adeline's health was troubled, her prospects for wealth were marginal, and Joe's wish to share the "same bed" was wishful thinking—something to hope for, not something he could be sure of.

Three final letters were kept as evidence in the court case, one from the summer of 1885 and two from July of the following year. All three were written on Lafayette Fire Insurance Company stationery, and all were written while Joe was in Abita Springs, Louisiana, where he had gone to take advantage of the purportedly curative powers of the water. When Joe wrote to Adeline on August 25, 1885, Dr. Olliphant, into whose house Joe had moved in late 1884, had just left for New Orleans after spending almost two weeks with Joe at Abita Springs. Joe had decided to stay on a few additional days and told Adeline to expect his return about noon the following Friday. He concluded, "The day after tomorrow will be two weeks since I left you, but it seems so many months. . . . I have not written to Louis only a postal card stating that I had arrived here. I haven't heard from him since I left— Goodbye old gal until next Friday. Remember me to all and oblige yours only, Joe."[73]

Court records and city directories from this period indicate that Joe was living at the Magazine Street address, but he spent at least some of his time with Adeline, and she was the first person he planned to see when he returned to the city. Most of the people who lived with Joe in the house at the corner of Magazine and Race Streets admitted in testimony that Joe regularly disappeared on Friday or Saturday and did not return to the house until Monday morning. Although none of them claimed to know Joe's whereabouts on the weekends, they all seem to have accepted his regular absences with little question. Why Joe chose to spend weekend nights with Adeline and not weeknights is a mystery. In its decision, the court would conclude that the only possible reason he had gone away for the weekends was to have sexual relations with her.[74]

This short excerpt also reveals continuing tensions between Joe and Louis. Joe had sent only a postcard to Louis, to which Louis had made no reply. Apparently, the situation between the brothers remained much the same in the summer of 1886. Like the boarders at Dr. Olliphant's house, Louis was willing to ignore Joe's weekend excursions to Adeline's, and the two seem to have reached some sort of wary standoff on the subject. Yet Joe's letters to Adeline seemed to grow even more affectionate the following summer. The first preserved letter from 1886, written on July 20 from "Long Branch House" in Abita Springs, began with the salutation, "My Dear, Dearer, Dearest Addie." He apologized for writing in pencil and indicated that he had been there less than a week; although he had been forced to share a room with three other men at first, he had finally gotten a private room. He went on to describe conditions at Long Branch House as very crowded and a bit too casual for his liking:

> There are 26 rooms and 46 boarders, mostly men and a few old women and no style we run around in our shirtsleeves and the women in their Mother Hubbards and to meals in the same costume. The Bosmer House is the stylish one but it and the other houses are not full. It is a pity that some enterprising men (Northern men) don't come here and build and keep the place in order, it could be made a beautiful resort, cottages built, gardens, walks and parks laid out, trees planted, and grass mowed down as it would have to do it. As it is now whenever it rains you cannot go to the spring for the weeds and not walk but for the weed and tall grass. I have enjoyed splendid health. I eat more in one meal here than I do at home in three and sleep like a top, the nights are pleasant and mornings very cool, I sleep under a quilt, the day is a little warm where there is no breeze blowing which is seldom the case. I did not intend to write for a week but could not resist the temptation of writing you, this is my first letter as I have not written to Louis and don't intend to for at least a week.[75]

The most interesting element from the passage above is Joe's association of "enterprising men" with "Northern men." That assertion suggests that it was not only northerners who considered southerners less enterprising and meticulous than themselves. Joe, who had spent his entire life in the South with the exception of his sojourn to California, connected industriousness with northerners. That is especially curious when one considers that in his own family there were at least two examples of industrious men who had made good for themselves in the South. Joe's father had worked his way up from newly arrived immigrant to substantial property holder and "capitalist." When Joe wrote this letter, Louis was among a handful of the most industrious and successful businessmen in New Orleans. Whatever Joe's personal assessment of his brother's business acumen, it is clear that tension remained between the two brothers; while he could not resist the temptation of writing to Adeline, he had not written to Louis and did not "intend to for at least a week."

The final letter preserved in the Court record was written nine days later, and reads in part:

> Abita Springs, July 29th 1886
> My Dearest Old Woman
> I received yours of the 26th inst. this morning and I hasten to respond. I am sorry to hear that you are not feeling well no doubt you are worrying yourself too much and the house [illegible] roomers leaving and not knowing what to do, Anaise sick and a thousand thoughts (troubles) it also makes me unhappy.
> There is no place nearer than Covington to accommodate Anaise. I got information from a colored man who chops wood around here there is a colored family living within one mile of the Spring but it is too swampy to be healthy only one room for 5 to sleep in. I will be home in about 2 weeks then you and Anaise can make a trip to Covington 3 miles from Abita Springs.
> I wrote to Louis the other day but have not yet rec'd an answer. I have a very slight touch of rheumatism in my neck otherwise I feel very well.[76]

Joe's last surviving letter to Adeline ended much the same way the first one had begun, with a reminder of his affection for her, but other information in that letter suggests the increasingly serious troubles Adeline was experiencing. Both her own health and Anaise's continued to be a problem, and she seems to have had trouble retaining boarders in this period. Even more telling was Joe's admission that the very resort he was writing from would not extend accommodations to "colored" people. Although Adeline

Long Branch House, Abita Springs, Louisiana, where Joseph Mathis wrote his final
letters to Adeline Stringer in the summer of 1886. *Photo by the author*

and Anaise were both consistently described as griffe or mulatto, this section
of the letter suggests that by 1886 segregation had begun creeping into most
facets of life in New Orleans and its environs for all people of color. Although the landmark decision by the United States Supreme Court in *Plessy
v. Ferguson* was a decade away, the process of creating a bifurcated racial
order and formalizing the legal segregation of the races was already in progress. Although white people were still living in Adeline's house at the time
of Joe's death, some of whom would even testify on her behalf in 1888, it
seems clear that formalized segregation had begun to impinge on Adeline's
chosen postwar profession. For white people like Louis, who were beginning
to see formalized racial segregation as a necessary part of postwar culture,
and to see race in stark though artificial shades of black and white, living in
the home of a mixed-race woman would have seemed objectionable. This
shift would have given white boardinghouse operators an advantage over
mixed-race women like Adeline, based solely on their increasingly important
whiteness.[77]

"Affectionately yours" were the final words Joe wrote to Adeline in the
last letter preserved in the court case. It is clear from the context of Joe's

letters that Adeline also wrote to him during periods when they were separated, and the court records reveal that Joe, like Adeline, preserved those letters. Although her letters to Joe are not available as part of the court record, the length and complexity of Joe's letters indicate that Adeline not only knew how to write but could read at an advanced level. Whether or not those were skills she had learned while still enslaved, her literacy played a crucial role, not only in her relationship with Joe, but in the confident way she made her way in the world. The letters Joe wrote were taken from Adeline because the court demanded them as evidence in the case. The presence of those crumpled, discolored love letters in an archived court record more than a century after the case was heard is a poignant reminder of her powerlessness to regain them once the case was decided.[78]

As for Adeline's letters to Joe, they were not offered into evidence because, as Louis explained in court, he had decided it was best to destroy them. He testified that Dr. Olliphant had given him the letters after Joe's death. When his attorney asked him what had become of them Louis admitted that he had burned them. Asked why he had done so, Louis said, "because I did not want my brother's correspondence exposed. I didn't know they were of use to anybody and they were better out of the way." Louis added that he had not read all of the letters but had "glanced at them." If Louis simply "glanced" at the letters, he did a remarkably good job of absorbing their contents; he testified that they were written in "an extremely affectionate manner." According to him, their contents were "about the regret she experienced at being separated from him and one letter I thought I noticed something of her being jealous of another girl, probably about absence, state of health, writing about Tom, Dick, and Harry." He rationalized his actions by saying, "I didn't know that I had a right to look, after my brother's death, into his correspondence, but from the fact of his living in that state with a negro woman I thought I had a right to see something of that kind." Living in that state, as Louis put it, without marriage was known as concubinage, and the proof of its existence between Joe and Adeline was critical to Louis's defense in *Stringer v. Mathis.*[79]

Stringer v. Mathis

Louis clearly felt justified in destroying Adeline's letters to Joe. He was also no doubt responsible for the decision to keep Adeline from seeing Joe in his final days of life. Adeline did not testify at all during the trial, but testimony from two other witnesses confirms that both Adeline and Anaise were kept from seeing Joe in his last days. The decision to move from Adeline's house to his room at Dr. Olliphant's seems to have been Joe's alone. Dr. Olliphant testified that he had received a call about two weeks before Joe's death, and, in response, went to the house at 14 Dryades to meet him. He also testified that even though Joe was ill, he had insisted that they take the street car home rather than hiring a private carriage. Still, Joe was concerned enough about the illness to ask Dr. Olliphant and Dr. Ayres, another physician who had been treating him at Adeline's, to escort him back to the house on Magazine. One of the reasons he may have returned to Magazine Street is so that Louis could visit him.[80]

During Joe's final days, Anaise went to the house at Magazine Street. Her stated purpose was to collect Joe's laundry. Mrs. Torre, a white woman who, like Adeline, rented the house from its owner Dr. Olliphant, and acted in the capacity of boardinghouse keeper, testified that she and a servant made Anaise wait outside while they gathered Joe's laundry. Apparently, the women were familiar enough with Anaise to give her the laundry; but that familiarity did not extend to letting her into the house, much less allowing her to see Joe. She was told that he could not be disturbed. Anaise was effectively locked out of the house. Adeline had probably sent Anaise to the house; thus the rejection extended to Adeline as well.[81]

Another witness, a Miss Emma Thompson, testified on Louis's behalf at the trial. She recounted the story of a disagreement she and Adeline had had some time earlier. Thompson recalled that she had been talking to Joe outside the offices of the Lafayette Fire Insurance Company. As she walked away, she said, Adeline had accosted her and accused her of being involved with Joe. Joe, according to Thompson, had intervened and sent Adeline on her way. But although Adeline had felt ill will toward Thompson before Joe's death, she apparently was desperate or distraught enough to reveal her heartbreak about having been unable to see Joe as he lay dying. Thompson testified that Adeline had told her that she believed that if Thompson had been nursing Joe she would have allowed her to see him on his deathbed.[82]

It is clear from testimony given in court that both Louis and Dr. Olliphant had face-to-face contact with Adeline on more than one occasion. Both of them were also certainly aware of her enduring connection with Joe. But particularly in Louis's case, their familiarity with Adeline seems only to have bred contempt. There is no way to know whether Joe asked to see Adeline; if he did, the request was not honored. Joe's feelings, intentions, actions, and desires in those final days will probably remain a mystery. But he became the subject of a great deal of official attention following his death on the morning of April 1, 1887.

Louis moved quickly to consolidate his inheritance of Joe's estate. He claimed that Joe had died intestate; with no will to consider, the succession was settled before the end of April. Louis was not even required to submit an inventory of Joe's property because the court concluded that he was the only and obvious heir. Although no inventory was prepared, Louis testified in court that, at the time of Joe's death, his estate was worth approximately twenty thousand dollars. He also testified that the aforementioned sum represented almost all of the original inheritance from their parents. If Joe had been squandering money on Adeline, he, or perhaps Louis, had ensured that his alleged profligate spending never diminished their overall property holdings.[83]

Given the overwhelming evidence of Joe's financial conservatism and meticulous record keeping, his failure to prepare a will is puzzling. Most "book keepers," as Joe had once described himself, would not be guilty of such an oversight. Perhaps Joe had made a conscious choice not to make a will. But given his obvious devotion to Adeline and his possible paternity of her daughter Marie, such a decision is difficult to understand. It is possible that Joe had prepared a will and that it was among the effects that Dr. Olliphant turned over to Louis after Joe's death. Did Louis destroy the will in the same way that he destroyed Adeline's letters? By all accounts, Louis was a tough and exacting but honest businessman. Still, by burning the letters Louis demonstrated that he was, at the very least, capable of destroying evidence of Joe's connection with Adeline.

Adeline believed that Joe had made a will, and she pressed Louis about it in person. He testified in court that he had told her there was no will and sent her away. Adeline apparently was not satisfied with this explanation. Meyer Levi, a storekeeper who testified for Louis, apparently knew both Louis and Adeline well. In fact, the Mathis brothers owned the building in which Levi ran his store. Levi testified that Adeline had had an account in his store since at least 1875 and that Joe had always paid the bill. Levi said that Adeline came to him after Joe's death and told him to charge her bill to Louis; she also told him she planned to bring suit. Levi advised her against it and apparently offered or was persuaded to act as an intermediary between the two. He testified, "I went to Mr. Mathis time and time again to compromise." The existence of the court record attests to the lack of success he met in those attempts. For Louis there could be no compromise. In an emotional outburst on the stand Louis made the following statement: "I want it understood that I don't concede that I owe anything to this woman, but if the succession of my brother owes anything to her whether strictly legally or in equity I am willing to pay to her whatever it is whether it is the sum of one dollar or $5000, and whatever the Court may find I will pay." But, he concluded "for the purpose of testing this matter I am not willing to resort to any legal niceties for the purpose of getting rid of that obligation if that is an obligation either legal or equitable I wish to pay all my brother's debts."[84]

According to Louis's testimony, not only was he unwilling to resort to "legal niceties" but he had also rebuffed attempts by Anaise to blackmail him into making a settlement with Adeline. He reported that Anaise had come to him and "threatened to publish him in the papers" if he did not make a settlement. Although Louis clearly disapproved of the relationship between his brother and Adeline, he did not seem particularly worried about the threat, recalling that he had told Anaise his name was an honorable one and he had no fear of its being put in the papers.[85]

Louis stood firm; given the laws on concubinage, his legal position was very good. Even if Joe had made a will that favored Adeline, legislation dating from 1870 would have severely limited the amount she could inherit, unless he had arranged for a confidante to transfer money or property to her surreptitiously. As Joe's concubine, Adeline would have been eligible to inherit only movable property. The law prohibited those who had "lived in open concubinage" from "making to each other . . . [a]ny donation of immovables; and if they make a donation of movables, it can not exceed one-tenth part of the whole value of their estate." The bulk of Joe's wealth was tied up in the real estate he and Louis had inherited together. He also had some stock in Lafayette Fire Insurance Company, and had invested three hundred dollars in "mineral lands in Mississippi" shortly before his death. Under the stipulations of the existing law on concubinage, none of that property could have been left to Adeline.[86]

And what about Marie Stringer? Even if Joe was the father of Adeline's daughter, the laws on donations to illegitimate children were even stingier than those directed at concubines. As it was, Marie was never mentioned by either side in the court case. If Adeline had claimed that Marie was Joe's child, Louis's charges of concubinage would have been proven beyond a doubt, undercutting Adeline's case. And Louis, if he was aware of Marie's existence at all and believed that Joe was her father, apparently had no interest in entering this information into the public record. The relationship of Joe and Adeline, at least as far as Louis was concerned, was mortifying enough.[87]

To secure a portion of Joe's estate, Adeline trumped up a claim that almost certainly had no basis in fact. Her petition to the court read in part: "The plaintiff, a lodging house keeper in this city, claims $1644.90 for room rent due by Joseph Mathis from May 1st 1884, to the date of his death, and $500 for services rendered to him as a sick-nurse during the same period." Adeline's total claim of $2144.90 amounted to almost exactly ten percent of Joe's total estate. Was this simply a coincidence? Joe's correspondence confirmed that he had been living at Adeline's when he wrote letters to her in May and June of 1884, but the court was also probably right in its opinion that "[t]he evidence in this case fully convinces us that there was no intention on the part of plaintiff to require, or of Mathis to make any payment for the occupancy of the room or for services." They also opined that "Mathis did not enrich himself at plaintiff's expense, but on the contrary, that he gave in other ways, a pecuniary quid pro quo for all the benefits received from her."[88]

As Joe had probably done in the agreement of 1878, Adeline had in 1887 constructed a ruse to help her secure a portion of Joe's estate. But her case defied logic in many respects. As many witnesses confirmed, Joe had spent only Saturday and Sunday nights at her house in his final years, leading the court to ask whether he had required nursing only on those nights of the week and not on any of the others.[89]

Louis was wise to engage Henry Plauché Dart to represent him, for Dart was an extremely capable and accomplished litigator. In fact, he had argued his first case before the Louisiana Supreme Court at the age of twenty-two. During his lifetime, he was considered the "foremost trial lawyer" in the state. He would go on to distinguish himself as a preservationist and local historian, serving as the editor of the *Louisiana Historical Quarterly* from 1922 until his death in 1934. Thirty years old at the time *Stringer v. Mathis* was adjudicated, Dart had been appointed five years earlier as counsel for the Lafayette Fire Insurance Company, a post he would hold until his death. He and Louis doubtless knew each other well, and Louis apparently trusted Dart with both his business and personal affairs.[90]

Adeline's attorney Branch K. Miller seems, in contrast, to have been less than completely committed to his client's cause. When the case was called into trial on June 28, 1888, the court record notes that Miller was absent.

Regardless of his performance, however, Miller expected to be paid. The case stretched on for nearly two years until the state supreme court gave its decision in December 1889. In January of that year, Adeline had been forced to sell one of the lots of ground that Joe had transferred to her at the time of the 1878 agreement. The deed of transfer claimed that she had paid him $400 for the property, although it is unlikely that any money actually changed hands. Louis testified that Joe had borrowed $600 from him to make the settlement with Adeline. Although that agreement noted that Joe had given Adeline $1,000 cash, it is more likely that the $600 borrowed from Louis was the only cash involved and that the other $400 had simply been assumed by Joe in exchange for the property. When Joe originally bought the two lots in 1867, he had paid $1,650 for both of them. When Adeline sold one of them in 1889, she got only $125 for it. Either she made a very poor deal, or she was desperate for cash.[91]

Adeline lost her case in Civil District Court in New Orleans. At the state supreme court level, Miller tried to argue that the letters entered into evidence did not prove that concubinage had existed between the two. This was, of course, a difficult case to make. Joe and Adeline's intimacy gleams through nearly every line of those letters, and the relationship revealed in them seems very much like a marriage minus only legal consecration.

Though his opposition was slight, Dart made a detailed argument against Adeline based on two issues. The first had to do with the character, veracity, and reliability of the witnesses who testified for each side. For instance, in considering the very favorable testimony Anaise had offered on Adeline's behalf, and the way in which it had contradicted testimony offered by Louis's witnesses, Dart asserted that, "against these witnesses of the highest social character, we have the testimony of Anaise Hutchinson, a colored girl of griffe complexion, who has been living with the plaintiff for some years and who calls her aunt, although she says she is no relation of hers." Dart's criticisms of Anaise were grounded in concepts of gender, class, race, and respectability. According to him, Adeline, a young woman of color, was no match for white male witnesses of the "highest social character."[92]

Dart used similar tactics to cast a critical light on the testimony of Mary Hobby, whom he described as "an aged negress." A boardinghouse keeper in the same neighborhood as Adeline, Hobby testified that she had often seen Joe at the Dryades Street house. Although Hobby noted that she had been in the rooming house business for thirty years, gave her age as seventy-three, and named several distinguished persons who had boarded in her house over the years, Dart contended in his brief to the court that "[h]er memory is not good as to dates." In this instance, Dart used Hobby's gender, race, and age to discredit her, although her testimony showed that she had a keen grasp on details and dates.[93]

Dart went on to review the testimony of three white men who had testified for Adeline, but he was more circumspect in his critique of their testimony. In his brief to the state supreme court, Dart first emphasized that F. J. Rodgers was "a white man" then scrutinized Rodgers's testimony, reviewing the claim that "he used to see" Joseph Mathis at the Dryades Street house "continually during '84 and until the latter part of 1886 every morning from 6 1/2 to 7, and that he frequently saw him in his shirt sleeves in the summer time and sometimes lying on the bed reading." F. Dezutter, a tailor, also testified that he lived in the neighborhood and had "upon ten or twelve occasions at Joseph Mathis' order . . . [s]ent clothes to" the Dryades Street house for him. Finally, Dart reviewed the testimony of Dr. Lewis, whose testimony on Adeline's behalf and stubborn refusal to confirm a sexual relationship between her and Joe had so frustrated Dart.[94]

Dart directly rebutted and discounted the testimony given by Anaise and Mary Hobby, but he was less willing to directly question the testimony given by the three white male witnesses. To rationalize his position, Dart wrote that the witnesses for the "defense are more nearly to the truth than those for the plaintiff, and this without reflecting at all upon the testimony of Dr. Lewis, Rodgers and Dezutter, because it is further evident that Jos. Mathis, when he left his home on Saturday evening, went to plaintiff's house and spent his Saturday and Sunday there." Giving the white male witnesses the benefit of the doubt, even though their testimony contradicted that of his own witnesses, Dart concluded that the men weren't lying but were just mistaken. He conceded that they had seen Mathis at the house but only on Saturdays and Sundays, the days Louis and his witnesses admitted Joe always spent with Adeline.[95]

Dart's brief to the Louisiana Supreme Court suggests that in the late 1880s, justice in Louisiana was neither color blind nor unbiased on the basis of gender. Dart felt free to impugn the testimony of two women of color, but, when the witnesses were white men, he was careful to suggest that they were mistaken rather than dishonest. The weight given to a witness's testimony, and its credibility, seem in this case to have been lodged in their gender, social class, race, and purported respectability. Of course, in the South of the late 1880s skin color automatically conveyed information about the quality of one's character—and, by extension, one's testimony. In Dart's brief, gender and color equaled character; he discounted out of hand the respectability of the female witnesses of color. He made this point in no uncertain terms when he asserted that Anaise's testimony was "flatly contradicted by gentlemen of irreproachable character."[96]

Neither Adeline's attorney nor anyone else in the case pointed out that the "gentlemen of irreproachable character" who testified for Louis were closely tied to him in business affairs. Dr. Olliphant, for example, was a stockholder and, eventually, a member of the board of directors of the Lafayette Fire Insurance Company. Godfried Gaisser, who had "known Joe all his life," was the company's secretary, a post previously held by Louis. Meyer Levi, the store proprietor who testified for Louis, ran his business out of a building that Louis owned. These circumstances either were not mentioned or did not elicit any comment at trial. After all, who would question white men who also had respectability and elevated social status to recommend them? It was enough to know that these were "gentlemen of irreproachable character," respectable white men in the postbellum South.

Dart's second argument focused on Adeline's decision not to testify, and he shrewdly shaped that decision into further proof of her concubinage with Joe. "It was," he wrote, "in her power to deny that she had been the concubine of the decedent. It was in her power to show that her association with Mathis was of a lofty and pure character; that her friendship was merely platonic. Above all, when she produced the letters written to her by Joseph Mathis, under the plaintiff's call, it was not only her privilege, but her duty, to explain away the allusions contained in these letters." Dart concluded that Adeline did not testify because she could not tell the truth about her relationship with Joe and sustain her case.[97]

Adeline would have had a difficult time on the stand if she denied that she had been Joe's concubine. Dart went on to review the profusely affectionate language used by Joe in the letters and concluded: "Tested by the ordinary understanding of what occurs between man and woman, there can be no hesitancy in saying that such letters written *by an unmarried white man to an unmarried griffe woman,* show a degree of familiarity which convinces the mind that they occupied concubinal relations."[98]

What Dart did not say was that the "ordinary understanding" of what occurs between men and women, was, in this case, directly related to their racial identifications. Dart even italicized the words *"unmarried white man"* and *"unmarried griffe woman"* giving them a sort of codified emphasis that reminds the modern reader that relations between a white man and a woman of color were assumed to be sexual in this period of New Orleans history.[99]

Ideas about respectability, and eroticized racial stereotypes that focused on light-skinned, mixed-race women, were not the only factors that figured in to the decision in this case, but they were significant ones. The outcome in another case with striking similarities to *Stringer v. Mathis* suggests that the gender, race, and assumed respectability of parties to a case could result in a very different decision from the Louisiana Supreme Court. Sixteen years after ruling in the case of *Stringer v. Mathis,* the Louisiana justices made a final decision in the contested succession of Sophie Jahraus. Jahraus, the sister-in-law and alleged concubine of successful hotel entrepreneur Anthony Monteleone, left her entire estate to him in a last will and testament that she wrote on her deathbed with Monteleone at her side.[100]

Jahraus, a white woman, was not married; many witnesses, including close family members, testified that she and her sister's husband had carried on a sexual affair for many years. Although Jahraus had a child out of wedlock (who some family members claimed was Monteleone's), and although another witness who lived with Jahraus gave explicit testimony about the sexual nature of her relationship with Monteleone, the court was exceedingly reluctant to conclude that they had been concubines. If they had, of course, Jahraus's bequest to Monteleone, which consisted largely of real estate, would have been invalidated. In their ruling, the justices went to great pains to explain why they had concluded that Monteleone was not Jahraus's concubine. Focusing on the word "open" in the state's concubinage statute, the court ultimately decided in Monteleone's favor. There was ample testimony to support the charges of concubinage but, the court opined, because "they hid their concubinage . . . under the cloak of an innocent relation," they had not engaged in "open concubinage."[101]

The testimony that there had been a sexual connection between the two was so compelling that the court had to accept it. But the justices did so reluctantly because, in their view, "the plaintiff's case is not benefited thereby, and to no purpose disrepute is brought to the defendant, Monteleone, and dishonor to the memory of the dead." The justices concluded, "whatever may be said of the relations of the defendant and the testatrix, they were not 'open.'" And because they were not, the court ruled, they did not fit under the rubric of the state's concubinage statute.

In Monteleone's case, he and other witnesses confirmed that he had escorted Jahraus home from work every night, spent Sunday afternoons at her house, and even moved her into his family home when she was pregnant with a child that many witnesses claimed was his. Yet because he was a respectable white man and, in the court's opinion at least, "had made attempts to cloak the affair in the guise of innocence," he could not be discounted as Jahraus's sole heir on the basis of concubinage.[102]

In contrast, although Joseph Mathis went to great pains to hide his ongoing relations with Adeline Stringer, including establishing two separate households, the court had no doubt that the two were concubines. In the case of *Stringer v. Mathis,* Adeline's race, gender, and presumed lack of respectability as a "colored woman," combined with Louis's unquestioned respectability as a successful white businessman, doomed her case from the beginning. Widely held stereotypes about the ubiquity of sexual relations between white men and light-skinned, mixed-race women in New Orleans only added to her presumed lack of credibility in the case.

Not surprisingly, in the case of *Stringer v. Mathis* the state supreme court reaffirmed the lower-court decision in favor of Louis Mathis. Concubinage between Joe and Adeline was undeniable, a fact that Adeline more or less conceded by failing to testify in her own behalf. But the original copy of the court's decision suggests that Dart's racist argument and sexualized stereotypes about women of color had a resonance with the members of the supreme court as well. In the court's official printed decision, digested in the *Louisiana Annual,* Adeline was described only as "the plaintiff, a lodging house keeper in this city." In contrast, on the court's original handwritten decision, she was described as "the plaintiff, a colored lodging house keeper in this city." At some point before the case was copied into digest form, someone must have crossed out the word "colored," ensuring its absence from the official decision that would appear in the *Louisiana Annual* digest of cases. Thus, while the court's decision officially appeared to have been color blind, the subsequent decision to remove the descriptor "colored" reveals a court that tried hard to pretend it did not take race or skin color into account. But the court's decision reflected the racist values and beliefs of the society in which it operated and which gave it legitimacy.[103]

Adeline's gender and color had everything to do with how her case was adjudicated and, in some cases, how witnesses testified. For example, when Dart questioned Fanny Brickell, who had been a slave in the Mathis household before the war, he became irate, pressing her to reveal information she had previously given to him outside the courtroom. Brickell refused to acknowledge whatever she had told Dart previously, and this exchange followed:

DART: I will ask you the direct question—I will ask you to repeat again what was it that Mrs. Stringer said in regard to the Mathis family not wishing to recognize her?
BRICKELL: She wondered what Mr. Mathis had against her that he didn't recognize her.
DART: As to what?
BRICKELL: She didn't say anything to that, and I told her "It's because you are a colored woman."
DART: I want to know if there was anything else said.
BRICKELL: No sir, nothing else.[104]

Perhaps, outside the courtroom, Brickell had confirmed Joe and Adeline's concubinage to Dart. Her testimony suggests that she and Adeline had been at least familiar enough to have a conversation about the Mathis family's failure to recognize her. But Brickell's refusal to divulge this information or repeat it inside the courtroom also suggests that, when push came to shove, her loyalties lay with Adeline, a former slave like herself, rather than with the son of her former master. Brickell's statement to Adeline about why the Mathis family refused to acknowledge her is striking as well: "It's because you are a colored woman." But that statement explains more than just the events surrounding the court case. Adeline's race had everything to do with the way in which her relationship with Joe was conducted. If she had been white, this story would have been significantly different. But because she was a colored woman she and Joe were forced to take actions and make decisions that were not necessary for those whose romantic relationships did not cross the color line.

In retrospect, it is striking how much Adeline and Louis had in common and how similar they were. Both of them loved Joe and were fiercely devoted to him. Both were ambitious in their business dealings, and both were determined to exercise influence over Joe's affairs when he was alive. Both laid claim to his estate after his death. But the chasm across which Louis looked at Adeline—the ever-widening chasm of race—made it impossible for him to appreciate the finer points of Adeline's character or to see the love and commitment that gleamed through his brother's letters to her. Besides Joe and Adeline themselves, Louis was probably the only person who had been privy to both sides of that correspondence. But the only thing Louis could see when he looked at Adeline was his brother's "colored" concubine, and the only feelings he could register were shame and disgust.

After the state supreme court ruling, Louis went on to solidify his place in New Orleans as a respectable and prosperous businessman. Months after the court rendered its final decision in December 1889, he purchased a large, impressive mansion with extensive grounds on St. Charles Avenue—the city's most fashionable and sought-after address. Coming as it did on the heels of the court's decision, the purchase of the house must have been made possible in part by the court's confirmation that Louis alone would inherit Joe's estate. When he died suddenly in 1903, Louis left the St. Charles property and a sizable estate to his second wife and his surviving children.[105]

Adeline was not listed in the city directory of 1888, but she reappeared in 1889 as a keeper of furnished rooms at 58 Baronne Street. She was still at that address through 1892, after which she disappeared from city directories entirely. But in the U.S. Census for 1900, a sixty-seven-year-old woman named "Adline Stringer" was enumerated in Clark County, Alabama. The name and age are right for Adeline, but she was no longer the head of her own household. Instead, she lived in the home of William Bradly, whose occupation was listed as "farmer." Bradly was forty-six at the time, making it conceivable that he was the "Capt. Willis" Joe had written about in his letters to and from Mobile in the late 1870s. Stringer's relationship to Bradly was listed as "mother-in-law." Bradly's wife, enumerated as "Betty E," could conceivably have been Adeline's older daughter. With a birth date of February 1867, she would have been born just before Joe's return to New Orleans from California. The name Betty suggests that her full name may have been Elizabeth, which could have been in honor of her mother Adeline Elizabeth Stringer. There is no "Marie" enumerated in Bradly's household but, as Adeline's daughter Marie would have been thirty by this time, she may have been married or living on her own. One detail from the census data is problematic: although the name and approximate age are right for Adeline, the entire family is classified as "white."[106]

Had Adeline gone to live with relatives in Alabama, and had the family decided to pass for white? Perhaps William Bradly *was* white, and perhaps Elizabeth was light enough to pass. The decision to pass for white would certainly be understandable. In the Deep South, with Jim Crow on the rise and lynching an all too common punishment for a dizzying array of "offenses" against white supremacy, it was certainly safer to become white. And "because she was a colored woman" no one would have known this better than Adeline Stringer.

The changing nature of race relations in the period between the Civil War and the rise of Jim Crow in the 1890s is mirrored in the relationship between Joe and Adeline. For a brief period that pre-dated and then coincided with Radical Reconstruction, there were significant openings for African Americans in many facets of New Orleans's social, political, and economic life. But as white supremacy became the rule in all of those arenas by merit of force and later by law, those gains were first scaled back and later obliterated. Although fleeting sexual forays across the color line continued, reaching their symbolic peak in the Storyville era, long-term relationships across the color line became increasingly problematic. As the requirements of white supremacy sought to dehumanize African Americans, raping or paying for sex with a woman of color continued to fit within the privileged sexual parameters white men set for themselves. But, as Joe and Adeline's story reveals, openly conducting a committed and meaningful relationship with a woman of color on the basis of equality and mutual respect did not.

Evolving ideas about gender, race, and the links between sexual behavior and respectability played critical roles in Joseph Mathis and Adeline Stringer's story and in the outcome of Adeline's court case. As committed relationships across the color line became less acceptable, a central institution in the city's antebellum sexual culture gave way to the rising imperatives of white supremacy. The economic agreements that had characterized plaçage before the Civil War all but disappeared as concubinage laws tightened and racial prejudices hardened. Sex across the color line continued, but it took new forms and increasingly occurred in physical spaces that, like the act itself, were derided and stigmatized by those who deemed themselves respectable.

The Business of Pleasure

CONCERT SALOONS AND SEXUAL COMMERCE
IN THE ECONOMIC MAINSTREAM

In January 1887, just three months before Joseph Mathis died, *Harper's New Monthly Magazine* published a flattering feature article on New Orleans written by Charles Dudley Warner. The author touted the city's potential as a tourist destination and emphasized its numerous natural attractions, its romantic reputation, and its heterogeneous population. According to Warner, New Orleans was "the most cosmopolitan of provincial cities." In his view this heterogeneity had both positive and negative ramifications. On the one hand, he suggested, the city's "comparative isolation . . . had preserved the individuality of the many races that give it color, morals, and character." Yet he also assured his readers that crossing the color line, both socially and sexually, was a remnant of the city's past rather than a feature of its present.[1]

Warner conceded that "no other city of the United States so abounds in stories pathetic and tragic . . . growing out of the mingling of races . . . especially out of the relations between the whites and the fair women who had in their thin veins drops of African blood." Yet, after admitting that relationships between white men and light-skinned women of color were both historical reality and "the staple of hundreds of thrilling tales," he concluded that this long history of racial amalgamation was at an end.[2]

It seems that Warner, like Louis Mathis, dealt with his own discomfort about sex across the color line by degrading its importance while simultaneously, if improbably, eradicating it from the city's current sexual culture simply by denying its continued existence. "I believe there is an instinct in both races against the mixture of blood, and upon this rests the law of Louisiana," he wrote. Warner was wrong on this count, apparently unaware of, or stubbornly impervious to, the fact that interracial marriage was, in fact, legal in the state at the time.[3]

As Joseph Mathis and Adeline Stringer's experiences attest, crossing the color line sexually, at least within the confines of a committed relationship, had become problematic in New Orleans by the 1880s. But, problematic or not, sex and socialization across the color line remained a constant, though contested, feature of the city's culture of commercial sexuality for decades after Warner's article. Reflecting this reality, and in response to Warner's claims, at least one of the city's newspapers was not content to let his assertions pass without challenge.

Although Warner had noted that there were "plenty of *café chantants,* gilded saloons, and gambling houses, and more than enough of the resorts upon which the police are supposed to keep one blind eye," his coverage of such haunts was deemed dubiously paltry by the editors of the city's muckraking weekly, the *Mascot* which dedicated its January 22 issue to "Sights of New Orleans, The Harpers [*sic*] Did Not See." In a clear challenge to the notion that racial amalgamation was at an end, the *Mascot's* coverage focused on "the slums and dives of Franklin Street," home to what it called "the most loathsome, filthy, hotbeds of vice and debauchery ever permitted to befoul the moral or physical atmosphere of any city." Prominent among the paper's complaints was the promiscuous racial mixing that took place in the "abominable hovels" and "palaces of sin" that dominated two blocks of the thoroughfare. These "shanties" were the sites of incredible "orgies" and places where "male and female, black and yellow, and even white, meet on terms of equality and abandon themselves to the extreme limit of obscenity and lasciviousness." To emphasize this point, the cover illustration (which the paper claimed was "not at all exaggerated") showed the cross-racial socialization that took place in the Franklin Street "slums and dives." The image included an integrated band playing for African American dancers and a white policeman seated between and receiving the affectionate attention of two women of color.[4]

Although the Franklin Street dives troubled the *Mascot,* they were located where respectable people, whether citizens or visitors like Warner, only had to encounter them if they chose to. But the Franklin Street dens and dives were not the only ones of their kind. They had an equivalent in the city's controversial and more centrally located concert saloons. In fact, the same kind of criticism aimed at the Franklin Street dives was also commonly leveled at concert saloons and their patrons. As early as 1884, the *Mascot* had

SIGHTS OF NEW ORLEANS, THE HARPERS DID NOT SEE.—The Gambling Hells of Franklin Street.

This *Mascot* cover (Jan. 22, 1887), captioned "Sights of New Orleans, the Harpers Did Not See," depicts Franklin Street "Gambling Hells." *Courtesy Louisiana State Museum*

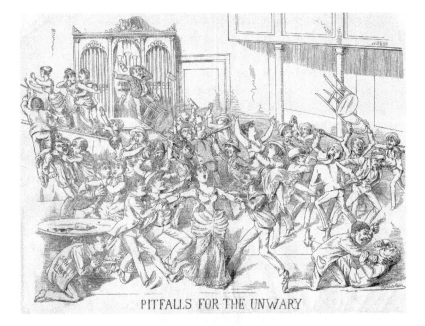

PITFALLS FOR THE UNWARY

This *Mascot* illustration of a concert saloon (Jan. 12, 1884) depicts "Pitfalls for the Unwary."
Courtesy Louisiana State Museum

opined that "very little difference . . . exists between the two localities. . . .
The proprietors of both enjoy the protection of the laws and the friendship
of its guardians by paying for the privilege. Both use women as decoys to
attract custom." The illustration for this story, captioned "Pitfalls for the
Unwary," depicted a scene from a concert saloon on Bourbon Street patronized by white men, mostly working class and recent immigrants. But according to the paper, "if the color and costumes were triflingly [*sic*] varied the
design would hold good for a row in a nigger dive on Franklin Street."[5]

Like the racially integrated Franklin Street dives, concert saloons shared
a reputation for disorder and an association with badly behaved, lower-class
persons. Both received a great deal of journalistic disapprobation, but there
was at least one critical difference between them. The Franklin Street establishments were still on the margins of the developed city in the late 1880s,
while concert saloons had moved boldly into the city's geographic and economic center. Concert saloons began to appear on major downtown streets
as early as the 1870s and in the next decade came to dominate several prominent blocks along Royal Street.

The explicit comparison between concert saloons and "negro dance halls" mirrors the way conceptual and behavioral boundaries, like crossing the color line, were joined by emerging geographic constraints as New Orleanians struggled to sort out their city and its contested culture of commercial sexuality in the years after 1865. Both kinds of boundaries, behavioral and geographic, played a role in the rise, development, and ultimate geographic segregation of the concert saloon.[6]

Although popular writers have often portrayed the city's culture of commercial sexuality as uniquely outrageous and outside the national norm, in this instance New Orleans's struggle to deal with the rapid growth and proliferation of sexually oriented businesses was shared by nearly all other American cities in the same period. As historians John D'Emilio and Estelle Freedman observe, in the second half of the nineteenth-century sexuality "moved into the world of commerce" and "American entrepreneurs began to trade in sexual fantasy and sexual experience."[7]

Certainly New Orleans, like virtually all other American port cities, had tolerated vice and prostitution districts before the Civil War, and many of those districts endured or reemerged after the war. Although significant aspects of the city's pre-war policy on and geography of prostitution remained in place, the meanings and practice of prostitution changed in both form and substance after the war. Brothels and assignation houses remained common places of resort for prostitutes and their clients. At the same time, the concert saloon reshaped and repackaged sex for sale in ways that changed its economic impact and social import, and it moved prostitution and commercial sexuality from the geographic margins squarely into the city's rapidly developing center and its economic mainstream. Although they are all but forgotten today, concert saloons were wildly popular, widely discussed, and extremely controversial urban-entertainment venues in the three decades after the Civil War. These rollicking resorts pushed the boundaries of probity and propriety, both behaviorally and spatially, for men and women of all classes in America's rapidly growing and modernizing cities. Debates about concert saloons and their locations also reveal how ideas about respectability, sexuality, and appropriate behavior for men and women were undergoing significant change in these years.

As concert saloons began to appear on the city's main shopping and business streets, people noticed, and some protested vigorously. The centrality and visibility of these rowdy entertainment venues, and the prostitution that went on within them, troubled critics, who suggested that they might be better placed elsewhere. But where would they go, and what did sex, race, and respectability have to do with answering that question for concert saloon patrons and their critics in the Great Southern Babylon? A close look at the experiences of an obscure but influential immigrant entrepreneur named Otto Henry Schoenhausen helps to answer those questions.

"An Illegal, Immoral, Lascivious, and Disorderly Business"

In December 1893, a group of Royal Street property owners and business proprietors sued their neighbor Otto Henry Schoenhausen, claiming that his business, a concert saloon called the Tivoli Varieties, was a nuisance that depreciated their property values and damaged their business prospects. In response to the charges, Schoenhausen claimed that the only effect his establishment had on his neighbors was to make them, in his words, "immensely rich." Litigation continued for nearly two years, and testimony in the case exceeded six hundred pages. In the course of that testimony, a variety of voices was recorded. Self-proclaimed progressive businessmen—such as lead plaintiff James A. Koehl, president of a sprawling gourmet grocery and wine store and part owner of a great deal of Royal Street real estate—squared off against disreputable and allegedly corrupt policemen, machine politicians, and other Royal Street businessmen who supported Schoenhausen. The other key plaintiffs, all of whom ran or owned nearby hotels and restaurants, claimed that concert saloons like Schoenhausen's and the prostitution that went on within them, disturbed or otherwise negatively affected their clientele. But as testimony proceeded, defense witnesses charged that all of the plaintiffs either supported or profited from prostitution themselves. Koehl, the outspoken lead plaintiff, even admitted on the stand that he personally was a generous patron of some of the women who entertained in the Royal Street concert saloons or worked in nearby brothels.[8]

Despite the many surprising twists and turns of this case, one conclusion emerges clearly. The compiled testimony and records in *Koehl v. Schoenhausen* reveal significant disagreement and concern about the prominence of sexually oriented businesses and entertainment venues in late-nineteenth-century New Orleans. The plaintiffs who sued Schoenhausen claimed that the Tivoli Varieties was "an illegal, immoral, lascivious, and disorderly business," and that its presence jeopardized their economic success. But Schoenhausen and his attorneys argued that Royal Street had been "dedicated to avocations usually regarded as disreputable and illegitimate" for many years. In addition to concert saloons, brothels, and assignation houses, "coffeehouses, 'gambling hells' and places where the sporting fraternity" gathered were common in the "immediate neighborhood."[9]

The arguments, testimony, and timing in this case give us a rare chance to listen to contending voices from the past as they debate the appropriate place for public sexual expression and commerce in the city after the Civil War. Those voices demonstrate how reform-oriented businessmen who saw themselves as progressive sought to draw new boundaries, both geographical and behavioral, that improved the city's moral landscape and simultaneously enhanced their own economic interests and social standing. While this case was undertaken to decide whether Schoenhausen's business was a nuisance that damaged the business prospects of his neighbors, several other issues clearly concerned the litigants and witnesses. While not explicitly connected to legal definitions of nuisance, these issues played a part in generating the plaintiffs' suit, preoccupied witnesses on the stand, and had an impact on the opinion that the Louisiana Supreme Court ultimately rendered in this case.

The first and most important of these issues was the question of where sexually oriented entertainment venues ought to be located. Many witnesses, particularly those for the plaintiffs, gave lip service to the idea that concert saloons were immoral. Yet some of those same witnesses admitted to frequenting such establishments or testified that they were willing to accept and even do business with concert saloons as long as they were situated in what they deemed to be appropriate locations. By late 1893, the plaintiffs and their supporters had determined that Royal Street was no longer an appropriate location for these morally compromised establishments. Questions about how to allocate public space at a time when sexual titillation was increasingly being sold in combination with good times and hospitality—a business with which the first three blocks of Royal Street had become commonly identified after the Civil War—were addressed at length.

A second issue central to the case was the question of respectability, particularly the respectability of men who frequented concert saloons. Lawyers and litigants repeatedly raised questions about the social class and character of the overwhelmingly male concert-saloon clientele. A lawyer for the plaintiffs asked, "Is it not a fact that [Schoenhausen's business] is frequented by people of the very lowest class and very lowest order?" He added, "Of course, there are occasions where gentlemen go there, but those are exceptions." From the plaintiffs' point of view, concert saloons were frequented only by disreputable men or by respectable men who were risking their reputations.

Even a witness for the defense testified that he did not frequent concert saloons because he had "a good reputation" and did not "want to lose it by going to places of that kind."[10]

On the witness stand, Schoenhausen suggested that the disdain directed at his patrons had more to do with their social class and ethnicity than it did with the character of his concert saloon. He defended his patrons, many of whom were recent immigrants like himself, and noted that "the people that frequent [my establishments] are first class people. I consider also all of them good hard working men, they don't wear high standing collars—I can't help that—they are nice men though; they are law-abiding men."[11]

Many witnesses in the case posited a direct relationship between social class and respectability, especially when it came to sexual behavior. The idea of respectability that was bandied about frequently but imprecisely by witnesses in *Koehl v. Schoenhausen,* has been defined as "civilized morality" by Mark Thomas Connelly. One key to the attainment of civilized morality was sexual self-control and the connected belief that " 'progress,' as well as personal economic and social advancement, depended on this control of the potentially dangerous sex drive." Thus the indulgence in the ribald behavior and sexually explicit entertainment presented to the mostly male patrons of concert saloons, clashed with the requirements of respectability posited by middle-class proponents of the code of civilized morality.[12]

The conflicting testimony of witnesses in this case mirrors conflicting ideas about manhood that were vying for predominance throughout America in this period. The kind of behavior that was tolerated and even encouraged in concert saloons grew out of the " 'rough' code of manhood" formulated by "many working class men" and stood in opposition to the allegedly more civilized "moralistic manliness of the middle class." These two conflicting models of manhood were celebrated or denounced by many of the male witnesses in this case, and, not surprisingly, were reflected in their opinions of concert saloons.[13]

Testimony in *Koehl v. Schoenhausen* and similar cases also leaves no doubt that the requirements of respectability were much less stringent for men than they were for women. Just as ideas about manhood were in flux during this period, so were ideas about female respectability. Not surprisingly, questions and concerns about the respectability of women—the women connected with concert saloons as employees and those who came into inadvertent contact with the establishments—also preoccupied witnesses in this case. Most witnesses seemed to assume that the women who worked in the Royal Street concert saloons were involved in immoral activity; some made the charge of prostitution explicit. Thus, according to the plaintiffs, the most pressing problem was how to separate and distinguish respectable women from their fallen sisters in the public areas adjacent to concert saloons. How, they asked, could respectable women be assured that their reputations would not be sullied by shopping or eating in restaurants in the first few blocks of Royal Street, where concert saloons and their female employees were so prevalent?

This concern was heightened because concert saloons appeared and gained popularity at the same time that women of all classes began to move more freely in the public sphere. The obvious advantages and freedoms gained by women as they moved into the mainstream of urban life were complicated by the dangers any respectable woman faced in the turn-of-the-century city. Chief among these was the danger that she might be mistaken for a public woman instead of simply a woman out in public.[14]

By necessity, working-class women—many of whom in New Orleans were either immigrants or African–Americans—were among the first to break down the barrier between the public sphere as a male space and the private or domestic sphere as a female space. In the process, as historians Christine Stansell and Kathy Peiss have so amply demonstrated, these women created a cultural and sartorial style of their own. Ultimately that style, and their ability to achieve it through the meager rewards of wage labor, changed the way all women dressed and navigated public space in the nation's cities. One result was that, by the late nineteenth century, "it was becoming more difficult to distinguish a respectable woman from her opposite based on appearance alone." Historian Robert Allen points out that in a controversial but increasingly common move, many women at the end of the nineteenth century "had shed their drab colors and simply cut dresses for a more assertive, colorful style." In many cases, they borrowed these bolder styles from working-class women, actresses, and prostitutes. This development exacerbated the problem of ascertaining a woman's character based solely on her appearance.[15]

Feminine clothing styles began to relax at the end of the Victorian era, but feminine respectability remained a critical imperative in polite, middle-class society. According to the plaintiffs in *Koehl v. Schoenhausen,* women who mixed too freely in public spaces with known prostitutes or "fast women," even if by necessity rather than choice, were taking a risk with their own reputations. As women in New Orleans and other cities moved into the public sphere to shop, to dine, to socialize, and to work, they routinely came into contact with people from all classes, races, and ethnic identities. The clear lines of demarcation posited by the doctrine of separate spheres were trampled under the feet of the often anonymous men and women who rubbed elbows in the city's increasingly diverse and sometimes dangerous streets. And while women could move about New Orleans unescorted by the 1890s, particularly during the daytime, they were assumed to be at risk or simply risqué if they ventured out alone after dark. The plaintiffs made continual reference to the dangers concert saloons presented to their respectable female clientele, but those dangers were as much conceptual as they were physical. The notion of female respectability was always under siege in the increasingly complicated social geography of late-nineteenth-century New Orleans.

The issues of *Koehl v. Schoenhausen* provide an illuminating perspective on sexual commerce and culture in turn-of-the-century New Orleans, but this case was not the only one of its kind. Several similar cases filed throughout the 1880s and 1890s also offer important clues that help us understand how diverse members of New Orleans society felt about concert saloons and the rapid expansion of sexualized commerce in their city in the late nineteenth century.

The Emergence of the Concert Saloon

In the years after the Civil War, a handful of newspaper writers and reporters described the interiors of concert saloons and the racially integrated dives to which they were often explicitly compared. Lafcadio Hearn, who came to New Orleans in 1877, made his mark as a journalist by chronicling a "world that respectable America rarely encountered and hardly understood." In fact, the year before he came to the Crescent City, he wrote about a racially integrated tavern in Cincinnati that bore striking physical similarities to descriptions of integrated dives and concert saloons in New Orleans:

> The attractive novelty of theatricals at old Pickett's tavern . . . by real negro minstrels, with amateur dancing performances by roustabouts and their "girls," has already created considerable interest in quarters where one would perhaps least expect to find it; and the patrolmen of the Row nightly escort fashionably dressed white strangers to No. 91 Front street. The theater has two entrances, one through the neat, spotlessly clean bar-room on the Front street side; the other from the sidewalk on the river side. The theater is also the ballroom, and when the ancient clock behind the black bar in the corner an-

nounces . . . the hour of 12, the footlights are extinguished, the seats cleared away, and the audiences quickly form into picturesque sets for wild dances.[16]

Hearn's rich description of Pickett's Tavern echoes the kind of chaos and disorder depicted so well in the *Mascot's* illustration of a concert saloon. But at the time Hearn wrote, not everyone agreed on exactly what a concert saloon was or—perhaps more important—what distinguished it from similar but less controversial theaters and taverns. New Orleans venues that resembled Pickett's Tavern in Cincinnati included not only the Franklin Street dives and concert saloons, but low-cost variety theaters and beer gardens that attracted working-class immigrants and were scattered around the city. All of these venues offered theatrical entertainment. But unlike so-called respectable theaters, which had been cleansed by antebellum reformers of disorderly and immoral behavior and the patronage of prostitutes, these emerging venues promoted various levels of informality and the kind of audience interaction and participation that the legitimate theaters had banned.

Many persons who ran such establishments bridled at the notion that they were concert saloons. Perhaps they did so only to avoid the stiff licensing fees to which concert saloons were subject, but their cases are often very revealing about what took place in these establishments. Henry Wenger, for example, whose establishment the *Mascot* had criticized and caricatured in 1884, actually went to court in 1887 to argue that his business was not a concert saloon. In pressing his case, Wenger suggested there were three important elements that distinguished his establishment from a concert saloon. First, he maintained, his patrons were in general more respectable than those who visited the Royal Street venues. Second, he argued, the women who were present in his place were better controlled than those on Royal Street. According to one witness, on Royal Street women had the run, "the freedom of the whole place." Wenger, in contrast, kept his female performers confined to an upstairs gallery, where, they could drink with customers in semiprivate boxes but only if they were invited by male patrons to do so.[17]

Wenger also provided a separate "ladies entrance" for his performers, but, according to witnesses, many of the women who frequented Wenger's were not ladies. Otto Schoenhausen testified that everybody "knows that from ten to fifteen women of that class go there every night." Two policemen corroborated his testimony, one testifying that "lewd and abandoned women" frequented the place while another claimed that the majority of the women in the place were "sporting women." Whether he kept them con-

This illustration from the *Mascot* (Oct. 27, 1883) shows that the
attire of "waiter girls" and "beer jerkers" in concert saloons was
both brief and scandalous. *Courtesy Louisiana State Museum*

fined to the upstairs or not, many witnesses suggested that Wenger's female
employees and patrons were engaged in prostitution—an activity intimately
linked with concert saloons.[18]

In his third argument Wenger claimed that the entertainment in his establishment was more professional and less degraded than that featured in
the Royal Street concert saloons. To prove it, he entered into the court record a set of instructions that he claimed he gave to all his performers. Chief
among them was the directive that "vulgar expressions or actions on the
stage will be met by instant dismissal. No excuse will be accepted." He and
other witnesses also emphasized that he did not allow blackface minstrelsy
in his establishments, while concert saloons did. According to one witness,
concert saloons had "black face performers" which was not the case at

"Wenger's." Another witness put it more bluntly, noting that he had seen "nigger singing" on Royal Street but never at Wenger's.[19]

The testimony about the presence of blackface minstrels in concert saloons is intriguing given the comparisons the *Mascot* made between Franklin Street dives and concert saloons. Blackface minstrels, white men who used burnt cork or grease paint to blacken their faces and who mimicked the allegedly comical and rowdy behavior of African American men in songs and sketches, rose to prominence in the antebellum North, where it was popular mainly with male, working-class audiences. Blackface minstrelsy had become more common in the South after the Civil War, but it was still considered a disreputable and dangerously lower-class form of entertainment. According to witnesses in Wenger's case, the mere presence of blackface minstrels could help to define a venue, like the Royal Street concert saloons, as disreputable.[20]

But blackface minstrelsy was not the only kind of mimicry that took place on concert saloon stages in New Orleans. In fact, impersonation and mimicry seem to have been a central feature of entertainment in the city's concert saloons. During Wenger's trial, witnesses recalled many varieties of ethnic mockery including a "Mexican contortionist," "Hebrew impersonators," "Chinese impersonators," "Irish singers," a "Tyrolean Troupe" of dancers and musicians, and an allegedly astounding impersonator named "Moore," who could go into the audience, choose any person, and, in a few seconds, distort his face to look just like theirs. Adding a slightly different twist to all of this ethnic homage and mimicry were men who dressed as women. According to legal documents these were men who sang, danced, and dressed in "imitation of the action and manners of women" and were known as "female impersonators." Wenger's stage, and the stages of other concert saloons also occasionally featured women who dressed in scandalous flesh-colored tights and played and sang men's roles in a new and controversial form of entertainment called burlesque.[21]

Although Wenger tried to convince the court that his place and his patrons were more respectable than many other venues termed concert saloons, the state supreme court was not convinced. In May 1890, the court declared his business a concert saloon and held him liable for paying the attendant licensing fees. Although the moniker "concert saloon" invited controversy and some avoided it, other entrepreneurs like Otto Schoenhausen adopted it eagerly. They were aware, no doubt, of the great pecuniary

benefits to be derived from running such lucrative though morally questionable establishments.

According to witnesses in *Koehl v. Schoenhausen,* concert saloons first
began to appear in New Orleans in the 1860s, most prominently in the first
three blocks of Chartres and Royal Streets in the French Quarter. Coinciden-
tally, this is the same time Schoenhausen arrived in the city. Described on
his passport as a slight man, five feet, eight inches tall, with gray eyes and an
aquiline nose, Schoenhausen is not mentioned in the histories of legitimate
theater in New Orleans, but he was a dominant figure in the development
and management of concert saloons in the city. Although he originally
worked for other people, first as a bartender and later as a manager, by the
mid-1880s Schoenhausen owned several concert saloons of his own.[22]

Hailing from Alsace-Lorraine, like many other German-speaking immigrants to New Orleans (including Joe and Louis Mathis's father), Schoenhausen came to America near the end of the Civil War and began his career
in New York City by opening a music hall. According to one of his obituaries, "his relatives there objected," so he moved to the South, first to Galveston where he directed a tent show, and later to Shreveport where, in
partnership with a man named Jules Socha, he opened another music hall.
According to the same newspaper account, the two "made money so fast
that they grew tired of the town and decided to enter a larger field." The
"larger field" they chose was New Orleans. Although he does not appear in
city directories until 1873, Schoenhausen testified that he was in New Orleans
by 1867, when he worked in a concert saloon, the Bismarck. The following
year he worked as a bartender in the rotunda of the St. Louis Hotel, which
was the site of a concert saloon operated by the firm of Krost and Voegtle.
Ironically, Joseph Voegtle, Schoenhausen's former employer and a man who
had been in the concert-saloon business himself, was one of the plaintiffs
suing him in 1893. While concert saloons were at the center of litigation in
1893, their presence had always incited criticism, controversy, and court
cases.[23]

What distinguished concert saloons from legitimate theaters or common
barrooms, and why did they generate so much controversy? According to
theater historians, concert saloons first appeared in American urban centers
in the late antebellum period; they were common in many "cities across the
country in the 1860s, their nature and longevity dependent on the accommodations proprietors could make with local authorities." Specifically, such
establishments were among the first to consciously market "an entertain-

ment package of music, drink, and sex." Added to this volatile combination
was a dizzying array of theatrical forms, ethnic and cultural antecedents, clientele, performers, and—most scandalously of all, according to contemporary observers—men and women.[24]

Antebellum theater proprietors had joined with moral reformers to rid
their establishments of elements and behavior they considered low or immoral. In contrast, the postbellum concert saloon welcomed—in fact, was
expressly for—the kinds of people and activities eschewed by legitimate or
so-called respectable theaters. In fact, nearly "all of the features of the theatrical experience that had been excluded in the creation of a 'respectable' theater were reconstituted in the concert saloon."[25]

Concert saloons shared many similarities with ordinary theaters, bars,
and restaurants, but four critical factors set them apart from their respectable competitors. First, in contrast to the city's elite, family-oriented theaters, in which alcohol sales were limited or nonexistent and patrons were
expected to behave with decorum and passivity, concert saloons made
drinks available to patrons throughout the premises and during performances. A promotional article for the Eden Theater, a concert saloon that
Schoenhausen opened on Royal Street in 1886, made clear reference to these
differences. In "the theater or opera house . . . one was compelled to sit
during the entire three or four hours entertainment, under pain of violating
the proprieties rigorously exacted by arbitrary custom." In contrast, patrons
of the Eden could "indulge their appetite for refreshments, liquid as well as
solid, and . . . gleeful conversation could be carried on . . . without in any
way disturbing the performers on the stage, or one's neighbor."[26]

The second important difference between concert saloons and "legitimate theaters" was the overtly sexual nature of their performances. When
the Globe Theatre's management introduced the can-can to the city in 1875,
the dance was still quite controversial and officials threatened to close the
theater. But within a decade the formerly scandalous can-can was common
and was joined by other exuberant dances like the schottische and clodoche.
When performed by scantily clad females, these dances were classed under
the term "female spectacular performance" and they became standard fare
in local concert saloons. By the 1880s female performers routinely appeared
in tights or body stockings, kicked up their skirts, showed their legs, and, in
some cases, actually simulated sexual acts onstage or in back-lit silhouette.
A police corporal described a salacious skit performed in one of Schoenhausen's establishments: four or five women began with the can-can and

A drawing (ca. 1900) circulated in the Shreveport vice district
illustrates the association between concert saloon performers
and prostitution. *Courtesy Eric Brock*

ended "just the same as a man and woman going to bed. They work together, get pretty close to each other. The only difference is the skin tights
that they have got on."[27]

The sexualized nature of the performances was connected to a third distinction between concert saloons and other entertainment venues. So-called
"waiter girls" or "beer jerkers" (allegedly prostitutes) were at the core of
what made concert saloons so controversial in New Orleans and elsewhere
in the country. While virtually all male witnesses in this case and others like
it testified that various kinds of men frequented concert saloons, they also
agreed that the women employed in them were uniformly considered to be
public women or prostitutes. Joseph Dare, who had managed a concert saloon for Schoenhausen, testified that "all class of people visited. . . . The men
who composed this community visited there, different men, all sorts. . . .
The disreputable part about the house was the women." Reiterating this
theme in an article about Canterbury Hall, one of New York's earliest con-

cert saloons, a reporter claimed that without "the waiter girl feature, the Canterbury might claim to rank as a respectable place of public amusement, the performance on the stage being of average merit, the singing endurable, the negro business no drearier than usual, the dancing pretty good, and in character not much exceeding the usual license accorded to the ballet."[28]

The writer concluded that concert saloons constituted "nothing less than a portico to the brothel." In New Orleans, editorial commentary about concert saloons was similarly negative; one newspaper referred to them simply as "beer brothels." Another reporter noted that, in an unnamed concert saloon at 57 St. Charles, "the frowsy waiter girls, formerly in worse places, behaved themselves tolerably well." But, he asked, "how long will they be on their good conduct?"[29]

The newspaper's question about the waiter girls' "good conduct" suggests that just as women's place in the metropolis was changing, so were ideas about what constituted "good" or respectable female conduct generally. The women who worked in concert saloons certainly had problematic reputations, but often the charge that they were prostitutes was circumstantial and based on their behavior on the job and on the reputations of the places where they worked. In the increasingly anonymous city, and outside the boundaries of brothel prostitution, it was hard to know for sure if someone was engaging in prostitution. As sex for sale took new and sometimes more subtle forms, female behavior and deportment in public became a critical crucible upon which definitions of female respectability were forged. Stepping out in public was becoming acceptable even for respectable women, but they had to be extremely careful not to overstep the newly important and in many ways even more restrictive behavioral requirements that their recently acquired mobility and forays into the heart of the city necessitated.

Clearly the presence of allegedly disreputable women in concert saloons lay at the heart of objections to them. In addition to their inherent cultural and social complexity, it was the mixing of men and sexually available women that so disturbed contemporary observers. The "women of the town," as one antebellum observer had described them, had been thrown out of legitimate theaters, but in concert saloons they spent time on the stage, in the audience, and (according to court testimony) after hours with their patrons as well. Even the term "women of the town," though certainly still a euphemism for prostitute, was called into question as women became more thoroughly integrated into the life of the late-nineteenth-century city.

Certainly concert saloons were the sites of sexual solicitation, and many of the women who worked in them did so with little compunction or concern about meeting the standards of middle-class respectability. Such a choice is more comprehensible when one considers how few occupational opportunities were available to women in the last half of the nineteenth century. Many young women in New Orleans and in other cities understandably opted for the relatively easy, occasionally exciting, and sometimes lucrative work available to them as waiter girls, beer jerkers, or concert-saloon performers when their only options were poorly paid domestic service or back-breaking, mind-numbing factory work. One can even argue that the dearth of economic options victimized women as a class during this period.

There is ample evidence that waiter girls and concert-saloon performers were sometimes victims in more tangible ways. On at least two occasions, newspaper stories charged Schoenhausen with luring women to New Orleans under false pretenses. In February 1891, for example, a seventeen-year-old girl named Jennie Reckwig signed a contract in New York City that promised her theatrical engagements in the Crescent City. On her arrival she was met by Schoenhausen, put into a boardinghouse of his choice, "provided with short clothes" (a euphemism for the short, skimpy dresses worn in concert saloons), and induced to go to work as a waiter girl in one of his Royal Street establishments. In the meantime, at her father's request, agents from the New York Society for the Prevention of Cruelty to Children launched an investigation into her "disappearance." Ultimately, with the help of "charitable ladies in New Orleans," Jennie was found and returned to New York, along with her belongings. (In a tactic often used by brothel madams, Schoenhausen unsuccessfully attempted to hold Jennie's "respectable" clothes and other belongings as security for what she owed him for her transportation.) According to a newspaper account, Schoenhausen claimed that Jennie and several other girls "had come here to lead an evil life and had used him as a tool to pay their passage." Schoenhausen faced similar accusations in 1893, when a singer named Anna Lassen claimed she had been misled by Schoenhausen about the nature of his business. Although she worked for him for a week to repay her train fare, she refused to "hustle with the men" like the other performers.[30]

Criminal behavior in concert saloons was not limited to the mistreatment or illegal solicitation of waiter girls. In fact, the routine presence of criminal activity constitutes the fourth distinction between concert saloons and respectable theaters. Concert saloons were often the sites of illegal behavior, ranging from simple drunken rowdiness to organized and premeditated assaults and thefts, sometimes perpetrated by or with the knowledge of their proprietors. Newspaper accounts, and the handful of court cases on the books involving Schoenhausen alone, suggest that concert saloons could be dangerous not only to the morals but to the health, wealth, and well-being of their clientele. According to the *Daily Picayune*, "men are drugged and robbed, and strangers visiting the city are decoyed into these places only to leave fleeced of their last dollar and oblivious of what has occurred." The story concluded with the question, "are these dens to continue their predatory and demoralizing offense, making night hideous and the neighborhood intolerable?"[31]

When such incidents were confined to marginal neighborhoods and lower-class populations, the local press was unlikely to notice, much less complain. According to one source, even the police hesitated to enter an area known as the Swamp, preferring to let criminals prey on one another within the boundaries of that tolerated district. Certainly disorder and crime were not new to New Orleans, but the establishment of concert saloons along main thoroughfares and in otherwise respectable neighborhoods meant that all residents were aware of, if not directly threatened by, the violence that took place in and around them. The men who frequented concert saloons might well fall victim to violence perpetrated by their fellow patrons. Even more troubling, corrupt concert-saloon owners and employees sometimes preyed on their own customers.

One of Schoenhausen's experiences during his first few years in New Orleans illustrates how the violent culture of the concert saloon could affect those in their immediate vicinity. In 1869, when he was a bartender at the concert saloon in the St. Louis Rotunda, Schoenhausen murdered an elderly doctor named Henry L. Nelson over a perceived insult. According to subsequent reports, in the early morning hours of April 30, 1869, Schoenhausen left work accompanied by a male friend and two women who worked as waiter girls. On their way home the foursome entered a nearby saloon where Dr. Nelson offered the party a drink. Schoenhausen reportedly considered the offer an insult and answered, "We are not beggars." A brief verbal exchange ensued and, according to witnesses, without further provocation, Schoenhausen shot Nelson "in the heart and in the face." This appalling act carried the violent culture of the concert saloon into a common tavern, with tragic results.[32]

Dr. Nelson died almost immediately, and a coroner's inquest was held on the premises that night. One newspaper account quoted from the inquest;

all witnesses agreed that Schoenhausen was responsible for the murder, but little legal action seems to have followed the incident. Although he was apprehended that night on the scene, he was not named as a defendant in a murder case. (Records for the coroner's jury are missing, but newspaper accounts quoted from them.) Schoenhausen seems to have literally gotten away with murder. Perhaps a large bribe or an influential friend made the matter disappear—a feat made less difficult by the chaotic and sometimes corrupt postwar political context in which concert saloons emerged and Nelson's murder took place. According to historian Joe Gray Taylor, this was "an era when many men preferred to settle their own difficulties with knife, pistol or shotgun rather than depend upon the law. Law enforcement left much to be desired, [and even] white killers of white men were seldom convicted." The absence of even a perfunctory charge and trial is curious, but the violence and chaotic circumstances that prevailed in New Orleans at the time help to explain why Schoenhausen was neither tried nor punished for the cold-blooded murder. His later court testimony makes clear that there was no interruption in his career as an up-and-coming concert-saloon entrepreneur as a result of the killing.[33]

Schoenhausen's first few years in the city's concert-saloon industry were eventful ones. After working at the St. Louis Rotunda for the partnership of Krost and Voegtle, Schoenhausen became a proprietor or partner in many of the city's earliest concert saloons, including the Bismarck and the Napoleon on Royal Street. By 1873, he was proprietor of his own saloon at 44 and 46 Baronne Street, but he was also heavily involved in that year with the opening of a large and apparently troublesome concert saloon on Chartres Street. His partner was Jules Socha, the man who newspapers claimed had joined Schoenhausen in earlier ventures in Galveston and Shreveport.

Socha, who first appeared in city directories in 1869, had been running a saloon at the corner of Chartres and Conti Streets since at least 1870, when he was listed as the proprietor of the Conclave Concert Saloon. According to a twentieth-century source, this establishment included a bar that "was fitted up as an exact replica of a section of [the city's characteristic] burial ovens or vaults, complete with marble slabs on which were chiseled 'Brandy, Whiskey, Gin,' etc. The bartenders were clad as undertakers and when one of them served a customer he opened a vault in the back bar and pulled out a small silver-handled coffin filled with bottles of the desired liquor." The Conclave's faddish appeal was short-lived; although Socha was listed as proprietor at this site from 1870 on, the Conclave disappeared after just one year. In March 1873, Socha was again in partnership with Schoenhausen. The Crystal Palace, as they called their new establishment (no doubt in reference to the great iron-and-glass exhibition hall erected for the 1851 London Exposition), was loathsome to many of its neighbors. It ultimately proved unlucky for its owners as well.[34]

Many in the immediate neighborhood complained about the noise, rowdiness, and ribald behavior at the Crystal Palace, but the customers seem to have been the intended targets of Socha and Schoenhausen's criminal misdeeds. In May 1873, Schoenhausen was charged with stealing a gold watch and a fifty-dollar check from a customer named John Daly. Although the facts of the case are murky, it seems that Daly had been brutally beaten during a fight that began inside the Crystal Palace, suffering injuries from which he eventually died. Although Schoenhausen was not charged with his murder, he was accused of perpetrating the robbery after Daly had been beaten into unconsciousness. In this instance, criminal charges were filed against Schoenhausen, but he was found not guilty. For the second time in four years, Schoenhausen had been clearly associated with an atrocious crime but escaped conviction. His luck would soon end.[35]

Five months after Daly's death, Schoenhausen, Socha, and the Crystal Palace exploded onto the pages of the city's newspapers. For the next two months, their names, and discussions about concert saloons in general, appeared frequently in the city's major newspapers, which were in uncharacteristic agreement about the trouble such establishments were causing the larger community. This wave of publicity was touched off by yet another robbery allegedly perpetrated by Schoenhausen and members of the Crystal Palace staff on October 5, 1873. The victim, Edmond Keith, claimed that $2,050 had been stolen from his vest pocket after Schoenhausen drugged his drink and moved him to another location in the hope that he would not remember where he had been robbed. Schoenhausen, Socha, a waiter girl identified as Bella, and "Columbus Smith, a colored boy who waited in the saloon," were all charged with robbery and larceny. Joining them as a defendant was Jacob Haberlin, a metropolitan policeman who, ironically, had been detailed to keep order inside the Crystal Palace.[36]

Journalistic outrage led to action by the mayor, Louis Wiltz. Even though newspapers claimed that citizens had been complaining about the Crystal Palace since its opening in March, Wiltz paid no attention until the robbery of Keith generated widespread public anger. His inaction can be better understood when one considers the tenuous political situation he faced. From

December of 1872 through 1874, the city's finances were in a shambles and New Orleans, then the state capital, was the site of intermittent street warfare between rival militias representing factions fighting for control of the state government. But Wiltz was finally forced to address the problems at the Crystal Palace. On October 9, in conjunction with metropolitan police superintendent A. S. Badger, Wiltz suspended Socha and Schoenhausen's license to operate. By the next day, however, Socha had found a judge who was willing to place an injunction in the way of the mayor's order. According to the *New Orleans Republican*, by the evening of October 10 the Crystal Palace was again operating at "full blast."[37]

Although the mayor had attempted to close the Crystal Palace by using his power to grant and suspend licenses, the *Republican* complained that under the terms of Ordinance 416, which had been adopted in 1870, the Crystal Palace had been operating illegally since its opening. This ordinance required that the keepers of concert saloons obtain a license that cost three hundred dollars per year. This Socha had done, but, according to the paper, he had failed to observe sections two and three of the ordinance. Section two required that all music and theatrical performances cease by midnight—a clause the Crystal Palace routinely ignored. The third section required the proprietor of a concert saloon to obtain "the written consent of the owners or lessees of one-half of the frontage on both sides of the street of the square where" the business would be located. According to the newspaper, Socha could not have secured approval from any of them even if he had tried. In fact, many of his neighbors had signed a petition asking the city to close the Crystal Palace. Finally, the *Republican* reminded the public that when Socha had previously been found guilty for running a disorderly ale and tippling house, a conviction that the Louisiana Supreme Court had upheld along with a five-thousand-dollar fine, the governor had pardoned him. Apparently Socha had friends in high places.[38]

While the newspapers continued to blast the Crystal Palace and its proprietors, and its neighbors signed petitions asking that the establishment be closed for good, Schoenhausen's trial for robbery began. His lawyers worked vigorously to clear him, but Schoenhausen was found guilty of robbing Keith and was sentenced in mid-November. Although he had escaped punishment for his earlier misdeeds, the judge in the Keith case took them into consideration. In handing down his sentence, the judge "referred to the killing of Nelson [and to] the part he took in the proceeding that led to the miserable end of the unfortunate Daly" and sentenced Schoenhausen to "ten years imprisonment at hard labor in the State Penitentiary." According to a newspaper account, Schoenhausen took "his sentence very hard, turning pale and trembling perceptibly."[39]

The city chose not to prosecute Columbus Smith and the waiter girl Bella, but Socha and Officer Haberlin's trial, which took place after Schoenhausen's, seemed, at least according to one newspaper, to move toward a foregone acquittal. Socha's lawyers managed to disallow Schoenhausen's testimony, but they could not keep his wife Rose off the stand. In lengthy and seemingly candid testimony Rose Schoenhausen admitted that her husband had participated in Keith's robbery and said that even he had been surprised by how much money he had taken from Keith, including a thousand-dollar bill. Schoenhausen and Haberlin had secretly shared this money, and Socha had appeared angry when he discovered their deception. She also maintained that, in her presence, Socha had said to her husband, "Take the whole on your shoulders. Plead guilty and I will get you a pardon."[40]

Eventually Schoenhausen did receive a pardon, but it seems to have been no thanks to Socha, who left New Orleans some time before 1875. Schoenhausen's pardon came only after he had served nine and a half years of his ten-year sentence. But even without these two notorious entrepreneurs, the concert-saloon issue did not go away. In fact, even as Schoenhausen's trial proceeded, newspapers reported that a new concert saloon had sprung up on St. Charles Avenue, one of the city's finest and most prominent thoroughfares.[41]

The Evolving Reputation of Royal Street

Whenever and wherever concert saloons emerged, newspapers ran stories criticizing the activities that went on within them. Editors also expressed a great deal of concern about the effect concert saloons had on the neighborhoods that surrounded them, particularly because they were being established on some of the city's finest and most prominent streets. For instance, in June 1869, the *New Orleans Times* reported that the proprietors of two concert saloons on St. Charles had been charged with "disturbing the peace and being a nuisance to the respectable portion of the community residing in their vicinity." The recorder who heard the case took particular umbrage at the "obscene language and songs" that constituted the entertainment. But the central concerns of the article were the issues of location and respectability:

We can state that in an experience of some years, we have never observed in
any of the dance houses of Gallatin and Barracks streets or the ball rooms of
the demi-monde further down town, the utter abandon which has characterized these places. St. Charles . . . which at one time was a thoroughfare for the
wives and daughters of the most respectable gentlemen in this community, is
now nearly deserted.[42]

In 1893, plaintiffs had similar objections to the location of Schoenhausen's Tivoli Varieties. In particular, they complained that the concert saloon was "within a block of Canal Street and Clay Statue, [on] . . . one of
the most important thoroughfares of the city . . . a street which would be
frequented by almost all the travelling public, or residents of the city of New
Orleans were it not for the character of said establishment."[43]

The plaintiffs were correct that Royal Street was one of the most important thoroughfares of the city, but the character of the street was neither as
static nor as exalted as the plaintiffs in this case contended. Royal had experienced its most important days as a center of retail and banking in the years
before the Civil War. Antebellum travelers like James Davidson commonly
identified it and Chartres Street as the city's most important shopping and
commercial thoroughfares. Royal Street was also the city's banking center
and home to its earliest financial institutions, including the Bank of the
United States and the Banque de la Louisiane.[44]

There were other important structures on Royal, the most important
being the legendary St. Louis Hotel, which took up an entire block between
Royal and Chartres. The hotel was famous as a site for elite social events and
rituals, but it also housed one of the city's primary exchanges or auction
houses. Hewlett's Exchange in the hotel's rotunda shared economic functions with nearby banks and traded in property that included estate goods,
real estate, and human chattel. This mix of economic and social functions
ensured the area's commercial and cultural predominance through the period of the Civil War.

Joseph Roach describes the hotel and its environs as a "kind of homosocial pleasure dome with overlapping commercial and leisure attractions." I
believe Roach uses the term homosocial to convey the male-dominated
commercial and leisure activities that supposedly governed use of the space.
But a closer look reveals that women also played an important role in deline-
ating Royal Street's character and importance. Both travelers' accounts and
slave narratives remind us that women were always in the area, albeit under

rigidly controlled conditions, as both commodities on the auction block and as privileged free women, both white and of color, who were consumers of upscale goods in the adjacent shopping areas. The presence of women in and around the first few blocks of Royal Street was both necessary and problematic for men engaged in business and leisure pursuits there. On Royal Street slave women were exchange goods in the same vicinity where respectable white women and known courtesans exchanged goods. On the one hand, ownership of slave bodies, male or female, conferred privilege upon the males who purchased them. On the other hand, an elite male's prosperity was demonstrated by his ability to indulge his wife or mistress (and sometimes both), in the fine fabrics, furniture, and other goods found on Royal Street. It is little wonder that the idea of female respectability was such a valuable commodity in an area where so many different kinds of women congregated in such close quarters. In the increasingly anonymous and heterogeneous postwar city, without the formal institution of slavery and the unquestioned assumption of white female inviolability to map the social terrain, ideas about female respectability became even more important. Thus the concern with making sure the streets were safe for the "wives and daughters of the most respectable gentlemen in this community" was also a concern about reestablishing white male control over the rules and rituals of the city itself.[45]

If, as John Chase wrote, the first few blocks of Royal before the Civil War were a "stag street hemmed in by petticoats," the exchange of political power would join male leisure as the area's identifying pursuits during and after Federal occupation. Throughout Reconstruction the blocks in and around the St. Louis Hotel were figurative and sometimes literal battlegrounds in the struggles for political power that characterized state and local politics in this era. Between 1874 and 1877, the St. Louis Hotel even served intermittently as the seat of state government. It also housed a concert saloon in which Schoenhausen was employed in 1868.[46]

The area's fortunes took a turn for the worse in the 1860s and 1870s, when many of the banks that had built impressive headquarters on Royal either failed or moved uptown to Canal Street and beyond. Many former bank buildings were converted to concert saloons, which moved into the economic mainstream just as they were moving into the city's physical center. For example, the former headquarters of the state's first bank, The Bank of Louisiana, at the corner of Royal and Conti, housed a concert saloon from 1871 until 1873. Two blocks closer to Canal, the building that had served as headquarters for both the Union and Citizens' Banks housed two different concert saloons. In addition to two others he had on Royal Street, Schoenhausen operated the Tivoli Varieties at this location from 1884 through 1891. Schoenhausen remodeled the building following a fire in 1891; between 1892 and 1893, he operated it as a saloon called the Bank. In December 1893, he converted it back into a concert saloon. That decision would set off the chain of events that culminated in *Koehl v. Schoenhausen.*[47]

Certainly, there had been entertainment establishments in antebellum New Orleans that resembled concert saloons. One thinks of unruly ballrooms like the Louisiana and the Globe, both of which had been associated with prostitution and promiscuous racial mixing. There were also the dance halls of Gallatin Street, in which prostitutes mingled with customers in what one reporter referred to as a state of "awful nudity." Yet the brothels and dance halls of Gallatin Street, while they may have been disorderly and lascivious, were confined to and geographically concentrated in a few blocks that had been given over to similar kinds of establishments and groups of disreputable people. Concert saloons made a sharp departure from the physical segregation or, at the very least, from the perfunctorily covert nature of the sexually oriented businesses that had come before. Not only were concert saloons now regularly established in mainstream retail and business neighborhoods, but on their premises sexual "solicitation was open and public. Privacy was typically confined to the specific act of intercourse upstairs or around the corner in a nearby brothel."[48]

The evolution of legislation aimed at regulating and taxing concert saloons helps to chronicle the controversy that surrounded their emergence as an important part of social life, particularly for males, in postbellum New Orleans. If city officials, whose views on concert saloons varied widely, could not or would not keep them from proliferating, they taxed them at a rate that made clear the city's concern about their morality. In the late antebellum period, all entertainment venues that served alcohol anywhere on the premises paid an annual tax of three hundred dollars. Under this system, taverns, cabarets, cock-pits, theaters, ballrooms, clubrooms, and pleasure gardens were all taxed at the same rate. In 1878, however, the city adopted a taxing and licensing scheme specifically for concert saloons. It required that their proprietors buy a license and pay a fee of twenty-five hundred dollars annually plus an additional fifty dollars designated for the Charity Hospital. In contrast, theaters that ministered "to the intellectual tastes by scenic exhibition, music, etc. . . . without furnishing drinks" were taxed at a rate of two hundred fifty dollars per year, while "coffee-houses doing no other business than that of retailing beverages" were required to pay only seventy-five dollars.[49]

A few years later the state, in this case unabashedly following the lead of New Orleans, decided that heavy taxation of concert saloons was also in the public interest. In Act No. 4 of 1882, the legislature made the level of concert-saloon taxation dependent upon the size of the city in which such establishments were located. For cities with more than twenty-five thousand inhabitants, the tax was one thousand dollars, while it was half that rate for smaller cities. The state tax penalized concert saloons in New Orleans by charging them double the rate assessed those in any other Louisiana city.[50]

Given such high levels of taxation, it is not surprising that the state and the municipality sued many New Orleans concert-saloon proprietors for nonpayment of licensing fees. In every one of these cases the courts found in the city or state's favor, but this did not stop some of the proprietors from suing the city in return. In 1879, for example, a plaintiff named G. S. Goldsmith argued that the license fee was unconstitutional because it exceeded "the aggregate amount exacted from keepers of coffeehouses and theatrical plays where these different occupations and businesses are carried on in separate and distinct places."[51]

The city's legal counsel countered this claim by arguing that the concert saloon's volatile mixture of "music, wine, and women" was explosive, comparing it to "keeping gunpowder, petroleum, and nitro-glycerine in one and the same building." The city attorney's assertions reveal once again an important and persistent theme that runs through criticism directed at concert saloons. Their danger lay in the mixing of potentially incendiary elements. Concert saloons were disorderly spaces that encompassed a mixture of theatrical forms, ethnic and cultural antecedents, people from different social classes, and perhaps most explosive of all, men and women who flouted the rules of respectability brazenly and in public. While gentlemen could occasionally visit concert saloons without sacrificing their respectability, women who frequented or worked in them were assumed to be sexually available, socially compromised, and incapable of achieving the status of respectability.[52]

During the period that it became linked with concert saloons, Royal Street also gained the sobriquet "the Monaco of North America" in reference to its many gaming establishments—or "gambling hells," as they were called at the time. In addition to gambling and the sexually charged atmosphere of concert saloons, one other activity sealed the reputation of Royal Street as a sporting enclave for males during the last two decades of the nineteenth century. During this period New Orleans was "coming to the fore as a Mecca of prize fighting." Not surprisingly, the energetically entrepreneurial Schoenhausen seems to have had a hand in this development. According to one of his obituaries, he "was among the first to introduce glove fighting in the city" and scheduled "pugilistic exhibitions in his dance hall." The article concluded by noting that "the deceased may be said to have been the pioneer of prize fighting as far as this city was concerned."[53]

Concert saloons, "gambling hells," barrooms, and prize fight arenas were four places sporting men could be found in late-nineteenth-century New Orleans, and the first three blocks of Royal Street teemed with such attractions. The street's reputation was surely tarnished by the promiscuous mixing of disreputable women and rowdy men whose class, ethnicity, and behavior marked them as less than respectable. But what about the question of racial mixing in concert saloons?

Testimony from *Koehl v. Schoenhausen* and related cases yields few clues in this regard. In fact, the lack of evidence about interracial sex and socialization in concert saloons suggests that the mixing that concerned city leaders was not racial in nature. In fact, aside from the presence of blackface minstrelsy in concert saloons, race was almost never mentioned in this case or other cases like it. The records from *Koehl v. Schoenhausen* include references to only two people of color. The first, Columbus Smith, was described as "a colored boy" who worked in the Crystal Palace.

The other person of color in this case looms larger but was actually deceased by the time testimony began in this case in May 1894. That man, Thomy Lafon, was one of the city's wealthiest men of color and had been free prior to the Civil War. When he died on December 22, 1893, he left the rental proceeds from many of the commercial buildings he owned to charitable organizations. This was the case with the former bank building that housed the Tivoli Varieties in 1893. The proceeds from the rent of that building, the former home of the Union Bank, were willed to the Thomy Lafon Asylum for Boys. Thus, according to the executor of his estate, the rental proceeds from the Tivoli Varieties went directly to support orphaned boys of color in the city. In one of the many ironies of this case, a sizeable chunk of the proceeds from Schoenhausen's morally questionable business was going to support a home for wayward and orphaned boys of color. (Although he was a man of color, Lafon was so distinguished that one local newspaper referred to him as a "wealthy colored gentleman," suggesting that race could be mitigated by economic accomplishment and class standing, at least posthumously.)[54]

Lafon and Smith aside, individual African Americans seem to have been tangential to the case of *Koehl v. Schoenhausen* and to the controversies over concert saloons in general. Although there were several state statutes in place that guaranteed African Americans unrestricted access to public accommodations in this period, Taylor argues that "segregation was enforced by custom and public opinion, rather than by law." He concludes that, "any commingling of races on any sort of basis of equality was regarded as an enormity." Although race mixing did occur in some leisure venues, like the Franklin Street dives to which concert saloons were compared, it was roundly and consistently criticized. Thus the silence on this issue in *Koehl v. Schoenhausen* suggests that concert saloons were not major offenders when it came to crossing the color line. Otherwise, their critics would have emphasized this infraction.[55]

Many witnesses in *Koehl v. Schoenhausen* testified that the neighborhood in and around the Tivoli Varieties was populated with sporting men and lewd women and that their presence was responsible for the neighborhood's bad reputation. In contrast, concert-saloon critics and the plaintiffs in the case argued that Royal Street was a place for respectable men and women and that the concert saloons were a cancer that had to be extracted. Yet the mere presence—not to mention the proliferation, success, and toleration—of so many risqué amusement establishments indicated that the city's engines of commerce were going to be fueled by decidedly different enterprises after the Civil War than they had been prior to it, at least on Royal Street. As testimony in *Koehl v. Schoenhausen* makes clear, concerns about respectability ranked alongside economic interests as opponents sparred over the fate of the Royal Street concert saloons.

The Matter of James A. Koehl et al. v. Otto Henry Schoenhausen

When Koehl and his fellow plaintiffs filed suit against Schoenhausen in early 1893, the reputation of Royal Street was a central point of contention; but, as testimony makes clear, many other issues were at stake. Certainly the perceived economic interests of the plaintiffs played a role in the timing of this case, but so did their beliefs about respectability or "civilized morality," social class, and ideas about what constituted proper behavior for men and women. As witnesses in this case reiterated, respectability was an increasingly valuable commodity, especially as women moved more assertively in urban spaces. The arguments made by both sides in this case suggest that women—both respectable ladies who made forays into public and public women who worked in Royal Street's concert saloons—were at the center of changing definitions of respectability and ideas about what constituted acceptable social geography. By the early 1890s, changing ideas about female respectability were making both physical and conceptual imprints on the social geography of New Orleans.

While the outlines of the city's emerging economy and broad social geography were still vague in these years, two fires in 1892 helped to clarify the picture considerably, at least for the first few blocks of Bourbon and Royal. On the evening of February 17, 1892, a fire began on Canal Street that damaged or destroyed more than two million dollars in property and merchandise. Among those burned out was Henry Wenger, proprietor of the Bourbon Street beer garden and concert saloon that the *Mascot* had compared to a Franklin Street dive.[56]

Less than two months after Wenger's establishment was destroyed, another spectacular fire did substantial damage to buildings in the first three blocks of Royal. Schoenhausen and other concert-saloon proprietors were prominent among the victims. At least one newspaper editor saw a bright spot in the damage and celebrated the fact that the fires had consumed several concert saloons. "Royal and Bourbon streets, two of the most important streets [in the city], have been purified by fire of these objectionable establishments. Let them remain so, and in the future if we are to have any more of these dives, let them be removed and confined to some less objectionable locality." In their call to "remove and confine" concert saloons to some other locality, the editors of the *Daily Picayune* had begun to argue that separating neighborhoods based on social class, and on the kinds of activities allowed in them, was an idea whose time had come.[57]

Concert-saloon proprietors soon found themselves at the mercy of this increasingly popular belief. For example, in the months following the 1892 fires, Henry Wenger considered reopening his concert saloon on Royal Street in the same location Schoenhausen had occupied from 1884 to 1891. Wenger was discouraged in this attempt by two men, Richard Venables and James A. Koehl, accountant and president respectively of the firm A. M. & J. Solari Ltd. In 1894, Venables took credit for Wenger's ultimate decision to move his business to Burgundy and Customhouse rather than to Royal Street following the 1892 fires. While testifying in *Koehl v. Schoenhausen* Venables recalled, "I fought against Wenger and was the cause" of his subsequent move to the back of the French Quarter. Venables also offered the opinion that Wenger was now "in a proper place." When Wenger had been on Bourbon Street, the firm of A. M. & J. Solari had purchased large advertising spaces in his printed programs. But now, although they had formerly supported Wenger with advertising revenues, Solari's directors believed that their business interests, not to mention their personal reputations, would be better served by separating themselves from their former associate.[58]

James A. Koehl, the driving force behind the case against Schoenhausen, testified that he was not opposed to concert saloons in principle. In fact, he was a great frequenter of such establishments and a generous patron of their performers and employees. Two female concert-saloon performers testified that they had been intimate with Koehl, and he admitted to affairs with several others. When Schoenhausen was asked about the number of encounters he had had with concert-saloon waiter girls and performers, he replied that "like Mr. Koehl," he would need "to get me a great big book to remember." While Koehl did not deny his visits to concert saloons and brothels, his lawyers took pains to point out that he was unmarried. But Koehl's admissions gave Schoenhausen's lawyers an opportunity to argue that Koehl,

> One of the moralists in this case, who is seeking to suppress concert saloons, is a frequenter of such establishments, and an associate of the women who are employed in [them]. . . . [I]t is not because of Schoenhausen's concert saloon that [Koehl's] place of business is not frequented by the most reputable ladies in New Orleans, but it is because of the associations of this gentleman that the most reputable ladies of New Orleans avoid his society.[59]

Koehl's ability to press this case and simultaneously continue to patronize concert saloons demonstrates yet again that the requirements of respectability were much less rigid for men than they were for women. This was especially true for unmarried men like Koehl. But as Schoenhausen's lawyer suggested, Koehl may have paid a price, both social and economic, in being snubbed by the "most reputable ladies of New Orleans."

Whatever the ultimate worth of the lawyer's assertions, there was a great deal more at stake in this court case than the reputations of the principals. Following the fires of 1892, extensive rebuilding and new construction took place in the first two blocks of Royal. Two new hotels were among the most impressive and costly additions to the street. J. B. Solari, who was Koehl's uncle, had begun construction on one of those new hotels in 1891. In May of that year, he told reporters that his new hotel would be "an edifice worthy of the age of progress in which we live." He concluded by noting that the new Cosmopolitan Hotel would "solicit the patronage of commercial travelers, not solely drummers, but capitalists, men of means, solid men who will come to New Orleans either on a tour of business or pleasure." Although the new hotel was owned by the firm of A. M. & J. Solari, Koehl's family business, it was being leased and managed by Joseph Voegtle when it opened in February 1894. In his capacity as manager of the Cosmopolitan, Voegtle was a party to the suit against Schoenhausen, although he had employed Schoenhausen at the St. Louis Rotunda and was himself a former concert-saloon manager. Questioned on the stand about this apparent contradiction, Voegtle said that when he had been involved with concert saloons they were "not carried on the way these saloons are carried on now." But if concert saloons had changed in the intervening years, so had the city itself. As public spaces became less exclusively male spaces, accommodation had to be made for the novel presence of respectable women in public spaces. Sexually oriented businesses like concert saloons presented politicians and property-owners with particularly difficult dilemmas.[60]

The design and layout of the new Cosmopolitan Hotel, for example, expressed in three dimensions many of the issues raised by witnesses in *Koehl v. Schoenhausen*. J. B. Solari had envisioned a hotel that would solicit the patronage of "men of means" who would come to New Orleans for "business or pleasure." He did not mention women, but when the hotel was completed in early 1894, it had a ladies' restaurant and even a separate entrance for ladies on Bourbon Street. The hotel cut through the entire block, and guests could enter the hotel on either Royal or Bourbon Street. According to a guidebook published the year it opened "the Royal Street front [was] devoted to its transient business, and the Bourbon Street side to family and permanent guests." The guide went on to note that its location was "centrally situated—convenient to all the places of amusement and business and . . . street car lines."[61]

In his testimony Venables, the accountant for Solari's, maintained that the company had been forced to build the Bourbon Street annex "in consequence of the locality of our place on Royal Street in proximity to Schoenhausen." On the stand, he maintained that the Cosmopolitan's location near Schoenhausen was a costly liability, but other witnesses suggested that the opposite was true. A former hotel employee testified that messenger boys were routinely sent over to Schoenhausen's from the Cosmopolitan to solicit girls for hotel guests, presumably for purposes of prostitution. Even Voegtle admitted that his information about the reputation of Schoenhausen's business had come from his own customers, especially visitors to the city. While Voegtle and other prosecution witnesses tried hard to portray their proximity to Schoenhausen as an economic liability that discouraged respectable patrons from visiting them, their own testimony and that of their guests and employees raised significant doubts that this was the case. Perhaps the contradiction is explicable in part because the requirements of respectability for female patrons were different from those for male guests. In the case of the Cosmopolitan, these separate standards resulted in separate male and female entrances, meeting places, and of course, expectations about how respectable women, at least, would behave.[62]

Anthony Monteleone, who a decade later would be accused of concubinage with his sister-in-law Sophie Jahraus, built the other new hotel that opened on Royal Street around the time the suit against Schoenhausen was first filed. An impressive five-story building at the corner of Royal and Customhouse, the Hotel Victor was directly across the street from Schoenhausen's Tivoli Varieties. The building was managed by Louise Bero, whose husband Victor ran a locally famous Bourbon Street restaurant that also bore his name. Like the Cosmopolitan, the Victor was a "favorite resort for travelling commercial men." While on the stand in the matter of *Koehl v. Schoenhausen,* Mrs. Bero testified that the noise from the concert saloon made it impossible for her guests to sleep, but other testimony suggested that sleeping was not on the minds of many of them. Many witnesses for the defense and some for the prosecution implied that some registered guests, as well as men and women who came directly from the concert saloons, used both hotels as houses of assignation. One employee of the Victor testified that he had been corrected sharply by Mrs. Bero when he had raised a question about a male guest who seemed to have a different "wife" every time he checked in. In this case Mrs. Bero, presumably a respectable woman herself, was protecting the sexual double standard while at the same time looking out for her business interests.[63]

Although Monteleone was not formally a party to the suit, he was one of the prosecution's most enthusiastic witnesses. He maintained that he had invested most of his money in the new building only after he had received assurances from the former mayor that no more concert saloons would be allowed in the area. Schoenhausen's attorney reminded Monteleone that concert saloons had been in the neighborhood for as long as he had owned property there. Monteleone's answer was brief but revealed the role that economic interests played in the timing of the suit: "Yes, but I had no building up [then], a new building." More to the point, in the new tourist and leisure economy that was developing in New Orleans and elsewhere, hotels hoped to draw unfamiliar, even anonymous, people to their doors. In some cases, the patrons' anonymity allowed hotel proprietors to plead ignorance when renting their rooms for less than respectable purposes. But they also sought to attract a respectable trade, and that was difficult to do with the concert saloons so near. None of the plaintiffs, including Monteleone, argued for the obliteration of the concert saloons. They simply wanted them out of their vicinity so that their own reputations and the reputations of their businesses would be above reproach.[64]

The final plaintiff, Lawrence Fabacher, proprietor of Fabacher's Restaurant and Hotel, had the same mix of economic and conceptual concerns. Like the other plaintiffs, Fabacher had added substantially to the seating capacity of his restaurant following the 1892 fire. Yet he bristled at suggestions that his restaurant and hotel had profited from the presence of concert saloons on the street. Predictably, Schoenhausen and witnesses for the defense disagreed. Women who worked in the concert saloons testified that Fabacher's, which ran a separate ladies' restaurant that was open late into the night, had routinely helped them complete a maneuver they referred to as "the Great American Shake." As the women explained it, after they dined at Fabacher's with men who had escorted them there from the concert saloons, restaurant employees would allow the women to go out through a back alley to "shake" the men with whom they had come in. (Perhaps these women wanted a free meal but did not want to bother with their escorts once the check was paid.) Fabacher and his employees hotly denied the women's claims, but he could not deny that in 1888 he had signed a petition approving the presence of three of Schoenhausen's concert saloons on Royal.[65]

Fabacher was not the only one who had previously had business dealings with Schoenhausen. Prior to 1893, cordial and even cooperative business relationships had existed between Schoenhausen and most of the plaintiffs. For instance, after a fire on Royal Street in the 1880s, Schoenhausen had subleased space in a former concert saloon to Solari's so that they could keep their business running while their own building was repaired. There is no smoking gun in the ashes of the 1892 fires that conclusively connects the moral indignation of the plaintiffs to their recent real-estate improvements. But by the time rebuilding and new construction were complete, all of them

As shown in this early-twentieth-century photograph, the intersection of Royal Street and
Customhouse (now Iberville) had been cleansed of concert saloons but not entirely of
male leisure establishments. The building in the left foreground that housed the Tivoli
Varieties concert saloon in the 1890s had become a billiard hall by this time.
Courtesy Historic New Orleans Collection, acc. no. 1974.25.9.192

owned or managed much more valuable property on Royal Street than they
had prior to the fires of 1892. As their new buildings rose in 1893, so did the
moral indignation of Koehl and his fellow plaintiffs. Yet their moral indignation was enhanced by their new economic imperatives. Their new upscale
hotels required upscale, respectable patrons. They might be able to accept
some trade on the sly from concert saloons, and their male patrons could
always visit the saloons with no problem, but their new buildings made respectability all the more important for them and the client base they hoped
to attract. Single men might reasonably stay in a hotel with a compromised
reputation, but gentlemen would never take their wives or families to one.
In this new, less sex-segregated economy, respectability was a valuable commodity indeed.

Monteleone testified that he had built his new hotel only because Joseph
Shakespeare, the previous mayor, had assured him that there would be no

more concert saloons on Royal. By the time his hotel was completed however, there had been a change in mayoral administrations. The new mayor, John Fitzpatrick, was a machine politician, boxing referee, and friend of Schoenhausen's. If Shakespeare, a reform mayor, had been averse to concert saloons, his successor had no compunction about permitting them. In fact, on December 10, 1893, the city officially recognized concert saloons as lawful establishments. The ruling by Mayor Fitzpatrick made it clear to Koehl and his allies that city hall would not be on their side in the matter of concert saloons. Koehl appealed to the courts, begging them to intervene on the grounds that concert saloons were a nuisance and financially damaging to nearby businesses. Schoenhausen and his attorneys disagreed vociferously with the second assertion. According to them, "no injury whatever, in a pecuniary point of view, has been sustained by the plaintiffs. . . . On the contrary, property in the immediate vicinity of this concert hall (which is only carried on in the night-time) has greatly enhanced in value."[66]

Why had Fabacher and the other plaintiffs who had co-existed with, and in some cases supported, Schoenhausen's establishments in earlier years suddenly turned on him in 1893? Obviously, part of the answer is connected to the expansion of their holdings and costly improvements to their properties on Royal Street. With so much more to lose, they reacted more strongly to any perceived threat to the health of their greatly expanded businesses. This reaction could only have been exacerbated by a nationwide economic crisis that began in 1893. A third factor that helps to explain the plaintiffs' desire to reform Royal Street is that during this same period many reform campaigns were bearing fruit in the state, chief among them the drive to rid Louisiana of its notoriously corrupt lottery. Yet the less tangible but no less important issue of the plaintiffs' own respectability also played a role in their changing attitude.

Moral judgments were intertwined with economic concerns and beliefs about social class in the testimony offered by witnesses in this and similar cases. For instance, ideas about social class and respectability merged in the testimony offered by Victor Bero. When prodded by Schoenhausen's lawyer, Bero admitted that there was not much substantive difference between the "ballet at the French Opera House" and the performances given in concert saloons. But, Bero opined, "the difference is that the French Opera House is the temple of art and the other one is a dive." The lawyer responded, "One is the rich man's opera, and the other a poor man's opera, is that it?" Bero disagreed that this was the case, but the language of class and respectability linked both men's statements. Hotel keepers like Bero, Fabacher, and Monteleone sought respectable patrons, and, in turn, had to adopt the requirements of civilized morality as their own.[67]

For Bero, the critical difference between the two lay in the fact that "in the French Opera women are not allowed to come in and sit in a man's lap and ask to treat and call him darling and so on." In this response, Bero also tied the issues of gender and respectability together and agreed, like most witnesses in this and similar cases, that the women who worked in concert saloons did not behave as respectable women should. In fact, when Henry Wenger fought the designation of his establishment as a concert saloon, the behavior of the women who frequented his establishment was the focus of most of the testimony. Most witnesses agreed that the women who went to Wenger's were the same kind of women who worked in or visited other concert saloons—"lewd and abandoned women," according to one of them. Other witnesses focused on the women's behavior, noting that they smoked in public or came into the establishment without escorts. A local reporter summed up the prevailing attitude about the women by testifying that their predominant characteristic was that they were "loose" or "women of the street." The witnesses' use of slang terms for prostitutes was no mistake. Further, nearly all of them agreed that they would not take their wives or sisters to such a place. As such, the doors of the concert saloon constituted a dividing line between respectable women and women who, if they were not prostitutes, behaved as if they were. The debate over the kind of women who frequented concert saloons also reveals that definitions of women's respectability were themselves in flux. Thus, respectable women on the street had to be careful not to be mistaken for women of the street, just as liberated women had to be careful not to appear lewd and abandoned.[68]

There was less certainty about the character of the men who visited concert saloons, especially if they just visited "out of curiosity." The plaintiffs' lawyer opined that "of course gentlemen go" to concert saloons from time to time. But he asked several witnesses to tell him "as a rule, what is the class of people who go to Schoenhausen's place?" Koehl responded that "the class of people that sort of business caters to . . . are not . . . the best." He called some of them "toughs" and said that one, a prize fighter named Kid Wilson, was "not a gentleman." Other witnesses—who, like Koehl, occasionally visited concert saloons but thought themselves respectable—agreed that the male habitués of concert saloons were "not first class citizens" and "not of the best class." Clearly, social and economic class mattered when it came to determining who was a gentleman and who was a "tough" among the concert saloons' heterogeneous patrons.[69]

For the plaintiffs in this case, being identified as respectable mattered a great deal. Nearly all of them were first- or second-generation immigrants. As they made their way up the ladder of economic success, they understood that being accepted by the best people in New Orleans also meant embracing their definition of civilized morality. Thus, economic interest was an incentive to embrace respectability and to eschew their former friendly relations with the avowedly disreputable Schoenhausen. Yet their quest to drive him from Royal Street did not require that his concert saloons close or that patrons not visit them. The plaintiffs were willing to profit from concert-saloon clients and employees, but they did not want to share urban space with them any longer.

In addition to promoting their own respectability, the male plaintiffs were eager to identify themselves and their businesses with progressive changes in the city's economy. For example, all the plaintiffs and their businesses were featured in a splashy city directory published in 1894. The opening page claimed that in New Orleans "Progress is making prodigious breaches in the Old order, letting in the New." This directory echoed the sentiments of J. B. Solari who had claimed in 1891 that the new Cosmopolitan Hotel would be an indicator of the "age of progress" in which he believed he lived. In the 1894 directory, the words "progress" and "prosperity" appeared many times, as did pictures of the plaintiffs and their establishments. It should come as no surprise that Schoenhausen and his concert saloons were not mentioned or depicted at all. In the progressive vision of the directory—and of the plaintiffs— there was no longer any place for businesses like Schoenhausen's, at least not on Royal Street.[70]

Not everyone agreed, however, and many persons testified in Schoenhausen's defense: ten policemen, two municipal authorities (including Mayor Fitzpatrick), and three present or former female performers from his concert saloons. The testimony of other Royal Street businessmen like W. G. Tebault, who owned a furniture store and other real estate on the street, was the most directly damaging to the plaintiffs. Tebault maintained that his Royal Street properties had actually increased in value despite their proximity to concert saloons; one of his buildings actually housed a concert saloon. Tebault did admit that he believed concert saloons were immoral, but he rented space to one, he said, because "I consulted an old friend, a very pious gentleman . . . and he told me I couldn't control the morals of this town, and as [the building] was a theater, I had better rent it. He would. I took his advice."[71]

James McCracken, a property owner called as a witness for the plaintiffs, actually changed his mind on the stand. He testified:

> I find that his place is differently conducted from what it was formerly. It is more closed, not so open, not so public. For those reasons I have changed my mind. I was very much opposed to his opening his place in the first place. I subscribed to a fund to prevent him and signed a petition . . . [but] my mind has underwent a change.[72]

A. M. Aucoin, recorder for the Second District, also testified for Schoenhausen. He defended concert saloons, although he admitted they were "not convents." Perhaps more tellingly, Aucoin recalled an occasion when he and three gentlemen friends had taken three burlesque performers out after their show at one of Schoenhausen's concert saloons. He recalled taking the women to a brothel where "they stripped them naked and made them dance. They wanted to see the town and we showed them the town."[73]

The notion that concert saloons and sexually explicit behavior such as Aucoin described were characteristic of the city in the 1890s was provocative and, to many New Orleanians, troubling. But the plaintiffs were more troubled by the location of concert saloons than by their existence. In their concern for the reputations and fortunes of their businesses, Koehl and the other plaintiffs rejected the contention that Royal Street had a long-standing reputation for prostitution and other rowdy leisure pursuits. In the process of suing Schoenhausen, Koehl and the others also challenged their specific locale's reputation for sexual liberality. But the very existence of their lawsuit suggested how prominent and successful sexually oriented businesses like Schoenhausen's had become by the mid-1890s.

With undisguised reluctance and no small amount of disgust, the Louisiana Supreme Court ruled in favor of Schoenhausen. Their opinion read in part, "the judgment of the lower court enjoins defendant from conducting the business of a concert saloon. But his licenses authorize that business. As long as that legislation is on the statute books, it is obligatory on the courts. The statutes suppose the concert saloon business to be reputable."[74]

The state's highest justices did not think Schoenhausen's establishment was respectable, and they called on local police authorities to monitor the Tivoli Varieties closely. But that would soon be unnecessary. Schoenhausen's legal victory was apparently both hollow and costly. The Tivoli Varieties

closed before the state supreme court's ruling was a year old, perhaps because the court fight had depleted Schoenhausen's financial resources. By
1898, he had sold his home on fashionable upper Canal Street. (In 1905, an
obituary noted that "his entire fortune including [the] beautiful home in
Canal Street, was swallowed up in a vain fight against the reform of Royal
Street.") By 1900 he was managing a saloon at the corner of Customhouse
and Burgundy in the same building that his former competitor, Henry
Wenger, had been forced to occupy after the 1892 fire and the campaign to
keep him from relocating to Royal. Although Schoenhausen disappears from
city directories after 1900, his 1905 obituaries claimed that he spent the last
five years of his life working as a bouncer in a Storyville dance hall. Ironically, the dance hall was in the same neighborhood as the Franklin Street
dives the *Mascot* had criticized and compared to concert saloons as early as
the 1880s.[75]

Schoenhausen's obituaries fashioned his life story into a morality tale. In
the newspaper versions of his rise and fall, he was portrayed as a bright
young man full of promise who, though prosperous for a time, ultimately
fell victim to his own criminality, vanity, and promotion of immoral pursuits. Schoenhausen was a murderer, a thief, and probably an alcoholic. He
was, by his own admission, often intoxicated, and, according to newspaper
accounts, a habitual criminal who was crude in both speech and manner.
But in one important respect he was a visionary. Schoenhausen was one of
the first people in post–Civil War New Orleans who consciously promoted
the "let the good times roll" attitude for which the city would become so
famous (or infamous) in the years immediately after this case was decided.
Schoenhausen not only recognized the profit to be gained from sexually oriented businesses, he also saw how the appeal of illicit sexuality permeated
and enriched the businesses of others, even those who were suing him. The
restaurant and hotel proprietors, although they wanted him off their street,
did not hesitate to serve and house the women who worked in his concert
saloons, and the men who were their patrons. Testimony from *Koehl v.
Schoenhausen* leaves little doubt that nearby hotels served as assignation
houses or meeting places for men who wanted to enjoy the company of the
concert-saloons' waiter girls.

Ironically, one of Schoenhausen's obituaries appeared next to an article
headlined "Talk of More Hotels." The story discussed the city's growing appeal as a tourist destination and noted the acute need for new hotels to accommodate all the visitors. Although the plaintiffs in this case would have

been loath to admit it, the sexualized entertainment venues developed by Schoenhausen and others like him played a significant role in making New Orleans such a popular tourist destination. This would continue to be the case long after Royal Street was purged of its concert saloons.[76]

The legal losers in this case were the long-term financial winners. Anthony Monteleone eventually acquired the building that housed the Tivoli Varieties. More notably, he ultimately expanded the Hotel Victor into a sprawling hotel that bore his own name. Today the Monteleone hotel covers the entire block of Royal Street between Iberville and Bienville and remains in family hands. In recent decades, the Monteleone has been joined by another looming multistory hotel, a Holiday Inn that sits directly across from the now dilapidated Cosmopolitan Hotel building. The Cosmopolitan later became the Astor Hotel, which closed in the early 1970s. The building, though no longer a hotel, remains in the Solari family.[77]

In its heyday, Fabacher's Restaurant claimed to be the South's largest. The restaurant no longer exists, but until his death in 1923 Lawrence Fabacher was one of the city's and the hospitality industry's most successful and respected businessmen. He "amassed a fortune in the restaurant business, and was successful later in his direction of the Jackson Brewing Company." His home on St. Charles Avenue, "one of the show places of New Orleans," included a casino, stables, and "a marble swimming-tank with Roman baths surrounding it." Solari's, the firm run by Koehl, ultimately became a noted Royal Street restaurant. Today the Solari building houses the restaurant Mr. B's, which is owned by the Brennan family, and an upper-level parking garage.[78]

In his testimony in *Koehl v. Schoenhausen,* W. G. Tebault reasoned that he could not "control the morals of the town." Neither could Koehl or any of the other plaintiffs in this case, but they did object to the idea that sexually oriented businesses were characteristic and therefore legitimate features of their section of Royal Street. Their lawyers wrote, "To hold that this locality in the very heart of the city . . . is dedicated and given up to establishments such as defendant conducts, would impede the march of progress, improvement and enterprise in the city of New Orleans."[79]

Progress was an important word and theme for the plaintiffs in this case. At the end of the century, they and other like-minded businessmen hailed the city's progress and worked hard to portray New Orleans as a clean, efficient, pleasant, prosperous, and respectable place of resort. Other men, like Otto Schoenhausen, saw a great deal more potential for profit in appealing to those who had a taste for Venus, Bacchus, and the Sirens. In the mid-1890s, sexually oriented businesses like concert saloons were under fire, and progressive businessmen like Koehl, Fabacher, and Voegtle had decided that they belonged in the back of town rather than in their back yards.

The plaintiffs in *Koehl v. Schoenhausen* sought to separate their businesses spatially from the morally compromised concert saloons and, in the process, to separate themselves from their less respectable neighbors. This same drama was played out citywide two years later. In the next municipal elections, a reform administration headed by Mayor Walter C. Flower came into office. Even though Koehl and his fellow plaintiffs had warned that to turn a "locality in the very heart of the city" over to sexually oriented businesses would impede "progress, improvement, and enterprise," Flower's administration oversaw the adoption of just such a process. Although in retrospect it may seem strange that a reform administration created a vice district, the case of *Koehl v. Schoenhausen* helps explain how reformers' economic concerns and beliefs about respectability conditioned their calls for the spatial segregation of sinful businesses. Finally, this case demonstrates that the creation of the city's last and most notorious vice district was the result of a process in which individuals took the stand, took sides, and took careful inventory of their own interests before deciding what ought to be done about "illegal, immoral, lascivious, and disorderly business[es]."

Koehl v. Schoenhausen shows us that the seeds of a segregated district were sown well before 1897, when Sidney Story introduced his now infamous vice-district ordinance. When city leaders considered where to place the boundaries of that district, they were drawn, as the *Mascot*'s writer had been ten years earlier, to the area of "Negro dives" and dance halls on Franklin Street. While it is generally known that this final vice district was established to control prostitution, it is less well understood that sexualized entertainment outlets like concert saloons were also required to do business within its boundaries. The conceptual and behavioral equivalence that the *Mascot* had noted between concert saloons and Franklin Street dives would become a legal requirement and a physical reality after 1897.

"Where the Least Harm Can Result"

SEX, RACE, AND RESPECTABILITY
IN A SINGLE NEIGHBORHOOD

On March 18, 1896, Dr. Samuel Olliphant presided over a rowdy meeting focused on controlling the spread of smallpox in New Orleans. Olliphant, who had been the friend and physician of the late Joseph Mathis, had recently become president of the state board of health. Those present at the meeting agreed that the disease was most likely to originate among Negroes; one person noted that of "160 cases now in the pesthouse, 154 cases were negroes." The alleged association between African Americans and the disease led one doctor to suggest that the board should have the mayor close the "negro dance halls" on Franklin Street as they were a central site for the spread of the contagion. That plan was rejected, however, because of the fear that the closure "would only result in the unclean blacks being disseminated among corner groceries and clean drinking dens, thus widening the influences of contamination." The board did, however, limit the movements of African Americans into and out of the city for a brief period, hoping to control spread of the disease.[1]

Exactly two months later, the United States Supreme Court issued its ruling in the case of *Plessy v. Ferguson.* That landmark judicial decision led to the legal principle of separate but equal and facilitated myriad forms of racial segregation that would dominate life in the South for the next six decades. But segregation was not always enacted on the basis of race. The very next year, for instance, the city of New Orleans adopted ordinances that forcibly segregated more than a thousand women, both black and white, in a neighborhood that was also home to the morally objectionable and, according to some observers, disease-ridden Franklin Street dives. Prostitution ordinances were the city's first residential segregation ordinances—enforced not on the basis of race but on the basis of gender, occupation, and the public identification of a woman as a prostitute.

It is no coincidence that this vice district was created the year after the Supreme Court's final decision in the *Plessy* case. As the suggestions made at the 1896 board of health meeting indicate, physical segregation was a popular solution to a range of social problems at the turn of the century, including the spread of disease, race relations, and prostitution. And just as the board of health temporarily limited the mobility of African Americans in mid-1896, city leaders sought to control the movements, the domiciles, and the lives of thousands of women they deemed lewd, abandoned, and disreputable in the years between 1897 and 1917.

When city leaders selected the boundaries for New Orleans's last, smallest, yet most notorious vice district, they were drawn to the same area that the *Mascot's* writers had criticized in 1887 and the board of health had focused on in 1896—the area surrounding the Franklin Street dives. That decision, and the events that followed, led to an extremely contentious court case, which, like *Plessy,* went all the way to the Supreme Court. Testimony and arguments in the new case tackled many of the same issues and raised many of the same concerns that had permeated the case against Otto Schoenhausen and his concert saloons. This time, however, the municipality itself was being sued for creating what some citizens called a nuisance. Specifically, plaintiffs objected to the designation of a single neighborhood as the city's officially recognized vice district. This newly defined district, sometimes called the segregated district, also came to be known as Storyville, in mocking homage to the sponsor of the ordinances in question, a native New Orleanian named Sidney Story.

The case filed against the final version of the vice-district ordinance, and the events leading up to its adjudication, reveal a great deal about the variety of attitudes about prostitution in turn-of-the-century New Orleans. The testimony and arguments in court records also reveal how conceptual beliefs about prostitution merged with ideas about race and respectability and contributed to the decision to segregate prostitutes and sexually oriented businesses spatially within the city's boundaries. In fact, looking back at these events through the prism of interrelated ideas about sex, race, and respectability offers important new insights into the city's notorious culture of commercial sexuality at the turn of the century. This same constellation of

ideas also helps us to understand why, in late 1897, the city's leaders chose
to resize and resituate the city's vice district one last time.[2]

Shortly after the July 6 adoption of Ordinance 13,485 C.S., which stipulated the final boundaries of a new vice district, George L'Hote filed suit
against the city of New Orleans in September 1897. A respected white man
and successful business owner, L'Hote based his complaint on the damage
the new vice district would do to the reputation of his neighborhood and to
the presumed respectability of his wife and family, who would be forced to
live in close proximity to the new district. Two other parties who owned
property inside the revised district, joined L'Hote in his suit. Bernardo Galvez Carbajal, a Spanish immigrant known commonly as B.G., claimed that
the value of his properties inside the new boundaries would be damaged if
the Story Ordinances were enforced. Yet his testimony made clear that Carbajal's real economic concern lay in retaining prostitutes as tenants in the
numerous properties he owned outside the boundaries of the newly delineated district. Although they disagreed on the particulars, both L'Hote and
Carbajal argued that the boundaries of the new vice district would damage
their personal, business, and real-estate interests. The second intervener to
L'Hote's suit was the Union Chapel, a thriving Methodist Episcopal Church
(MEC) congregation. Although the church had a large membership, its
members and leaders, who were all African American, lacked meaningful
political influence. Moreover, testimony and the arguments deployed by the
city against the claims of the Union Chapel provide numerous examples of
how whites assumed that African Americans as a class were sexually immoral. In part, this belief led city leaders to place both sections of the city's
vice district in areas heavily populated by African Americans. The arguments
pursued by each of these plaintiffs, and by the defendants, have something
critical to tell us about the case and about commercial sexuality in late-
nineteenth-century New Orleans. But it was L'Hote, at least initially, who
was the central force behind pressing the suit. As the case wound through
city and state courts and, by 1900, to the Supreme Court, its testimony and
pleadings created a rich and varied record of opinions about prostitution
and sexualized entertainment in the Great Southern Babylon on the eve of
the twentieth century. *L'Hote v. City of New Orleans* demonstrates how evolving ideas about sexuality, race, and respectability collided with one another
in the city reputed to be the South's most sinful. The substantial legal debris
allows us a glimpse of New Orleans's culture of commercial sexuality at the
moment of Storyville's creation.[3]

Storyville in Context

Popular writers and local lore have consistently portrayed Storyville and its era as the zenith of outrageous commercial sexuality in New Orleans—if not the entire nation. Yet a closer look at the historical record suggests a much different scenario. It was not at all unusual for American cities to grapple with the problem of prostitution after the Civil War. In fact, most cities made some kind of accommodation with prostitution in this period. Methods of accommodation included simply ignoring the problem, protecting prostitution through informal agreements and graft, or allowing prostitution to be carried out in certain informally recognized districts. What set New Orleans apart was the frank and direct way the city's leaders chose to delineate its vice district through municipal ordinance.

But the 1897 Story Ordinances were not the first of their kind passed in New Orleans, as the 1857 Lorette Ordinance reminds us. Nor did they differ in practical effect from decisions made by many other American cities, large and small, in the same period. Certainly some aspects of the city's 1897 legal compromise with prostitution interests were unique. But the idea that prostitution was a problem best dealt with through some combination of residential segregation, registration, and intensive police monitoring was put into practice in cities all across America in the late nineteenth century. Storyville was outrageous, both in size and in the size of its regional and national reputation. It was also distinct in the specificity of its enabling legislation and in the long-term cultural impact of events that took place within and around it. Early practitioners of jazz, for instance, honed their craft and their musical style at approximately the same time—though not, as many believe, exclusively within the bounds of Storyville. But, as a solution to the problem of prostitution at the turn of the century, the city's decision to segregate its vice district was neither unique nor particularly innovative. As the city's experience with the rise of concert saloons demonstrates, New Orleans's well-known and problematic population of prostitutes made it more typical than atypical among American cities in this period.

According to David Pivar, "in the late 1860s and early 1870s many states and municipalities considered legalizing prostitution." In 1870, for instance, the St. Louis City Council passed an ordinance that mandated licensing, medical inspection, and police control of prostitutes "by using a loophole in state law." Controversy over the St. Louis Social Evil Law raged for four years, until a state constitutional convention removed the loophole, bringing

St. Louis's experiment with legally regulated prostitution to an end. Many other states and municipalities had similar debates, and, while most efforts to regulate prostitution, thereby giving it some measure of legal recognition and legitimacy, were defeated, "the national debate over regulation extended over a number of decades."[4]

By the time Sidney Story presented his ordinances to the New Orleans City Council in 1897, de facto toleration of prostitution in the nation's cities was the rule rather than the exception. According to Mark Thomas Connelly, "during the first two decades of the twentieth century there was at least one red-light district in virtually every American city with a population over 100,000, and in many smaller ones, too." Throughout the country some small towns and sprawling urban centers ignored the statutes that made prostitution illegal. In St. Paul, Minnesota, for example, "prostitution was illegal under both state law and city ordinance, but enforcement took the form of arresting each of the city's madams at monthly intervals and fining them according to the number of inmates in their houses—in effect taxing their operations." In Atlanta, officials and most of the city's population turned a blind eye and "permitted the breaking of city and state laws against prostitution . . . for more than fifty years."[5]

While in some cities municipal authorities simply ignored prostitution, in others the accommodation with prostitution interests was explicit. In New Orleans the pattern of formal legal accommodation with prostitution interests dated to 1857. In the forty years between adoption of the Lorette and the Story Ordinances, the city acted at least eight other times to control prostitution through a variety of means. Municipal authorities did not try to subdue Satan in the way that Ted Ownby suggests was characteristic in the rest of the largely rural South. Certainly the attachment to place or "home sentiment" that Ownby describes as being central to southern culture between 1865 and 1920 was present in New Orleans. But the evangelical piety that he identifies as being typically or generally southern was not, providing at least part of the explanation for why Catholic New Orleans was considered so different from the rest of the South. In 1897, in an extremely direct and decidedly non-Protestant fashion, New Orleans city officials, acknowledging their belief that sins of the flesh were inevitable, looked Satan in the eye, cut a deal, and gave him his own address.[6]

This bold municipal maneuver had a number of subsequent imitators. While Storyville was one of the largest vice districts in the nation, in Louisiana alone Shreveport, Alexandria, and Crowley adopted ordinances that

mimicked the Story Ordinances after the court battles surrounding their legality were complete. In 1908 Houston, Texas, also passed a similar vice-
district ordinance when changes in state laws threatened the city's former
system of toleration. In short, prostitution districts, whether formally legislated or informally tolerated, were a typical American way of dealing with
what many claimed was a "plague of prostitution" that threatened the nation's cities in the decades after the Civil War.[7]

While Storyville was by no means a singular phenomenon, during the
twentieth century it gained a reputation as unique. This is partially due to
the parochial nature of what has been written about it, and also to the widely
held notion that New Orleans is *sui generis,* unique among American cities.
The rose-colored, though myopic, view of the segregated district by its popular chroniclers has combined with the city's long-standing reputation as
the Great Southern Babylon to obscure our view of what Storyville was in
fact. Even more obscure are the reasons why the city chose to revise its policy on prostitution in 1897. Before we can understand George L'Hote's objections to the district proposed by Story, we must briefly consider the
process and the precedents that led to the creation of the city's last, most
infamous, but surprisingly smallest legally recognized prostitution district.[8]

Although a local court overturned the licensing requirements of the 1857
Lorette Ordinance, many of its provisions were reiterated in future ordinances. On at least eight occasions in the next four decades the city council
adopted ordinances designed to regulate, control, or simply profit from
prostitution. Their provisions ranged from defining brothels as nuisances to
placing prostitutes and brothel owners under heavy taxation. Most commonly, they altered the geographic provisions set down in the Lorette Ordinance. Five of the eight ordinances passed between 1857 and 1890 included
some sort of spatial stipulation. Except for ordinance 3428 O.S., which expanded the Lorette limits three months after its original passage, and 6302
O.S., which simply reiterated the geographic provisions adopted in 1857, all
ensuing ordinances with geographic provisions further limited the areas in
which prostitution would be tolerated. These ordinances most often focused
on brothel prostitution and discouraged streetwalking by placing restrictions
on the movement and activities of known prostitutes.[9]

Ironically, as the city's population grew, its officially delineated vice districts shrank. By 1890, under the terms of Ordinance 4434 C.S., prostitution
was officially proscribed but unofficially tolerated in the geographic heart of
the city, bounded by the river and by Poydras, Claiborne, and St. Louis

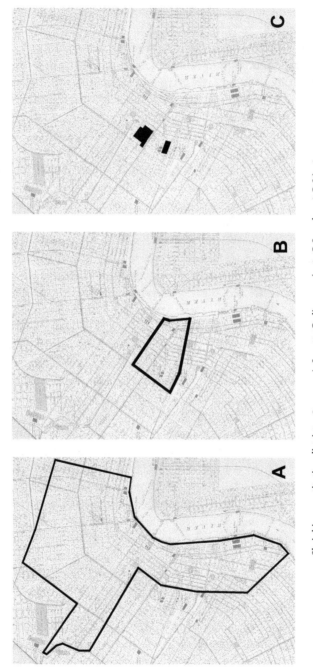

Shrinking prostitution districts, 1857–1917: A. Lorette Ordinances (3267 O.S. and 3428 O.S.), 1857.
B. Ordinance 4434 C.S., 1890. C. Story Ordinances (13,032 C.S. and 13,485 C.S.), 1917. *Sam Rykels*

Streets. Even within these limits, two important commercial and residential thoroughfares, Tulane Avenue and Canal Street, were declared off limits by specific ordinances passed in 1887 and 1889 respectively. Other streets or portions of them were free from prostitution by custom or through the dogged determination of influential residents.[10]

With this history in mind, it is easier to understand why, in 1897, a self-proclaimed reform administration chose to restrict the boundaries of tolerated prostitution once again. Until now, the Story Ordinances have generally been represented as a rupture in the city's previous policy on prostitution and as an outrageous example of the city's frank recognition of prostitution and the pursuit of pleasures of the flesh. But the historic record conclusively demonstrates that attempts to segregate prostitution and prostitutes had been a city policy for forty years by the time Sidney Story sought to revise and restrict the limits once again.

The Storyville Solution

To understand why the Story Ordinances appeared when they did, we have to consider the city's economic, social, and cultural landscape in the late 1890s. It is instructive to note that two of the same issues that preoccupied city administrators and prompted the passage of the Lorette Ordinance in 1857 were still germane when Story presented his vice-district ordinances to the city administration forty years later. First, in 1897 there was widespread concern in the city about the deleterious effect of brothels on residential property values, just as there had been in 1857. Second, in 1897 competing visions of how best to direct the city's economic growth and resources preoccupied and divided businessmen, just as they had forty years before. Concerns about residential property values and the city's broad economic development played crucial roles in generating the Storyville Ordinances. Both factors also played a role in George L'Hote's decision to file suit against a city administration he supported on many other fronts.

Sidney Story and the other men who led the 1897 drive for the restricted district had won office in the municipal elections of 1896. Although hotly contested, the election was between predictably aligned opposition factions within the Democratic Party. On one side stood "the Ring," whose leaders excelled at organizing voters (both dead and alive, according to their opponents) through patronage and personal appeals at the ward level. Ring supporters formed a "lower- and working-class coalition that included the city's traditional ward-based machine, organized labor, and some black support."[11]

On the other side stood prominent businessmen, many of whom were the scions of the city's most elite families. This self-identified reform party, which called itself the Citizens' League, was not the first of its kind. Until 1896, however, reform organizations such as the Young Men's Democratic Association or the Citizens' Protective Association, created in response to specific issues or before upcoming elections, had tended to disintegrate as soon as the issue was addressed or the election was over. Thus, even though they enjoyed electoral victories in 1880 and 1888, reformers tended to squander their momentum by failing to unite in an ongoing organization.

In late 1895, recognizing the need to create an organization that would stay in place after an election had been won or lost, a group of self-identified reformers "representing the best commercial interests of the city" gathered to discuss the upcoming 1896 municipal elections. The Citizens' League charter outlined the members' main platform: "the league is organized for the purpose of securing and maintaining an honest administration of affairs of the city of New Orleans, by officials chosen with reference to their character, capacity and efficiency, rather than ability to manipulate ward politics." Not surprisingly, many of the city's most prominent businessmen were elected to leadership positions in the league. George L'Hote was among them and was named to serve on the executive committee. His appointment was due, in part, to his own recent political experience, something most other members of the league lacked. L'Hote had served on the City Council from 1888 to 1892, when the Young Men's Democratic Association had dominated city government under Mayor Joseph A. Shakespeare.[12]

The league won the 1896 election and, caught up in the spirit of self-congratulations, its members published a celebratory volume the next year. Subtitled *A History of the Great Reform Movement in New Orleans, April 21st, 1896,* the volume began with the dubious declaration that "New Orleans has generally been considered as one of the most conservative cities in this country." While in hindsight this claim has more the ring of rhetoric than of truth, at least in terms of the city's long-standing reputation as the Great Southern Babylon it should be taken seriously; it indicates how the league planned to direct the city's development, both social and economic, as it entered the twentieth century. The boast about the city's reputation for conservatism may have been wishful thinking, but it was politically useful to graft the league's vision for the future onto the city's past.[13]

The history also featured "biographical sketches of those who took prominent part" in the league's victory. George L'Hote was described in glowing terms as "one of the leading lumber manufacturers in this city" and "a very active and enthusiastic man all around." His description concluded, "where there is anything affecting the interests of the city at stake, [he] is ready to do what he can." Clearly L'Hote's Citizen League peers respected and admired him. But months after this description was published, he was embroiled in a lawsuit against the administration he had helped to elect, and, even more curious, because of the adoption of restricted district ordinances he had originally supported. His story helps us understand how his personal economic interests led him to sue the city administration whose larger political and economic program he had helped to forge. The records from L'Hote's case also allow us to ponder how members of the reform administration and other individuals caught up in this case balanced their professed interest in improving public morality with their equally compelling desire to improve the city's economy.[14]

Sidney Story, born in New Orleans in 1863 to a prominent and privileged family, is also described in the volume. His father, General Clement Story, was a graduate of West Point while his mother, Amelie de Lesseps, was a member of another prominent New Orleans family. Sidney grew to adulthood in the city but after graduating from college he moved to Chicago. He remained there for ten years before returning to New Orleans in the early 1890s. Back home he engaged in the import/export trade, but at age thirty-three he had yet to make a name for himself in his hometown. His relative obscurity was about to change in spectacular fashion, thanks to the vice-district ordinances he would champion. While the league history noted rather coyly that he was "responsible for several important measures," the only one it specified was his recent "ordinance to prevent fortune tellers and clairvoyants from practicing their vocation" in the city. He was also described as "a gentleman of pleasing address [who] knows just what the city is in need of." In 1897, L'Hote, Story, and a great many other people agreed that the city was "in need of" a redefined vice district. As a newly elected council member Story presented his plan for vice-district reform on January 4, 1897, to the other council members who made up the Committee on Public Order.[15]

At the time of his death four decades later, one of his obituaries claimed that Story's ordinances were based "on his study of vice regulation in large European cities." This may have been partially true, but at least two factors discredit the claim that Story's ordinances were either all his own or completely inspired by European models. First, the raw material for Story's pro-

Sidney Story, sponsor of the 1897 vice-district ordinances.
The largest section of the vice district created by Ordinance
13,485 C.S. was dubbed "Storyville" in mocking homage
to the councilman. *Courtesy Louisiana State Museum*

posals had been in place in the city since 1857. In fact, the language of the
Story Ordinances is similar to that found in the Lorette Ordinance and in a
number of the other ordinances that followed. The 1897 ordinances differed
significantly from their predecessors only in the drastically reduced geographic boundaries they stipulated and in their absence of formal requirements for either licensure or taxation. Otherwise, much of the legal language
was modeled on the earlier ordinances.[16]

Second, they contained no requirement for medical examination of prostitutes. This omission clearly distinguishes Story's ordinances from European models. The requirement that prostitutes be routinely checked for
venereal disease was the most significant, characteristic, and controversial
element of European urban vice regulation in the nineteenth century. In
France, an entirely independent bureaucracy called the *police des moeurs*
grew out of the medical-examination requirements of vice legislation, while
in England the Contagious Disease Acts set off a storm of controversy in the
1860s and were repealed. In the United States, Union officers mandated that
local prostitutes be subject to medical inspection in Nashville, Tennessee,
during the Civil War, and the St. Louis Social Evil Law had included similar
requirements.[17]

Medical inspection of prostitutes was always an extremely controversial practice. The English Contagious Disease Act of 1869 was successfully opposed by a coalition that included "middle-class evangelicals, feminists and radical workingmen." A similar coalition of forces in America, joined by former abolitionists, actively opposed the medical regulation requirements of the St. Louis Social Evil Law and attempts to pass similar legislation in other states. This coalition of reformers based their opposition to regulation and medical inspection on the related beliefs that regulation did not inhibit the spread of venereal disease and that it constituted state or municipal recognition of a sexual double standard that they abhorred and believed was responsible for the widespread existence of prostitution in the first place.[18]

While New Orleans was short on evangelicals, and its formally organized women's reform groups were small in both number and influence in the years before 1900, a coalition of local women played an important role in discouraging the adoption of regulations that would require medical examination of prostitutes in their city. According to Dr. Isadore Dyer, who was a proponent of regulation and medical inspection of prostitutes, "in 1891, the police authorities of New Orleans proposed that a city ordinance provide for the compulsory medical examination of this class." In response "the women of New Orleans . . . held a mass meeting of indignant opposition, and this was the death knell of the movement." Although they could not vote, and were only sporadically organized into political-reform organizations during this period, a vocal and clearly influential group of New Orleans women was able to thwart an attempt to require the medical inspection of prostitutes in the Crescent City. While the sexual double standard remained in place through municipal regulation of prostitution, these women's refusal to adhere to the code of silence when it came to discussing sexual matters, at least on this occasion, kept New Orleans from adopting medical inspection and thereby providing further municipal regulation of a practice they clearly abhorred.[19]

The events of 1891 help explain why Story left medical-inspection requirements out of his 1897 ordinance drafts. He may have supported such measures privately, but there was absolutely no mention of venereal disease or of medical-inspection requirements in the ordinances as adopted in 1897. Nor do the records from the City Council's Committee on Public Order include any mention of medical-inspection requirements during the period of debate surrounding the adoption and refinement of Story's ordinances. Although fears about the spread of venereal disease would have a great deal to do with Storyville's demise, on the level of the detectable historical record, such concerns, officially at least, had little to do with the district's establishment.

Although the Story Ordinances did not explicitly address the topic of venereal disease, implicit social beliefs about disease in general, and venereal disease in particular, certainly contributed to the city's decision to restrict its vice-district boundaries yet again in 1897. Of course prostitutes, rather than their clients, were at the top of the list of presumed carriers of venereal disease. They were lumped in with the poor, immigrants, African Americans and promiscuous men of the lower classes as those among whom venereal infections were deservedly rampant. Thus, to the degree that adoption of the Story Ordinances was conditioned by beliefs about disease, it was probably considered sufficient to impose the common remedy of quarantining infected carriers, in this case prostitutes, without explicit public discussion of their assumed culpability in the spread of venereal disease. With this in mind, the headline "A Plague of Prostitutes," which ran on the cover of the *Mascot* in June 1892, represents more than a simple example of journalistic alliteration. Prostitutes, like African Americans as a class, were considered by many to be coterminous with the presence of disease, particularly venereal infection.[20]

During the course of the L'Hote case, several witnesses also used the terminology of disease when referring to the presence of prostitutes in a given area. For instance, a lawyer for the city asked Chief of Police D. S. Gaster, "Isn't it a fact, Chief, that when a locality or house becomes infected by the occupancy of lewd women that it ceases to be fit for any other purpose?" Gaster's reply included similar terminology when he noted that "Basin and Customhouse street back of Basin so long as I can remember have always been infested with prostitutes." The language of disease and the use of the terms "plague," "infection," and "infested" to refer to prostitutes reveal a clear link between social constructions of disease and prostitution.[21]

A request Story made to the Committee on Public Order on October 4, 1897, provides fragmentary evidence that he was interested in emphasizing the control of venereal disease as well as of prostitution generally in the adoption of his ordinances. On that date, he asked that "certain petitions previously adopted by the Council be forwarded to the Secretary of the Navy." Although the records do not indicate that these petitions were his vice-district ordinances, it stands to reason that the council may have wanted to make the Department of the Navy aware of the tight new geographic boundaries they had designated for the city's vice district. Elsewhere in the country, purity reformers were alarmed that recognition and regulation of prostitution was occurring around army encampments. In New Orleans, in contrast, it seems that Story was eager to present the city's new regulation scheme to the Department of the Navy as an example of how best to manage prostitution in an urban area.[22]

The involvement of Story's family in the shipping industry provides a tantalizing but unverifiable suggestion that personal economic incentives may have played a role in initiating the 1897 vice-district ordinances. Even though official United States involvement in the struggle between Spain and Cuba was months away, port cities were already vying for the privilege and economic advantages that would come from hosting military encampments and depots. Whether or not the city's decision to restrict its population of prostitutes had anything to do with it, during April and May 1898, approximately two thousand troops were temporarily stationed at the City Park Fairgrounds.[23]

Although medical-inspection requirements did not play a prominent role in the adoption of the Story Ordinances, the sexual double standard permeated their construction. The ordinances sought to control women "notoriously abandoned to lewdness" or "public prostitutes," but they did not penalize discreet kept women, or the hotels, like those on Royal Street, that served informally as places of assignation for seemingly respectable visitors. Nor did the ordinances even consider the possibility that men could be prostitutes. Moreover, the ordinances completely ignored the men who most certainly would serve as the customers of the city's lewd and abandoned women. Yet men's political, social, financial, and sexual desires, and their ideas about the requirements, privileges, and prerogatives of respectability lay squarely at the center of the impulse to create a segregated vice district in the first place. The Storyville solution combined ideas about the protection of private property, and the protection of respectable white women, with ideas about the imperatives and privileges of male sexuality, especially for white men, and grafted them onto the city's geographic grid.[24]

The ordinances were able to withstand legal scrutiny because they went on to disavow knowledge of the district they had just created by including the proviso that "nothing herein shall be construed as to authorize any lewd women to occupy a house . . . in any portion of the city." White men wrote and passed ordinances that created a vice district primarily for their use. Yet, in the ordinances themselves, they disavowed playing an active role in legalizing prostitution. It was a crafty though predictable legal maneuver, but this transparent ploy withstood judicial review beyond the parochial confines of Orleans Parish courtrooms.[25]

Clearly, a complex set of factors contributed to the city's decision to revise the boundaries of its tolerated vice district in 1897, but the ever-present theme of respectability was reiterated by city officials and other witnesses once L'Hote's case went to trial. Echoing the arguments of the plaintiffs in *Koehl v. Schoenhausen,* newspaper writers and witnesses claimed that the city chose to segregate vice so that respectable people would not have to come into contact with it. The *Daily Picayune* expressed it this way: "The city government is trying to drive vice and immorality out of the most prominent localities and into obscure neighborhoods where decent people will not be constantly offended by [the] open and shameless flauntings" of prostitutes and their compatriots. Perhaps this was true in part, but many of the men (and they were mostly men) who drafted, passed, and supported the vice-district ordinances, would be more than happy to mingle with prostitutes from time to time in these new and conveniently obscure settings.[26]

The choice of the "obscure neighborhood" that would become known as Storyville was certainly conditioned by the class and race of the people who lived there. Low-lying and swampy, this area, sometimes called "back o' town," was largely populated by people without the resources to buy houses or pay rent in more desirable areas. The *Daily Picayune* noted the "obscurity" of the people in the neighborhood. The obscurity of the neighborhood was a function not only of its geographic inferiority but also of its poverty and powerlessness.

The claim that the creation of Storyville would protect certain areas of the city from the presence of overt prostitution connects the city's actions in 1897 to the arguments deployed by James Koehl and others who, just four years earlier, filed suit in opposition to the concert saloons on Royal Street. Widely differing opinions about the import and requirements of respectability dominated testimony in *Koehl v. Schoenhausen.* The same kind of debate was prominent in the testimony in *L'Hote v. City of New Orleans.* One witness even made an explicit connection between the two cases. Steve Ciolina was a substantial property owner in the area chosen to become the new vice district and, according to one source, "well known in financial and real estate circles." When asked about the character of the neighborhood destined to become Storyville, he said, "Well, it is as respectable as Royal Street now." The court transcript continues:

Q: Were there many people of bad character living in that neighborhood more than a year ago?
A: No more than on Royal or Bourbon street.
Q: Well, are there many people of bad character living on Royal or Bourbon street now?
A: Some.
Q: Well, are there as many in this district?
A: Not as many as on Royal or Bourbon.[27]

While this may seem like a mundane exchange, it actually touches on one of the key points at issue in the records of L'Hote's case against the city. Discussions about the character of the neighborhood chosen to become the new vice district appear often in the transcripts for good reason. The issue of how this neighborhood stacked up against others, and questions about the respectability and reputation of its inhabitants, were central to the adjudication of *L'Hote v. City of New Orleans* just as they had been in *Koehl v. Schoenhausen.* They were also critical in determining whether or not the city had chosen the kind of "obscure neighborhood" it sought for the new vice district—the kind that "decent people" sought to avoid.

Apparently, the city administration was convinced that it had chosen well, because Story's initial ordinance proceeded smoothly through the Committee on Public Order and was passed by the full council on January 29. The ordinance, numbered 13,032 C.S., established the new district in the squares bounded by Basin, Customhouse, Robertson, and St. Louis Streets. However, it also contained the proviso that "no lewd women shall be permitted to occupy a house, room or closet on St. Louis street" itself.[28]

This newly delineated district dramatically decreased the geographical area within which prostitution would be tolerated by the city. Moreover, because 13,032 C.S. stipulated that "it shall be unlawful for any public prostitute or woman notoriously abandoned to lewdness to occupy, inhabit, live or sleep in any house, room, or closet" outside the new limits, large numbers of women were actually required to move into the boundaries of the new district by October 1, when the ordinance was initially slated to take effect. The residency requirement, combined with the much smaller area stipulated, actually caused some to worry out loud about whether this new district had enough room to hold the city's prostitutes. Louis Cucullu, a Ring loyalist recently reelected councilman from the Sixth Ward and a member of the Public Order Committee, testified on L'Hote's behalf that "the new

limits are entirely too restricted to house the estimated 1500 prostitutes living in the city."[29]

As objections like Cucullu's reveal, instead of settling the matter, adoption of the dramatically decreased vice-district boundaries set off a chain of
protests and complaints by parties with a variety of interests. Story's vice-
district ordinances and issues related to them played a prominent role in
more than half of the Committee on Public Order's 1897 sessions. Many of
the agenda items were petitions from or presentations by individuals or
groups of citizens who, for a variety of reasons, wished to champion, challenge, or change the boundaries established by Ordinance 13,032. The contents of those petitions and letters reveal at least two different levels of
concern about what effect the new vice-district ordinances would have.
Some petitioners complained about the moral aspects of having prostitutes
for neighbors or being forced into daily contact with them. Other complaints seemed driven by economic interests. Often there was considerable
overlap between economic concerns and notions of morality.

On February 6, for instance, twelve property owners petitioned the Public Order Committee to keep Poydras and Lafayette Streets outside the new
limits. They argued that those streets constituted the main "avenues to the
Poydras Market by which all the families residing back of town walk to make
their daily market and other purchases." They also contended it would be
"creating a hardship . . . on these respectable people to place these unfortunates on their path." For these property owners, who wanted to ensure that
the Poydras Market and its environs remained a safe and inviting destination, good neighborhoods and good business went hand in hand.[30]

While some petitioners did not want their neighborhoods or businesses
to be included within the boundaries of the new vice district, other property
owners worried about the economic impact of losing prostitutes as tenants
and customers. Cucullu testified that the city had received several petitions
signed by property holders and merchants who opposed the new limits because their properties were excluded from them. Although the petitions
could not be located at the time of his testimony and do not exist in the
court record today, two other witnesses confirmed their existence. John St.
Paul, a local judge and practicing attorney, took the stand as a spokesman
for several property owners in the area "bounded by Dauphine and Rampart, Canal and St. Louis." The blocks inside those boundaries had been
densely populated with prostitutes since at least the 1880s. Even the chief of
police testified that "at one time fifty-two houses of prostitution" were on

Burgundy Street alone. Lawyers for L'Hote and the other plaintiffs reiterated the concerns of these parties in their brief to the court, recalling, "that almost all of the property holders and other persons carrying on businesses within the old limits previously established by the council protested and objected to any change or alteration in said limits and the removal of prostitutes therefrom." They concluded that the "enforcement of the ordinance in question would practically destroy the value of all property now occupied by this class of persons."[31]

The economic stakes for the landlords represented by St. Paul were high, but merchants were also concerned about the loss of trade they would experience if their prostitute customers moved *en masse* into the new district. Pierre Peret, a property holder in the same vicinity, had both concerns: one of his properties was "rented for a grocery and a coffeehouse" and another "to a woman of this class." He signed a petition asking the "city to retain the old limits." He claimed that more than one hundred others joined him, including "most of the Canal street merchants on this side of Canal." Thus, for some parties, holding on to prostitutes as tenants and customers outweighed whatever moral objections they had to sharing public space with women who engaged in prostitution.[32]

Bernardo Galvez Carbajal, the first party to intervene in L'Hote's case against the city, shared the concerns of the Canal Street property owners. Carbajal was a Spanish immigrant who had come to the city in 1866 at age fourteen. Arriving "a penniless boy," he went to work in his uncle's grocery store on Canal at the corner of Franklin—one block over from the neighborhood that became Storyville after 1897. According to one of his obituaries, good business practices allowed him to accumulate a large number of properties by the turn of the century. Carbajal owned at least two double houses inside the new district, and it was on behalf of these properties that he pressed his suit against the city. He claimed that his properties inside the smaller district would decrease in value by two thousand dollars if the new limits were enforced. But testimony made it abundantly clear that Carbajal stood to suffer no financial damage to his properties in the new vice district.[33]

He even admitted as much on the stand, testifying that by "January 1897 the rents had gone up from one hundred to three hundred percent higher in advance of the ordinance being passed" because there was "an expectation that [it] was going to go through." Before passage of the Story Ordinances, both of Carbajal's Bienville Street doubles had been rented to African American working men who lived in the houses with their families. These tenants paid him sixteen dollars per month. By the time the case actually went to trial, some of those tenants had been replaced by prostitutes who paid substantially higher rents. According to a police-department survey, most of the rents in the immediate area had risen significantly—some more than doubled—during 1897 as the ordinances were debated.[34]

Carbajal's testimony was surprisingly candid; he freely admitted that his real concern was his properties outside the new boundaries. He was particularly rich in properties on Gasquet Street, an area notorious for its high concentration of prostitutes prior to 1897. If prostitutes were forced to abandon their places on Gasquet, he testified, "as far as the revenue of the property is concerned it would be a complete confiscation from the owners." Like the French Quarter property owners and Canal Street merchants who petitioned the city to keep the larger limits in place, Carbajal stood to suffer significant economic losses if the Story Ordinances were enforced. In this respect, Carbajal was like many other property and business owners: any moral compunction they felt about geographically widespread prostitution in their city was outweighed by their narrow economic interests.[35]

But the reform-dominated city government had enough support among residents and business owners to press their solution forward. Their arguments in favor of the new district also had both moral and economic aspects. On the one hand, they suggested that isolating prostitution into a single locale would protect the largest number of citizens from constant exposure to the trade. They also argued that the new district would keep brothels out of most residential areas, thereby stabilizing property values for the majority of city homeowners. These broad economic and moral goals were appealing to a large number of citizens. The only question that remained to be answered was where precisely the boundaries of the new vice district would be.

Discussions about whether to include or exclude particular streets and neighborhoods in a revised version of Story's original ordinance occupied the Committee on Public Order until early summer. By July, however, St. Louis Street had become their focus. Recall that in ordinance 13,032 St. Louis was one of the boundaries of the new district, but prostitutes were not allowed to live on it. Many argued that including St. Louis within the allowable areas for habitation by prostitutes would alleviate concerns about overcrowding within the new district. The Public Order Committee received two petitions during July from thirteen property holders and one real-estate company, all of whom pleaded with the city to make St. Louis active within

the new limits. "This district," they argued, "is composed of the same element that inhabits the proposed limit now before your body and no harm
can inure to anyone concerned to include the above two sides of the street
in the proposed amendment."[36]

Although those who wanted to include St. Louis Street seemed to be in
the majority, George L'Hote vehemently disagreed with the contention that
"no harm would inure to anyone" if St. Louis were included within the district. Nevertheless, the committee was swayed in the other direction, recom-
mending inclusion of the street within the new limits. At the same time,
it added a second and entirely separate area to the city's new vice-district
boundaries. These additional blocks were just above Canal Street in a crime-
ridden area, largely populated by immigrants and African Americans, which
was sometimes referred to as "The Battlefield" because, according to Louis
Armstrong, "the toughest characters in town used to live there and would
shoot and fight so much."[37]

The full council passed the revised ordinance, numbered 13,485 C.S., on
July 6. A final addendum was made to this version of the vice-district ordinance on September 1. On the previous day, the full council passed Ordinance 13,604 C.S. On its own, this ordinance stipulated that, "it shall be
unlawful to open, operate or carry on any cabaret, concert-saloon or place
where cancan, clodoche, or similar female dancing or sensational performance are shown" outside the newly defined limits below Canal Street. The
first section of 13,604 C.S. was made an addendum to 13,485 C.S. on September 1. Thus, by September, the vice-district limits below Canal Street were
the only physical space inside the city where concert saloons and other sexually oriented entertainment establishments could legally be established. In
certain ways, this addendum represented a final settlement of the issues that
had been so hotly debated in *Koehl v. Schoenhausen*. In its final form, Ordinance 13,485 C.S. also provided the impetus for L'Hote to bring suit against
the city.

L'Hote v. City of New Orleans

The inclusion of St. Louis Street within the new limits led directly to
George L'Hote's decision to file suit. He made this point explicitly in later
testimony. "If the ordinance remained as it was, that is to come within the
depth of one block of St. Louis street, I had no objection to it, because I
appeared before the committee and favored the ordinance in that way." In
fact, his home was not on St. Louis Street itself but half a block away, at 520

North Liberty, a point the city would often make as the matter made its way through the courts. L'Hote responded that even though St. Louis was not his address per se, it did constitute the "chief and principal way of approaching his residence, and for ingress and egress thereto." Thus L'Hote's concerns were similar to the moral concerns expressed by the Poydras and Lafayette Street property holders who had complained months earlier that the city would be "creating a hardship . . . on . . . respectable people to place these unfortunates on their path." Even if he did not have to share a street with prostitutes, under the terms of 13,485 C.S., L'Hote, his wife, and their eight children would be forced to share public space with them and to confront them every time they left or returned to their home.[38]

Like those of his counterparts near the Poydras Street Market, L'Hote's moral concerns were connected to his economic stake in nearby commercial and residential properties. L'Hote had been born in the house next door to 520 North Liberty; along with several other members of his family, he owned many other residential properties in the immediate squares. The value of his family home was the primary basis of L'Hote's lawsuit, but he also owned and administered a tremendous amount of commercial real estate in the area adjacent to the newly delineated vice district. L'Hote's father, George Sr., originally established L'Hote and Company as a sash, door, and blind factory in 1847. He died in 1868, and eight years later, at age twenty, George Jr. took over as managing partner of the business. L'Hote was young but apparently precocious. Under his dynamic stewardship, the company became the largest facility of its kind in the city. With 250 men in its employ by 1892, L'Hote and Company had expanded well beyond sashes, doors, and blinds. In addition to selling dressed lumber, the company turned out fine interior elements, a variety of low-cost cottage furniture, and, perhaps most impressive, entire "cabins and dwellings framed for shipment" and ready to erect on delivery.[39]

L'Hote was a hands-on manager who routinely worked twelve to fourteen hours a day and was involved in all aspects of his business. He was also an innovator, credited with the invention of "several important milling machines" that increased productivity and profit. Another source noted that "the only fuel used in the battery of three boilers of 100-horse power each is the shavings [that] accumulate rapidly in the plant," giving another indication of L'Hote's commitment to economy and efficiency. His hard work and leadership resulted in impressive growth and equally impressive profits. By the early 1890s annual sales had reached $900,000.[40]

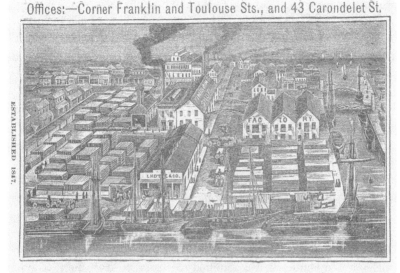

Offices:—Corner Franklin and Toulouse Sts., and 43 Carondelet St.

ESTABLISHED 1847.

LHOTE & CO.

BIRDS EYE VIEW OF LHOTE & CO'S FACTORY AND YARD.

The residential area adjacent to George L'Hote's residence and lumber company (pictured here in an advertisement in A. Boucherau's *Statement of the Sugar and Rice Crops in Louisiana 1883–84*) became a vice district upon passage of Ordinance 13,485 C.S. in July 1897. L'Hote filed suit against the city of New Orleans two months later. *Courtesy Louisiana State Museum*

L'Hote's home at 520 North Liberty was surrounded on three sides by his company's lumberyards, warehouses, and ever-expanding manufacturing facilities. The Sash, Door & Blind Warehouse was next door, while the lumber yards were directly behind and in front of the house. The company's holdings also extended across Toulouse Street where they dominated two additional squares fronting the Carondelet or Old Basin Canal. His extensive commercial holdings lead one to wonder just how far beyond his family home L'Hote's economic concerns about the new vice district stretched. But as a homeowner and family man he also evinced genuine concern about the reputation of the area.[41]

Questions about the character of the neighborhood in which he had been raised permeated arguments made by both sides in the case. L'Hote was the first to weigh in on the subject. In his original petition to the court, filed September 20, 1897, he made three main claims. First, he maintained that his neighborhood had "always been used for private residences, schools, groceries and other merchant establishments." Second, he claimed "that the people residing in said locality are now, and have always been moral, virtuous, sober, law-abiding, and peaceable." Finally, he insisted that his neighborhood was "not now and never has been dedicated to immoral purposes, or used for dwelling places and as a refuge of public prostitutes, lewd and abandoned women, and the necessary attendants thereof, drunkard, idle, vicious, and disorderly persons."[42]

Those three points were reiterated and disputed many times as testimony proceeded. Witness after witness was asked first about the character of the neighborhood in question, second about the character of the people who lived in it, and third and perhaps most important, about how long and how prominently prostitutes had inhabited the neighborhood before 1897. L'Hote was the first witness to take the stand when testimony commenced on December 20, 1897. Although his petition of September 20 asserted unequivocally that his neighborhood had never been identified with prostitution or immorality, his testimony under oath suggested a more ambiguous neighborhood landscape. He admitted that prior to 1897, the neighborhood's "character was mixed." But, he explained, this was true of every neighborhood in the city because "those women were not being particularly controlled to any neighborhood, they were all over."[43]

He also pointed out that whenever he became aware that houses in his vicinity had been "invaded by this class of people, by these women . . . I immediately had affidavits made and had them removed. . . . Some of these cases were fought very hard in the Recorder's Court, and I succeeded in removing them, but pending the litigation they remained." Even as stubborn and persistent a foe as George L'Hote had to admit that it was sometimes difficult and time-consuming to remove such residents once their presence became known. It was this dilemma and the ease with which a brothel or assignation house could be established in any neighborhood that, in part at least, motivated the city to establish the new district in the first place, and, presumably, garnered approval for the Story Ordinances among the public at large.[44]

In fact, in general terms L'Hote agreed with the city's decision to revise the boundaries of the vice district. He had even been a supporter of the new district, right up until the time it came within half a block of his home. When the city decided to include St. Louis Street within the boundaries of the new district, L'Hote ceased to support the plan, not because he believed it was a bad idea in principle but because, in contemporary parlance, the city administration had decided to place it in his back yard. L'Hote's disagreement with the city helps us to delineate further the economic and moral arguments for and against the vice district. Even L'Hote believed that effective segregation of the city's vice establishments and prostitutes was a good idea. But when the ordinances threatened the reputation of his real-estate holdings and the respectability of his wife and family, he had no choice but to withdraw his support of the Story Ordinances, although he could profit handily from having prostitutes as tenants.[45]

For L'Hote, the concept of his neighborhood seemed to be very limited and specific. His testimony and actions made clear that he was only interested in protecting those blocks that provided entrée to or were occupied by his residential and commercial properties. But, in pressing his claim against the city, L'Hote and his lawyers outlined three reasons why the neighborhood in question was an inappropriate choice for the new vice district. First, the new vice district was entirely too small to handle the city's entire population of prostitutes. The lack of adequate housing in the new district would lead prostitutes to ignore the rules and result in "scattering the prostitutes now residing in the old limits throughout the entire city, contaminating the public morals" even further, at least in geographic terms.[46]

Second, it was "difficult, if not impossible to change the destination [sic] of houses of prostitution." While L'Hote admitted that houses of prostitution had intermittently made their way into his neighborhood, he was right to suggest that other streets in the city were more heavily occupied by prostitutes and more readily identified with them before 1897. Even the city's superintendent of police, D. S. Gaster, confirmed L'Hote's point during his testimony for the city. In addition to pointing out the astounding concentration of houses on certain blocks of Burgundy, Gaster named Customhouse between Dauphine and Rampart, Bienville, Gravier, Basin between Perdido and Canal, and "Gasquet and Liberty Street particularly" as all having been heavily populated by prostitutes prior to passage of the Story Ordinances.[47]

Relying on the authority of the nineteenth century's two most important texts on prostitution, Dr. William Sanger's *The History of Prostitution,* and Alexandre Parent-Duchâtelet's *De la prostitution dans la ville de Paris,* L'Hote's lawyers pressed the argument that "a house which has once been leased to prostitutes loses its reputation, and can never afterward be put to any other use." Working from this assumption, they also claimed that enforcement of the new ordinances "would practically destroy the value of all property now occupied by this class of persons." According to their logic, the city had to retain its previous prostitution boundaries, not only to protect their client's interests, but to protect the value of prostitute-inhabited properties within the previous limits.[48]

Forging ahead in their brief, L'Hote's attorneys pressed their third argument against the new boundaries by pointing out that the new limits were home to one school, one church, and five cemeteries. Again relying on excerpts from Parent's influential study of the subject in Paris, the brief maintained that "it is a notorious fact . . . that prostitutes always avoid the neighborhood and vicinage of churches and grave-yards. It is the respect which vice pays to virtue." They concluded by referring to the city's decision to place prostitutes in the proximity of the city's oldest cemeteries as "a crime, a shame, profanation and disgrace." While their arguments were rich in hyperbole and apostolic bombast, it may have been the cemeteries that, in part, made the neighborhood such an easy target. After all, even if charges that the city's voting rolls were riddled with the names of dead New Orleanians were correct, corpses constituted only a minor portion of the New Orleans electorate.[49]

In their defense against L'Hote's suit, city attorneys also focused their case on the character of the neighborhood chosen to be the new vice district. The testimony of two policemen and one property owner disputed L'Hote's claims about the long-standing respectability of the area around St. Louis. Both police officers testified about specific brothels and assignation houses that had existed in L'Hote's vicinity for years, some for more than a decade. One claimed, "There has always been sporting houses and assignation houses all through there. I have taken down the census." A Mrs. Donally, who owned three houses near the corner of Franklin and St. Louis, testified that she had tried on several occasions to rent them "to respectable people, but they wouldn't live in the neighborhood," so she rented them to prostitutes or questionable characters instead.[50]

The city prepared a survey of houses "situated within 2 squares of L'Hote's residence," which proved even more damning to L'Hote's claims about his neighborhood's long-standing reputation for respectability. Sixteen houses were listed on the neatly printed and organized document that the city submitted into the court record. There were separate columns for categories that included "kind of house," "rent per month paid," and "length of time used for purposes of prostitution." All of the houses included were classed under "kind of house" as either prostitution, assignation, or "suspicious." L'Hote's lawyer strenuously objected to the submission of the survey, claiming that the recent upsurge of prostitutes in the neighborhood was a direct result of the newly passed ordinances. He claimed the city was not only "destroying the morality and virtue" of the neighborhood but, by "forcing a lot of prostitutes in[to] that area" before L'Hote's case was settled, city officials were contributing to the degradation of the neighborhood's "character" by "their own act."[51]

There is some evidence that this objection was justified. Although an injunction against the enforcement of Ordinance 13,485 C.S. was in place, two letters in the court record demonstrate that the mayor and his superintendent of police were actively stacking the deck against the character of the neighborhood by trying to force prostitutes to move into the new limits as quickly as possible, thus making the new district a fait accompli. Even while the case was being heard in December, the mayor's office sent letters to prostitutes who continued to live outside the boundaries of the new district. Under the authority of Section 8 of Ordinance 4334 C.S., adopted in 1890, the mayor used his power to evict a prostitute from her house on the grounds that it had become "dangerous to public morals, either from the manner in which it is conducted or the character of the neighborhood in which it is situated." The addresses on the two letters in the court record were squarely inside the tolerated limits specified in the 1890 ordinance. This helps to explain why the mayor chose to exclude those portions of the ordinance that would have contradicted the boundaries he specified in the letters he sent to Alice Chapius, Marie Flurry, and the women who lived with them. The judge ruled both the mayor and the superintendent of police, D. S. Gaster, in contempt of court for their part in this ploy. There is little doubt, however, that such tactics had encouraged if not forced some prostitutes into the new district, even as the legitimacy of the new boundaries was being considered in civil district court.[52]

Regardless of how long the new district's population of prostitutes had been in place, the city argued that the new limits were the best overall choice for the city. The city's attorneys even concluded their arguments with a quantitative flourish, showing on a carefully prepared map and chart that the limits specified in 13,485 C.S. contained within their boundaries fewer churches, schools, and public buildings than any of the previous limits had. While the chart failed to point out the proximity of the city's five oldest cemeteries to the new limits, attorneys for the city boasted that the newly delineated district contained "only one church, one school, and no public buildings." They also maintained that "the discretion of the City Council surely was correctly exercised" because "the new [district] is certainly the one where the least harm can result." The lawyers admitted that the boundaries of the new district might cause, "some citizens [to] suffer inconvenience or even loss," but this "is a sacrifice demanded of the few for the benefit of the many."[53]

Based on the city's quantitative evidence, the advantages of the boundaries selected for the new district were self-evident. But if, as city attorneys argued, this new district was so much better, the contention begs the question "better for whom?" Certainly George L'Hote believed his family would suffer because of their residential proximity to the new vice district, but other families, residents, and groups in the neighborhood would suffer as well. More than two thousand other people lived, shopped, and attended school or church in the neighborhood that was to become Storyville. Six hundred of them were members of the Union Chapel, a little-known African American Methodist Episcopal Church whose congregation's participation in this case provides a key to understanding the racial dimensions of the Storyville solution.

Table 1. *Number of Churches, Schools, and Public Buildings in Limits under (New) Ordinance*

	Churches	Schools	Public Buildings
6302 O.S. (1865)	41	16	17
4434 C.S. (1890)	9	2	10
13,485 C.S. (1897)	1	1	0

Source: Printed on back of map prepared by City Engineer's office showing same. Prepared Dec. 28, 1897, and submitted to Louisiana Supreme Court, March 8, 1898.

The Union Chapel Methodist Episcopal Church

Just as they had in 1857, concerns about widespread prostitution and its effect on residential property values, questions about the city's economic future, and a preoccupation with the requirements of respectability worried city leaders in 1897. New Orleanians and their leaders were also obsessed with racial issues in 1897, just as they had been four decades earlier. Although the Story Ordinances did not mention race, they were adopted the year after the United States Supreme Court's final ruling in *Plessy v. Ferguson,* and they did seek a solution to the city's prostitution problem through a territorial segregation scheme focused on neighborhoods with large African

American populations. Although prostitutes whom the city referred to as "lewd and abandoned women" were the parties to be segregated, they would come to share both physical and ideological space with African Americans in the city—and in the minds of many of the city's residents.

In fact, in years to come, the same kind of rhetoric that had been used to rationalize the residential segregation of prostitutes in 1897 would be deployed against the city's African Americans. Segregationists would argue that, like prostitutes, African Americans should be separated from respectable whites because of their natural propensity toward disorder, sensuality, immorality, filth, and disease. By 1908, reformers had begun to charge that segregation of the city's prostitutes was, itself, explicitly a racial issue. As historian Kathy D. Williams argues was the case in Louisville during these same years, in New Orleans "the segregation of prostitutes within the red light district eventually led to an ideological as well as [a] physical intersection of race and sexuality." In the second decade of the district's existence, New Orleans reformers focused on prostitutes of color and on sex across the color line as they sought to gain public support for their campaigns against Storyville. By 1908 reformers had charged that African American prostitutes and sex across the color line were the most offensive aspects of the city's vice district, but one African American church congregation played an important role in fighting the ordinances at their outset.[54]

The leaders of the Union Chapel provide the only African American voices heard in this case. Their concerns, like L'Hote's, had both moral and economic aspects. But for the leaders of the Union Chapel, the final plaintiff to intervene in the case, questions about the respectability of their neighborhood were complicated by and inextricably linked to questions about their own respectability as "colored" people. Like George L'Hote, the pastor and elders of the Union Chapel were concerned about the value of their property and the feasibility of maintaining their congregation in the midst of such morally compromised surroundings. But their pleas, while based on concerns about the future of their congregation and the value of its building, were heard and assessed through the filter of racial stereotypes and on the basis of the unevenly applied politics of respectability. While L'Hote and Carbajal were influential citizens with money and reputation to spare, the members and leaders of the Union Chapel were bound by their racial identity and by the white, middle-class presumption that African Americans, even those who strove to meet the requirements of middle-class respectability, were inherently immoral or sensual.[55]

In recent years, many historians have explored the political significance of portraying African American women and men in the years after the Civil War as inherently sexually immoral beings. Even as they argued against such contentions, African American writers and spokespersons conceded that, at the turn of the century, "sensualism" was reputed to be one of their "distinguishing racial characteristics." Among other things, the stereotype of inherent black sensuality provided a rationalization for the rape of black women by white men, purportedly at the invitation of the victims. Such sexualized racial stereotyping also provided a rationalization for the lynching of black men who, regardless of the facts in individual cases, were portrayed as voracious sexual predators from whom the community, particularly white women, needed protection. In New Orleans, the assumed link between people of color and sexual immorality also played a role in the city's choice of boundaries for its new vice district.[56]

Most accounts by witnesses in this case suggest that the neighborhood that became Storyville was complex—to use L'Hote's term, it was "mixed." In some ways, its "mixed" character made it a quintessentially New Orleans neighborhood. After all, the mixing of people within its tight antebellum boundaries was one of the city's distinguishing characteristics. Of course, many American cities shared similar levels of neighborhood heterogeneity as late-nineteenth-century immigration forever altered the ethnic landscape of the nation. This was certainly the case in New Orleans; even neighborhoods named for their primary inhabitants—the American section, the French Quarter, or the Irish Channel for instance—were rarely completely homogeneous racially or ethnically. While the creation of vast pumping stations that could drain the city's surrounding swamp lands did not occur until early in the twentieth century, improved drainage and construction methods had begun to expand the city's habitable areas by the end of the nineteenth century. It was at this moment, when meaningful residential segregation first became possible, that the Story Ordinances were adopted.[57]

While the city did not pass an ordinance that mandated residential segregation based on race until 1917, racial covenants had begun to alter the racial landscape as early as 1910. Even earlier, in the 1890s, the city's many distinct neighborhoods had begun to exhibit what Peirce Lewis calls a "curious racial geography." Lewis describes a racial distribution among neighborhoods that helps explain the subtleties of racial segregation and how it was beginning to take hold at the turn of the century in this otherwise notably heterogeneous city. Overlaying a grid on the neighborhoods, Lewis describes a pattern in which prominent commercial or residential streets establish the boundaries for a given area. Inside each of these "superblocks" is a discernible core or nucleus of African American population. Often these African American neighborhood cores were "multinucleated" or had "fuzzy boundaries." While even the cores of the neighborhoods were rarely all black, the main streets and prominent thoroughfares surrounding them were more affluent and almost always completely white. Lewis's schema certainly holds true for the two areas selected to become the 1897 vice district.[58]

The newly delineated vice district was bounded on its uptown border by Iberville Street, one block away from the thriving retail thoroughfare Canal Street. Looking toward the river, the district was enclosed by Basin Street which already encompassed a number of large houses, many of them upscale brothels belonging to elite madams or white male entrepreneurs. At the end of Basin, Saint Louis Cemetery No. 1, St. Louis Street, and the Carondelet Canal established the downtown boundary of the district, while the back-of-town or lakeside boundary was Robertson Street, which lay along the edge of Saint Louis Cemetery No. 2. Above Canal Street, four additional blocks were delineated. Within both sets of boundaries lay a distinguishable core of African American residents, particularly along Bienville, Customhouse, and Robertson Streets where, as one witness testified, "most all [the residents] are colored people."[59]

This thriving and lively African American neighborhood core was also home to a portion of the "Negro dance hall" district that so many residents and newspaper writers had complained about since the 1880s. According to an 1896 Sanborn map, there were four "Negro Dance Halls," one "Negro Club Room," and one "Negro Chop House" on Franklin in the blocks inside the new limits. Louis Cucullu testified that there was also "an extremely bad locality adjoining the district, which is that of the Franklin Street dens . . . one of the lowest in the city."[60]

Certainly much of the derision directed at these establishments was because of their largely African American clientele, but contemporary descriptions also suggest that these establishments had a great deal in common with the rowdy, ribald, and crime-ridden concert saloons that had plagued Royal Street in recent years. While these leisure establishments certainly contributed to the area's bad reputation, the immediate neighborhood was also home to many working-class African American families who went to work, sent their children to school, and attended church in the area destined to become Storyville.

Like L'Hote, the Union Chapel's leadership disagreed with the city's contention that their neighborhood was the one "in which the least harm can result." Theirs was the one church within the boundaries of the new district; like the single school chosen to share space with the city's prostitutes, the church was used and attended solely by African Americans. The city's assumption that "the least harm" would result by moving prostitutes into an area identified with African Americans came as no surprise to at least one writer for the *Southwestern Christian Advocate*, a Methodist weekly based in New Orleans. On March 10, 1898, a story titled "What Shall We Do with the Negro?" included a passage that seemed to refer, if only obliquely, to the new situation inside the area by then commonly known as Storyville. In reference to the issue of forced segregation, the unnamed writer argued "as it is, the two races do not touch except at the bottom, that is in the lowest grades of both, and then under such condition as licenses the one to prey upon the other without let or hindrance." If the writer was not referring explicitly to conditions inside Storyville, he may have been referring to events that occurred earlier in the district, particularly the displacement of working-class African American tenants to free up space for prostitutes, black and white, who could pay higher rents.[61]

Testimony on both sides of the case confirms that property values and rents inside the bounds of Storyville were rising at astonishing rates. B. G. Carbajal testified that rents "had gone up from one hundred to three hundred percent [even] in advance of the ordinance being passed." Stephen Duncan, a former pastor of the Union Chapel, testified that some church members had been forced to move because of this rent explosion. According to Duncan, "Around on Conti Street there was some two or three families moved out. They were paying twelve dollars rent, and they told me they would have to pay twenty-five dollars a month or move out." When the Reverend Henry Taylor, the Union Chapel's current minister, was asked, "How many of your congregation live in this tenderloin district?" he answered, "There are not many of them now because they had to get out."[62]

Testimony from these and other witnesses indicated that residential properties were being priced out of the reach of many African Americans who had lived in the neighborhood prior to passage of the Story Ordinances. The diminution of affordable housing within the new vice district exacerbated an already existing shortage of housing available to African Americans throughout the city. According to a newspaper article published a month before the Union Chapel filed suit against the city, "It is extremely difficult and may we say next to impossible, for a Negro to secure a decent house in a desirable portion of this city. There being, as far as we have been able to learn, only one party who builds houses to rent who will hire this class of property to Negro tenants." Certainly the Union Chapel's neighborhood had become extremely desirable to its property owners, who knew they could double their rents by taking in prostitutes as tenants. Some owners were even evicting their present tenants before the court had ruled on the legality of the new district, "in order to make repairs for this class of people that was coming in." Presumably not all of the evictions displaced African Americans, and some of the prostitutes who replaced African American and other working-class families were themselves African American. But in a housing market that was clearly biased against people of color, steeply rising rents and evictions from existing housing within the boundaries of Storyville made an already difficult situation worse.[63]

Although there was an increase in the value of rental properties, the Union Chapel's congregation did not share in the boom. A recently completed renovation had improved the church's sanctuary significantly, but the two-lot, two-story church building was not an ideal candidate for quick conversion into a brothel. The debts accrued by the local congregation in the course of making those improvements, and significant indebtedness to the Church Extension Society of the Methodist Episcopal Church, which held title to the building, also made selling the building difficult if not impossible. Thus, in their initial petition of intervention to the court, the Union Chapel's attorneys claimed "the value of its property would be destroyed, and the same would be wholly unfit for the purposes for which it was erected, and for which it is now being used, enjoyed and occupied." The lawyers did make a financial claim, contending that activation of the new district would decrease by half the value of the chapel's ten-thousand-dollar lot and building. But Reverend Taylor came closer to the crux of the matter when he testified that enforcement of the Story Ordinances would "destroy the value of the property for the purpose for which it was intended . . . as a place of worship." Just as in L'Hote's case, the Union Chapel's claims had both moral and economic aspects.[64]

Taylor testified that he and other church leaders had petitioned the Public Order Committee "three or four times, and went before" them to ask for relief in this matter. His testimony about those encounters is revealing. The exchange began with a question by his lawyer:

Q: Did they express sympathy with you?

A: Not very much.

Q: Did they grant you any relief? What did they tell you?

A: Well, the relief was they would appoint a committee and look after the matter and see how that district was situated and how our church was surrounded, and so on, but they never seemed to show us very much feeling in the matter.

Q: Did they suggest to you to move your church?

A: Yes, sir. They said we ought to get out, we ought to get out.[65]

Taylor also testified that he and others had gone to Mayor Flower seeking help. According to Taylor, the mayor claimed there were "so many letters coming into him from property holders designating that place to be the proper place for a tenderloin district that he didn't see then what he could do about the matter. He was sorry for us, but he thought we would have to go to work and preach and reform them."[66]

City attorneys repeated the glib suggestions made by Flower and the Public Order Committee in their brief to the United States Supreme Court. In answer to the charge that the city had discriminated against the Union Chapel and its African American congregation, the city responded by asserting, "How on earth an ordinance, which on its face simply prohibits prostitutes and lewd women from living outside of certain limits, can be considered a discrimination against a religious corporation that found a field of missionary labor in a portion of the city set aside for abandoned and lewd women we cannot perceive."[67]

Such arguments and suggestions by city officials revealed profound and perhaps willful ignorance about the history, mission, and contemporary position of the Union Chapel in the city's African American Methodist community. Although the city claimed the Union Chapel had been established inside a vice district to begin with, and therefore had no right to complain, that claim does not withstand scrutiny. The church that would eventually become the Union Chapel was established in 1846 in a house on "Marais Street, between Bienville and Conti," less than a block from its 1897 location. In its early years, the church building was held in trust for its African American congregants by a group of sympathetic white trustees. Even at the time of its founding in the 1840s, the immediate neighborhood was a less than completely desirable location. The congregation changed its name to the Marais Street Church in 1846. The new name was apt. Marais, which means swamp in French, accurately described the wet and marshy ground upon which the church was built. But even though the neighborhood surrounding the church was geographically inferior, it is worth emphasizing that at the time of the 1857 Lorette Ordinance, the church that would become the Union Chapel was located inside a vice district only as much as most other structures, since the boundaries it specified included virtually the entire city.[68]

During Union occupation, Methodist Church properties in the Department of the Gulf and several other Union-held areas in the South were deeded over to the MEC North. Although these claims were later disputed and in some cases overturned, the members of the Marais Street Church decided to cast their lot with the MEC North after the Civil War. Perhaps one of the most compelling reasons they chose to do so was the work of the MEC North's Church Extension Society (CES). Although the CES was chronically short of funds, and some Northern Methodists referred to it as "a corruption fund for the South," the CES nevertheless had a profound impact on the development of "Negro Methodism" in the South.[69]

Typically, the CES made loans and provided construction plans to African American congregations that wished to buy property and build churches of their own. Following this pattern, the CES helped the congregation of the former Marais Street Church, which by then was known as the Union Chapel, purchase two lots on Bienville Street in 1879. According to Dale Patterson, normally the CES "provided a small booklet of architectural drawings and some loans." Then "local architects were to take the basic plans" and make revisions to them to meet the building requirements of a particular area.[70]

Testimony in a subsequent court case reveals that the CES did not play a major role in the Union Chapel's day-to-day affairs. But when the congregation joined L'Hote's case against the city, it did so under the auspices of the Church Extension Society's local board. Although it is unclear whether they had the national board's permission to intervene in the case, the local trustees probably made the decision to do so because the CES was still the major lien-holder on the church building and property.[71]

While the city's lawyers were right in stating that the congregation's emphasis was on evangelization and missionary work, they were wrong to suggest that the primary targets of those efforts were prostitutes. The Union Chapel's focus was on the spiritual salvation and social elevation of its African American congregation. Contrary to the city's claims, it was not at its inception, nor at anytime during its coexistence with Storyville, a church that primarily aimed its efforts at converting prostitutes and their clients.

Court testimony and related contemporary documents reveal that before and during 1897, the Union Chapel was a thriving, well-attended church that had its sights set on the education and edification of its own. According to one source the Union Chapel's commodious facility was one of the largest and finest African American church buildings, surpassing most other "churches of color in the State in size and beauty." Prior to the adoption of the Story Ordinances, church leaders reported that the Union Chapel had three hundred active members and a total attendance of about six hundred that assembled regularly on Sundays, Tuesdays, and Fridays. They also noted that "one hundred and seventy children who receive religious instructions and teachings," attended their weekly Sunday School.[72]

The problems of ingress and egress that concerned L'Hote, whose house was on the fringe of the new district, were compounded for the Union Chapel and its members, since the church sat fully inside the newly delineated district. According to the chapel's supplementary petition of intervention, which was filed in late December after testimony had already begun, members of the congregation came from both the immediate neighborhood and from "different sections of the city." Thus church members were "compelled in going to and returning from religious services, instructions, and Sunday school, to pass through the several streets situated within the" new limits.[73]

This was also the case for hundreds of African American children who attended the Robertson Street School. The 830 students who attended the school in 1897, like the congregation of the Union Chapel, were not considered important or respectable enough to spare them from inclusion within the boundaries of the new district. Although the city and its attorneys repeatedly denied that the racial composition of the neighborhood and its institutions had anything to do with its choice, local opinion among African Americans, the leaders of the Union Chapel, and witnesses in the case suggests that race was indeed a factor in the city's decision.[74]

Race was also a factor in another ordinance that Story proposed in early 1898. This one, intended to keep local priests from establishing a school for African Americans, had significant conceptual and spatial links to his vice-district ordinances. The ordinance, and the debate that arose in response to it, suggests that ideas about race played a role in Story's plans to reform the city spatially and that the city's new sex district was considered an appropriate place for both prostitutes and African Americans. Details about the episode are found in an article revealingly titled "The Color Line on Esplanade Street." Story, whose family home was on Esplanade, led "the protest against the [proposed] colored school" and attempted to have it declared a nuisance. Some members of the Committee on Public Order suggested it was impossible to declare the school a nuisance before it had even opened. But other committeemen, Story among them, argued that the school was objectionable to local residents precisely because its student body was going to be African American. Story testified that the presence of a school for African Americans would be a nuisance because the students, "leaving the school in a body and passing along Esplanade," would be "boisterous and insulting." He concluded "there was no need to establish a school on Esplanade avenue to evangelize the negroes."[75]

Another member of the committee, identified only as Mr. Clark, argued that "prejudice never entered his thoughts upon the question," and that "if the colored people were right he would give them their due." In a statement that is strikingly similar to the arguments made by city attorneys in *L'Hote v. City of New Orleans,* Clark concluded that, "the citizens were on Esplanade [A]venue first and built their magnificent homes. They made their properties valuable and should not be damaged in their rights. . . . [T]he committee on public order had made it a rule to protect schools and churches from objectionable places of business, and the citizens, as residents, were entitled to as much protection."[76]

The irony of Clark's argument was probably not lost on the members of the Union Chapel or the parents of the children who attended the Robertson Street School, since their school and church were not "entitled to as much protection" as the property of the white residents of Esplanade Avenue. One committee member, a Mr. Hirsch, made an even more direct link between African Americans and Storyville when he noted that "he would object himself if the school were to be placed adjoining his property." But "if they [sic] were removed to Storyville he would make no objection."[77]

Storyville was designed as a segregated district that would serve to quarantine the city's undesirable population of prostitutes. By early 1898, some argued that it was the place where undesirable people in general belonged. Statements like Hirsch's, and the debate surrounding Story's limited segregation ordinances, reveal that sharing physical space with African Americans was becoming objectionable to many whites in the city's increasingly differentiated neighborhoods. This episode also demonstrates that the same kinds of arguments that had been used to rationalize the new vice district were deployed against African Americans months after the vice-district ordinances were passed. The debate over this ordinance reveals how the drive to segregate the sexually immoral women in Storyville was linked to emerging objections to any social contact between whites and African Americans, no matter how casual. Finally—and perhaps least surprising—it also makes clear that city officials treated powerful citizens like Story, and the white property owners for whom he spoke, with a great deal more deference than those whose race or economic condition put them at a disadvantage.

Of course, New Orleans was not the only city in which minority populations shared conceptual and physical space with prostitutes. The selection of boundaries for San Francisco's first post-Civil War vice district has profound parallels with events in New Orleans in 1897. According to historian Mary Ryan, "in San Francisco immigrants from Asia and prostitutes were singled out as the kinds of people whose place in the city demanded spatial confinement." Ryan notes that when the city's board of health took steps "to contain venereal disease and prostitution" it "attempted the first instance of de jure segregation" in Chinatown. She concludes, "the politics of Chinatown linked race, gender, and spatial segregation in ominous ways that were not unique to San Francisco."[78]

As with San Francisco's Chinatown, the objections raised by the leaders of the Union Chapel suggest a scenario in which the boundaries of a vice district were selected, at least in part, because of a given area's racial or ethnic composition. Growing disdain for blacks on the part of whites, combined with the precarious political position and relative social and economic powerlessness of the city's African American population in 1897, must not be overlooked as significant factors in the selection of the neighborhood that would become Storyville. In fact, in setting the boundaries of the new vice district Story was applying the new legal doctrine of "separate but equal," albeit in a perverse and distorted way.

In creating Storyville, the city sought to separate respectable New Orleanians from prostitutes. In the process, city leaders implied a rough equality between its population of "lewd and abandoned women," both white and black, and the African Americans who lived, went to school, and worshiped in the neighborhood. The Story Ordinances placed people of color on a plane with prostitutes and other sexual sinners, both conceptually and in terms of physical proximity.

Race is only part of the story here, but by focusing on the racial aspects of this case, we understand more about why the city chose the area it did for its new vice district in 1897. In the years that followed, the conceptual sexualization of African Americans provided much of the rationale for segregating blacks from whites in nearly every facet of life in the South. The adoption of the Story Ordinances was a dramatic step in this process and was, among other things, a physical and geographic expression of the growing ability many whites had to act on their racial prejudice against African Americans.

Conclusion

The lower-court judge rejected the city's contention that the plaintiffs in L'Hote had no right to contest the Story Ordinances, since none of them fell under its requirements. "In this case," he wrote, "quiet citizens and a large church congregation, who do not propose to violate any ordinance of the city, who cannot be arrested under the ordinance complained of, for it is not applicable to them nor intended to govern their conduct or residence, seek to protect by injunction their property rights, their families, [and] their house of worship from a threatened nuisance." Yet when he handed down his decision in January 1898, he ruled in favor of L'Hote and against the claims made by Carbajal and the Union Chapel. Judge Fred D. King's decision in the case was based on two crucial points. First, he concluded that Bienville Street between Marais and Villere, where both the Union Chapel and Carbajal's properties were located, had been an active part of the vice-district limits delineated in the 1890 ordinance. He also concluded that St. Louis between Franklin and Robertson had not. According to the judge, Act. No. 45 of the 1896 city charter gave the city the right to "regulate, police, close, and exclude houses of prostitution from certain limits." He argued, however, that the charter did not give the city the power "to include within the limits a street not [already] within the limits at the time" of its adoption. Thus judgment was "rendered in favor of the plaintiff, George L'Hote against the city, and in favor of the city against the intervenors." To add insult to injury, George L'Hote's court costs were to be borne by the city while the Union Chapel and B. G. Carbajal had to pay their own.[79]

The city appealed Judge King's decision to the state supreme court the following month. Records of the lower-court testimony and much of the same evidence was presented to the court for its consideration. When the justices rendered their verdict in November 1898, they explicitly questioned King's assertion that "St. Louis Street never was within the space assigned for" houses of prostitution. The justices opined that they had gained "a different impression" but concluded that whether or not the street had been active within previous limits was irrelevant in any case. The state's highest court ruled that the arguments pressed by L'Hote and the interveners were not sufficient to overturn the validity of the ordinance as adopted in July 1897, concluding that "on every aspect of the case . . . the ordinance is the exercise of lawful power and no ground exists to enjoin the execution of that which the ordinance proposes." Thus L'Hote's local victory was overturned, and the negative verdict against the Union Chapel and Carbajal was affirmed. The court also dissolved Judge King's injunction against the Story Ordinances, opening the way for the city to begin officially enforcing the ordinance, although it had been doing so informally for some time.[80]

Although B. G. Carbajal dropped out of the suit after this ruling, both L'Hote and the Union Chapel, once again under the auspices of the local board of the Church Extension Society, appealed the unfavorable verdict to the United States Supreme Court. The Court agreed to review the case and render a decision on the constitutionality of Ordinance 13,485 C.S. After reviewing transcripts and records in the case, the Court affirmed the ruling of the Louisiana justices on May 14, 1900, effectively exhausting all legal recourse in the case. A month later, Mayor Paul Capdeville ordered the police to begin enforcing the Story Ordinances and "to serve notices upon such women occupying quarters outside of the district to remove within them before July 1."[81]

At this point, the landlords of prostitutes who still lived outside the boundaries of Storyville asked the mayor to "withhold his order until September 1, when leases made would expire." The mayor refused to wait any longer, arguing that "all parties to such leases were cognizant at the time of making leases that they were acting in violation of one of the city's statutes." Some landlords appealed to the Committee on Public Order, asking the city to expand the limits to include areas in which they held property. Even though these interests were influential enough to gain a majority vote in the city council, Mayor Capdeville refused to approve any expansion or amendment to the Story Ordinances on the grounds that "an amended ordinance would not be the measure the Supreme Court passed upon, and if changed in one particular would be susceptible to change in other particulars. If one section had the right to be included in the limits, so had another, and it was quite certain one amendment would be followed by another."[82]

Thus the first efforts to reform the city's new vice district were under-

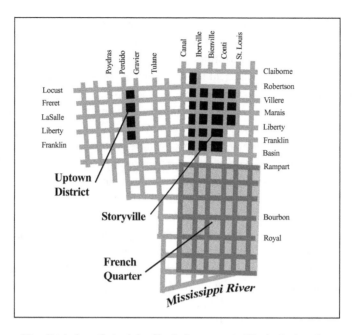

Vice-district boundaries defined by Ordinance 13,485 C.S., the final version
of the so-called Story Ordinance. *Sam Rykels*

taken by property owners outside the new boundaries, and were aimed at expanding those boundaries rather than doing away with the district. Capdeville, however, stood firm, and three and a half years after Story first presented his initial vice-district ordinance to the Committee on Public Order, and three years after the city council adopted it in final form, the legal battles over Storyville came to an end. At the end of June 1900, the *Daily Picayune* predicted that even though the mayor would be able to stave off amendments to Ordinance 13,485 C.S. through his veto power, "there will be further discussion, since the interests opposing the 'Storyville' ordinance[s] are very powerful." The paper's editors lauded the city's efforts "to gather in the lewd and depraved members of the population now infesting every quarter, and to consign them to a particular district," concluding that "nobody except interested parties, questions the wisdom and propriety of the act."[83]

Certainly parties on both sides of the debate would continue to question the wisdom and propriety of the Story Ordinances for years to come. But by 1900, with all legal appeals exhausted and little chance of the city administration's allowing further expansion of the approved limits, Storyville was a legal fact and an already active vice district. In the parlance of the day, it was "wide open." By 1900, the argument that the district was not large enough to house all of the city's prostitutes seems to have subsided. When asked by the mayor if there was sufficient room within the "prescribed territory," for all of the city's prostitutes, Police Superintendent Gaster replied that "he had a little list of all the houses [outside] the territory and the vacancies within it. There was plenty of room."[84]

Most of the city's population seems to have acquiesced in the decision, and several even wrote letters to the mayor asking him to make sure the order was enforced in their neighborhoods. Between June and December 1900, the mayor received at least ten such letters in which people complained that brothels or assignation houses still existed in their midst and requested that the women in them be moved to Storyville. One woman identified as "Mrs. Widow J. Dours" actually went to the mayor's office in person to report that her neighbor and a woman living with him "drink heavily and use obscene language, and commit obscene actions on the gallery of the house in public view." She believed "they should be in Storyville although their action[s] would not be permitted even there."[85]

Some prostitutes wrote to the mayor requesting that they be given additional time before moving into the district. Emma Johnson, who would later reign over infamous sex circuses in her House of All Nations on Basin Street, wrote to the mayor on June 29, 1900, asking permission to remain in her house at 923 Customhouse Street outside the district until July 15. Capdeville agreed and sent a note to the police asking them to "make sure she keeps her promise."[86]

Capdeville's correspondence also reveals that the mayor pressured police to enforce the ordinance. On August 1, for example, he sent a letter to the chief of police that read: "Some time ago a communication was sent to this office, giving a long list of inmates of furnished rooms houses on Rampart [S]treet. I returned this list with the request to note if the proper evidence had been secured against these people, in order to compel them to move. Since then I have received no information from you on this subject. Kindly let me hear from you."[87]

Perhaps Capdeville, like the citizens who lobbied him to enforce the new district's boundaries, felt the enforcement of the Story Ordinances could do the two things their advocates promised. One, they would provide an effective way to separate respectable people in the community, especially women, from their fallen sisters and the rowdy, sexually oriented business establishments like concert saloons and dance halls that featured casual prostitution on the bill of fare. Second, by moving prostitutes out of other residential neighborhoods, the ordinances would protect families and property values.

The subsequent history of the vice district, to which we will turn next, provides answers as to whether the hopes of these citizens were fulfilled. But the various outcomes for the plaintiffs in *L'Hote v. City of New Orleans* are revealing in their own right. Perhaps it is not surprising that among the three plaintiffs, the Union Chapel fared worst in the years to come. Church leaders had expressed fears about the long-term prospects of maintaining a large and active congregation within the boundaries of a vice district, but the process took years longer than one might expect. In fact, the Union Chapel continued to exist inside the boundaries of Storyville until 1914. Church conference records confirm that membership declined steadily over the first decade of the district's existence. The church reported 101 probationary members, 694 full members, and 160 Sunday School scholars in 1895, two years before adoption of the Story Ordinances. By 1899 the number of probationers had dwindled to 24 while full members had decreased by more than half to 331. By 1909 the number of full members had plummeted to 120, there were no probationers, and the Sunday School had only 68 children enrolled. Still the members held on, even though they were subject to harassment within the district. According to historian Walter N. Vernon, for example, "one Sunday, in about 1914, the members of Union Chapel were gathering with their children for Sunday school but were stopped by a police officer who told them that children were not allowed in the district." In the face of these difficulties, members of the Union Chapel merged with another struggling MEC congregation in 1915. "At first they were able to meet in a school building, but later a discarded 'horse stable' was obtained to rent. They began to meet there and to console each other with the thought, 'Since there was no place for us in the Inn, we went to the stable.' "[88]

Difficulties were nothing new to the members of the Union Chapel, who had been plagued by economic problems throughout Storyville's existence. In fact, a surprising party sought to put the Union Chapel building up for sale in 1904 to collect outstanding debts the church owed him. In February 1904, George L'Hote's lumber company sued the Church Extension Society for possession of the Union Chapel property. The case was heard before Judge John St. Paul, who had been a witness for the plaintiffs and spokesman for a group of property holders who wanted to keep the previous limits in place in *L'Hote v. City of New Orleans*. According to L'Hote, who was the only witness to testify in the case, he had furnished building materials used in the 1896 renovation of the Union Chapel. Between May 1899 and November 1901, the church made steady and substantial payments to L'Hote, but after 1901, he claimed, no more payments were forthcoming. Although the outcome of the case is unclear from extant records, it is unlikely that seizure ever took place since city representatives were unable to serve a notice on the Church Extension Society of the Methodist Episcopal Church or "anyone legally authorized to represent it" in New Orleans. Although the records are sketchy in this case, they provide a fascinating glimpse into the relationship between the Union Chapel and L'Hote at the time the church joined him in his suit against the city. Although the church had a great deal to lose in its own right, its financial vulnerability to L'Hote might have contributed to the decision to intervene in the case in the first place.[89]

George L'Hote was a shrewd businessman who, records indicate, was willing to protect his interests energetically whenever he felt they were threatened, even if that meant turning on his former legal ally. In the court case that bore his name, L'Hote and the Union Chapel objected to the new vice district on both moral and economic grounds. On the moral front, both were troubled by the fact that prostitutes and sexually oriented businesses would completely surround them once the new district ordinances were enforced. Once the case was closed, however, the congregation of the Union Chapel did not have the ability or the will to change its location. In contrast, by 1900 L'Hote had moved his family out of the district and its environs entirely. He vacated his childhood home on Liberty Street and moved to an upscale residential section of Canal Street.[90]

While the Union Chapel experienced a decline in its congregation once the Story Ordinances were enacted, L'Hote's business interests seem not to have been adversely affected at all by the proximity of the new vice district. In a glowing newspaper story dated August 31, 1902, L'Hote's lumber business was referred to as "one of the city's great manufacturing establishments." The article also noted, presumably based on information from L'Hote, that "the most marked growth in business and general prosperity which the company has enjoyed has developed during the past eighteen months." If the article's claims are accurate, L'Hote's business was actually thriving alongside the new vice district.[91]

Certainly it would not have been possible under such favorable business conditions for L'Hote to claim that Storyville was bad for his business, but did the presence of the vice district invigorate his business or general economic fortunes in any way? Direct evidence is hard to come by, but several property transfers in 1901 suggest that this might indeed have been the case. L'Hote's wife, Amanda Roca L'Hote, died in May 1899 at age 38. L'Hote purchased her half of their community property two years later, following the settlement of her succession. In that sale, dated May 29, 1901, L'Hote took full possession of eighteen lots that were either in or adjoining Storyville.[92]

In August of that same year, two additional acts of sale transferred another eighteen lots from L'Hote, his mother, and his fellow heirs to L'Hote Lumber Manufacturing Company. All of these lots were either inside Storyville or in the squares immediately adjacent to it. Perhaps the properties were transferred so that L'Hote could continue to expand his business. But there is also the possibility that these properties, some of them clearly residential, were transferred to the family company so that rents could be collected from prostitutes without the L'Hote family's having to be directly involved. As early as 1884 the *Mascot* had ridiculed and identified another group of what it called "high-toned owners" of brothel properties. According to the paper, all of these men were religious gentlemen who had very high standing in the commercial world. While direct ownership of valuable brothel properties could lead to criticism and public scorn, indirect ownership of brothel properties allowed New Orleanians to reap the financial fruits of prostitution without dirtying their own hands or reputations in the process. Thus, the L'Hote family's 1901 property transfers offer just one example of how monies generated by property ownership in the district might be laundered through business or other channels, separating the individuals from actual management of the property and relegating those duties to a business or property management company.[93]

B. G. Carbajal, the final plaintiff in this case, continued to speculate in real estate throughout his life. During the district's existence, Carbajal openly expanded his property holdings inside Storyville, and eventually ran and owned a bar inside the district that carried his name. When he died in 1920, his total estate was valued at more than $500,000. His son Nicholas Carbajal, a respected lawyer who had helped his father manage his properties, testified that his father's real estate holdings consisted of "seventy various titles. . . some of [them] covering three and four pieces of property." While the bulk of his holdings fell outside the boundaries of Storyville, Carbajal clearly profited handsomely from his property inside the district.[94]

Nor did Carbajal's interest in and advocacy of renting to prostitutes hurt his or his family's standing in the community in their own lifetimes. Carba-

In 1884 the *Mascot* ridiculed the respectable "high-toned" property owners who
profited from prostitution but refused to share physical space with brothels.
Courtesy Louisiana State Museum

jal was a respected businessman. One of his obituaries referred to him as a
"prominent figure in [the] city's business life" and noted that "for many
years" he had "been identified with the city's development." All three of Carbajal's sons were young men during the period of Storyville's existence and
none of them seems to have been tainted by his father's association with
the prostitution district. Nicholas's clients were "drawn from the larger and
representative corporations and prominent business men" of the city. His
two brothers, Facundo and Joseph, both became Catholic priests, indicating
that their father's interest in the prostitution trade did not hurt his family's
standing within the Catholic Church either. Two years after his death, John
Smith Kendall described Carbajal in his *History of New Orleans:* "His entire
career was an abject lesson in the value of the homely virtues of perseverance

and industry, backed by integrity and honor, and when he died his community lost a citizen who had done much to advance its welfare." While Carbajal may have done much to advance the city's welfare, Storyville had helped advance his financial fortunes in the process.[95]

Prostitution was unquestionably shameful for its female practitioners, and, on occasion, for the men who indulged in it as patrons or openly as district-business owners. But rental-property owners and absentee landlords seem to have been able to reap the monetary fruits of prostitution in a tightly defined restricted district while creating little or no sustained damage to their reputations in the community. As Storyville took shape in the years following 1900, such double standards—based on gender, class, and the concept of respectability—came to characterize the district and the role it played in the city's culture and economy. The district would also be characterized by the racism that had helped determine its boundaries in 1897.

4

"Unusual Situations and Remarkable People"

MARY DEUBLER, RESPECTABILITY, AND THE
HISTORY OF STORYVILLE

The twenty-year history of Storyville is replete with tales of colorful and often outrageous figures. Well-known procurers, prostitutes, and politicians all played active roles in the district's history. But so did thousands of ordinary and anonymous New Orleanians and visitors to the city who—through property holding, business ownership, occasional patronage, or nonsexual employment in the district's many bars, restaurants, dance halls, and service establishments—kept the vice district afloat and flourishing for two decades. Both prostitutes and patrons moved in and out of the district at a rapid pace. Proceeds from the district were filtered back into the community in the form of rent, monies, or real estate transferred from workers in the district to their families outside the district.

Because the intent of the reformers who created the district was to segregate vice and its practitioners from respectable people, the history of Storyville has often been portrayed as if the district were clearly separated and sealed off from the rest of the city. Nothing could be further from the truth. In fact, Storyville and the city had a symbiotic relationship that can be understood, in part, by looking back at their shared history through the lens of related ideas about commercial sex and respectability. The same analytical strategy also helps us to understand and appreciate the role Storyville played in the surrounding region and the rest of the nation.

In this chapter and the next, we will explore the subjects of respectability and race in the vice district by examining the lives of two of its best-known and most successful madams. Although far from typical, their careers illustrate how the city's culture of commercial sexuality was woven into the economy and how it affected the daily lives of the city's inhabitants. In the final chapter we will focus on the subject of race and Storyville, but for now our focus is squarely on the relationship between commercial sex and ideas about respectability, both within and outside the boundaries of the red-light district.

As the case of *L'Hote v. City of New Orleans* makes clear, many self-proclaimed respectable New Orleanians frowned on prostitution and considered its practitioners and patrons disreputable and dangerous. While many respectable citizens were willing to profit from prostitution indirectly, most did not wish to share physical space with brothels and other sexually oriented businesses. Al Rose astutely observes that those who did profit from property ownership or business investments within and around the vice district believed "their guilt would wash away if they refrained from actual physical contact with the women." Avoiding contact with the men who patronized Storyville was a trickier prospect, since so many of them lived in the city and were not confined by law to the boundaries of the district.[1]

Yet historical records demonstrate that many of the people who worked, lived, or ran businesses in Storyville, no matter what their gender, were vitally connected to the larger community through family ties and financial relationships. There is also substantial evidence that the allegedly disreputable people whose bodies and businesses were technically confined to Storyville were as preoccupied with the idea of respectability as those who sought to protect themselves by creating or advocating a segregated district in the first place. This was especially true in the case of the district's most successful madams and the men who served as Storyville's chief power brokers, promoters, and political fixers. The life, experiences, and relationships of one of these women demonstrates just how influential and pervasive ideas about respectability were, even among those who were shunned by the city's reputable and upright inhabitants. Her life story also provides powerful evidence of how permeable the boundaries of the vice district were throughout its twenty-year existence, despite the intentions of its creators.

To understand the relationship between commercial sex and respectability in Storyville, we will examine the experiences of a woman whose legal name was Mary Anna Deubler. Born in the city on February 8, 1864, Deubler worked as a prostitute under a variety of aliases and ultimately became a spectacularly successful madam and brothel owner. She was so successful, in fact, that a decade into the district's existence she was able to buy the trappings (but not the substance) of respectability; she lived out her life in relative ease and luxury on one of the city's most reputable thoroughfares. Deubler's life and her economic success were extraordinary, but her experiences suggest that there is much more to the history of Storyville than sex for sale, compelling anecdotes, and colorful characters.[2]

Much of what is known about Deubler's life has been gleaned from court records, especially those related to her succession. As was the case with Joseph Mathis's estate, a person who believed he had not received his due portion contested Deubler's will shortly after her death; the case ultimately went to the Louisiana Supreme Court. The legal issues revolved around questions of concubinage, just as they had in *Stringer v. Mathis.* In Deubler's case, however, it was her brother, not her concubine, who was unhappy with the will and sought to invalidate it. Deubler's life, like her succession, was extremely controversial. In the words of one lawyer, it was chock full of "unusual situations and remarkable people." But even a life as extraordinary as hers offers new and fascinating details of the quotidian history of Storyville. Her experiences also reveal how Deubler manipulated ideas about sex and respectability to make a fortune and how her designated heirs did the same in a battle to hold on to that wealth after her death.[3]

Born to German immigrant parents, Deubler later claimed that both parents had died when she was very young. She and at least two brothers fended for themselves, with intermittent help from extended family. According to her recollection, "her father died when she was about four years old, and her mother died when she was eight or nine." From that time on, she confided to her favorite niece, "she had lived a very peculiar life." Even though she went to live with her mother's sister, "she was made to go barefooted during the coldest days in winter, to sell apples on the street, and . . . would be unmercifully beat if she didn't bring [home] $1.50 a day." According to the niece, who gave these details in later court testimony, Deubler "had scars on her to show that this was true."[4]

Although the niece's retelling of Deubler's early life sounds like formulaic melodrama, it is evident that Deubler endured a short, hardscrabble, and impoverished childhood. Her lack of financial resources and educational opportunities was complicated by the overwhelming lack of economic choices for all women in this period, no matter what their circumstances or station. Deubler told her niece that she had begun to engage in prostitution at age ten or eleven. Although there is no documentation to support this claim, it is clear that by the time she was in her teens Deubler was working steadily as a prostitute. Like many other women who engaged in prostitution, Deubler

worked under several aliases. A police captain recalled that early in her career she had used the name Mary Nix. According to Herbert Asbury, by the
1880s she had adopted the name Josie Alton, under which she worked for
several years in "various brothels on Customhouse and Basin Streets." She
was first listed in a city directory in 1885 as Miss Josie Lobrano, residing at
31 N. Liberty Street. This listing, which indicates that Josie was head of the
household, suggests that by age twenty-one, Deubler had graduated from
prostitute to madam and was overseeing her own "house."[5]

Why she chose the name Josie is unknown, but her surname was taken
in homage to her concubine Phillip Lobrano. By 1888 they were living together in a house at the corner of Customhouse and Burgundy near the edge
of the French Quarter. Her brothel was in a neighborhood densely populated with saloons, bordellos, and boardinghouses that catered to both
whites and people of color. In fact, the house was just a few doors from
where Adeline Stringer had kept her first boardinghouse in the 1870s. Josie's
brothel was also within two blocks of the Royal and Bourbon Street concert
saloons. And once Henry Wenger moved his concert saloon to Burgundy
Street in the early 1890s, it was just across the street from Josie's brothel.

Like Royal Street and parts of Bourbon and Burgundy, Customhouse had
a compromised reputation in the period after the Civil War; it was one of
the areas police authorities and muckraking newspapers like the *Mascot* frequently commented on or complained about. But while the Customhouse
brothels troubled newspaper writers and respectable citizens, they offered
women like Josie a way to make steady money in amounts they could
scarcely have dreamed of otherwise. Although engaging in prostitution was
shameful enough to require a change of name, it did not necessarily alienate
women like Josie from their families. Throughout her life, she maintained
close ties with her brothers, a cousin, and their offspring. In fact, she provided members of her extended family with jobs, housing, ongoing financial
support and, upon her death, substantial economic bequests.[6]

Her first cousin Margaret Mclafflen, for example, worked as a seamstress
for Josie and for other madams and prostitutes she met through her cousin.
Mclafflen also helped oversee the Customhouse brothel when Josie took an
extended vacation in the early 1890s. In later court testimony Mclafflen recalled that "there was a woman who ran the house by the name of Effie
Dudley . . . and she used to turn the money over to me and I took it to the
bank, and that is all I had to do with it." Under cross-examination, however,
Mclafflen was forced to admit that she, too, had engaged in prostitution for

a time, even though she had been married since 1890. Mclafflen reluctantly testified that her husband had been sick and that, when Josie returned from vacation, she "wasn't ready to go to housekeeping." According to Mclafflen, "things turned a different way and I couldn't help myself." The lawyer also forced her to admit that she had given birth to two children prior to her marriage, both of whom had died, and that her oldest living son had been born in Josie's Customhouse Street brothel. Although the child's paternity was not specifically discussed, the implication was clear that he was a product of his mother's engagement in prostitution.[7]

Yet soon after her son's birth Mclafflen moved out of the brothel and established residence in a working-class area of St. Claude Avenue. The lawyers in the battle over Deubler's succession suggested that Mclafflen's promiscuity revealed her true character and thus undercut the reliability of her testimony. But her recollections also suggest how easy it was for any working-class woman, even one who was married, to slide into prostitution when economic necessity or preference prevailed and later move back into the community. Mclafflen's reputation was certainly damaged by her foray into the sex trade, but once she left her cousin's brothel she was able to live quietly in a working-class neighborhood and resume her former work as a seamstress.[8]

Mclafflen's stewardship of the brothel and Josie's long vacation in 1891 were probably both the results of a stressful and violent event that had occurred the year before. Like concert saloons, brothels troubled their neighbors because of the sexual services they packaged and sold and also because they were often the scenes of violent behavior. Fights were fairly common, both between prostitutes and between prostitutes and their customers. Asbury suggests that Josie herself had a reputation as a fighter in her early years. Sometime in 1886, for example, "she engaged in a fierce fight on Burgundy Street with a Negro prostitute [named] Beulah Ripley." A newspaper report suggested that "Ripley staggered from the scene of combat minus part of her lower lip and half an ear," while Josie lost a significant amount of hair in the fracas.[9]

Long hours of boredom, high levels of alcohol consumption, competition over patrons, disagreements with customers—all certainly contributed to violence in and around brothels. Whatever its source, the violence at Josie's brothel on Customhouse Street on the morning of November 29, 1890, came to a tragic conclusion. A disagreement that ultimately involved several members of the household came to a shocking end when Phillip Lobrano, Josie's

This photograph of Mary Deubler in a highly ornamented but respectably cut
suit was probably taken in the early 1890s, about the time she began to call
herself Josie Arlington. *From the Josie Arlington Collection, courtesy
Earl K. Long Library, University of New Orleans*

lover of at least five years, shot her younger brother Peter Deubler in the
face at point-blank range with a .32-caliber revolver. Peter lingered for nearly
ten days before dying on December 9 at 2:15 P.M. in the Hotel Dieu hospital.
He was twenty-five years old.[10]

A few days later the *Mascot* noted that Phillip Lobrano was awaiting trial
for murder and suggested that his relationship with Josie was the real source
of his troubles. In an article that lampooned Josie's physique and sexual promiscuity, the paper opined that "Phil ha[d] been a slave to the woman for
years and sacrificed every manly instinct for her. His infatuation . . . was of
such intensity that it almost deranged his mind." According to the paper,
Josie's power did not come from her looks: "Josie's face does not resemble

that of a Christmas doll, nor is her figure the kind that would attract the attention of an artist." But the story's headline, "A Wide Berth: This Is What a Score of Lovers Will Now Enjoy," suggests that Josie was sexually desirable even if she was a bit plump.[11]

Although court records of Lobrano's murder trial are scant, he was acquitted of the charge. His relationship with Josie, however, ended long before his trial began in January 1892. By the summer of 1891, Josie was on her way to Hot Springs, Arkansas, for an extended vacation with a man who called himself John Thomas Brady. A New Orleans native, he was born April 7, 1862, with the surname Hearn. By the time he was in his early twenties, he had changed his last name to Brady—an alias he would maintain all his life. His earliest jobs were on the riverfront, where he served as a low-level clerk for fishmongers, but by 1888, after a failed attempt to start his own business, he had become a ward leader for the Young Men's Democratic Association. Brady, whose role consisted of mobilizing voters in the Eighth Ward, was rewarded for his role in the organization's electoral victory of that year with a lucrative patronage appointment in the city treasurer's office. Although the pay was generous, the workload was apparently light enough to allow him to indulge in two of his favorite avocations—playing pool for money and betting on the ponies.[12]

Like Otto Schoenhausen and many other men who gambled and frequented the concert saloons and Customhouse Street brothels, Brady was a "sporting man." He and Josie no doubt moved in the same circles and knew the same people. Brady testified that he had known Josie since 1889, but their ongoing intimate relationship seems to have begun only after Lobrano murdered Josie's brother in 1890. Brady accompanied her to Arkansas in 1891 and would be at her side and at her service continually in the years that followed.

Hot Springs was a good choice for both Josie and Brady. Like New Orleans, it was a burgeoning tourist destination. The city's numerous hotels and its famous Bath House Row provided soothing treatments in the reputedly curative waters. In addition to the city's natural beauty and relaxing water cures, Josie and John probably engaged in legalized gambling, betting on the ponies, and socializing with the other sporting men and women who frequented the city. Although there is no record to confirm where they lodged, the largest and finest hotel in the city at that time was the Arlington. Built in 1875, the sprawling, beautiful, and commodious resort provided posh accommodations for travelers, many of whom stayed in the city for an entire season. Guests could take the water cures or lounge on the three-story hotel's verandas to catch the breeze and watch other visitors promenade up and down Bath House Row.[13]

Whether or not she was a guest in the hotel, Josie apparently admired the Arlington, for soon after she returned to New Orleans she added the hotel name to her brothel, and eventually she took it as her own. From 1892 on, her Customhouse Street brothel was called the Chateau Lobrano d'Arlington and she began to call herself Josie Arlington, the alias under which she would eventually become infamous and wealthy in the Storyville period. Yet her remaining six years on Customhouse Street were also well and industriously spent. Between 1892 and 1898 she continued to run a thriving brothel, but she also began to transform herself from a brawling bawd into a madam who understood, aspired to, sometimes ridiculed, but always sagely manipulated the idea of respectability that permeated American culture in this period.

After renaming her brothel the Chateau Lobrano d'Arlington, Josie "announced that she would fill her house with gracious, amiable foreign girls, who would be at home only to gentlemen of taste and refinement." She went to great lengths to project an image of sophistication for her boarders, even when the representation was a ruse. For instance, an announcement in the *Mascot* in 1895 noted that "society is graced by the presence of a bona-fide baroness, direct from the Court at St. Petersburg. The baroness is currently residing incog[nito] at the Chateau Lobrano d'Arlington." According to Asbury, "the baroness was exposed within a few weeks as a hoochy-koochy dancer and circus specialist who had performed on the Midway at the Chicago World's Fair, and several of Josie Arlington's other importations were likewise branded as imposters." Yet even these imposters had an appeal for men seeking to couple the erotic with the rare, refined, and exotic on their visits to Josie's brothel.[14]

In the same period, Josie developed an enduring friendship and business relationship with Tom Anderson. Like Brady, Anderson was a successful political ward leader and sporting man. He also had considerable business acumen and devoted his energies to developing saloons and restaurants. In 1892, about the same time Josie adopted the surname Arlington, Anderson opened his first saloon and restaurant on Rampart Street, just around the corner from Josie's brothel. Anderson called his establishment the Arlington as well; perhaps he, too, adopted the name of the Hot Springs resort. Some writers have suggested that Anderson and Josie were briefly lovers and that he named the place for her. Whatever the inspiration, both of them used the name, and their association with each other, to full advantage, making substantial amounts of money in the process.[15]

By 1897, when Sidney Story and the members of the Committee on Public Order began selecting the boundaries for a smaller vice district, astute and politically connected entrepreneurs like Josie and Tom Anderson bought property within the new boundaries as soon as they seemed secure. Basin Street, just one block from Anderson's Rampart Street business, was on the front edge of the new vice district; it would become its main thoroughfare and the location of its most spectacular showplaces.

Given subsequent developments, it is easy to forget that the men who originally created the vice district in 1897 believed that the strict segregation of brothels and sexually oriented entertainment venues would limit their visibility and their impact on the city's economy. The reformers also thought it would be easier for authorities to control undesirables, particularly public women, by forcing them to inhabit a tightly defined geographic space. Those men, whose economic hopes for the future lay in further development of the port, real estate, railroads, and manufacturing concerns, did not anticipate that the segregation of brothels, dance halls, and concert saloons would have exactly the opposite effect from the one that they had intended. Over time the district became an economic powerhouse that generated graft, enhanced the city's erotic reputation, and helped it become one of the South's most popular tourist destinations.[16]

The reform administration that created Storyville in 1897 was soundly defeated in the next municipal election. As political administrations changed, and the working-class, Democratic faction nicknamed the Ring regained control of city government, Anderson's connection to city leaders grew even closer—so close in fact that Anderson came to be known as the Mayor of Storyville. He was elected to represent the district and its environs in the state legislature between 1904 and 1920. For the next two decades, the Ring dominated city government. Perpetually successful mayoral candidate Martin Behrman, who was later credited with the statement, "You can make prostitution illegal in Louisiana but you can't make it unpopular," held that office continuously from 1904 to 1920. His single-term predecessor Paul Capdeville also supported the Storyville solution. Anderson's close connection with these men, especially Behrman, eased the way for the district to become a cornerstone of the city's economy through its appeal to tourists, despite its concomitant notoriety.[17]

In this advertisement for Tom Anderson's Arlington Café and Restaurant in the November 1900 issue of the *Southern Buck*, the prominent female nudes suggest that prostitution was on the establishment's unofficial bill of fare, available in the "private dining rooms upstairs."
Courtesy Louisiana Division, New Orleans Public Library

With so many brothels, cribs, prostitutes, dance halls, cabarets, and saloons crammed into such a concentrated area, the resulting landscape was a
crazy quilt of hundreds of colorful dens of iniquity. At the time it was established in 1897, the blocks that made up Storyville contained more than 360
structures. Over the next decade that number actually increased as prosperous brothel and bar owners like Anderson built flashy new establishments,
especially on Basin Street. In other less visible areas of the district, greedy
but astute property owners subdivided existing buildings into multiple narrow rooms called cribs that could be rented by prostitutes who did not live
in the district full time. In 1900, city officials reported that there were 230
brothels and 60 assignation houses in the district. These figures do not take
into account the dozens of cribs, saloons, dance halls, cafés, and restaurants
where prostitutes solicited and sometimes even did business while tourists
or local slummers looked on. Certainly a great many other American cities
had municipally legislated or unofficially tolerated vice districts in this era,
but few were as substantial in size or as concentrated in population as Storyville.[18]

Storyville or "the district," as many people called it, encompassed parts
of sixteen city squares and featured buildings that ranged from the modest
and run-down to the gaudily magnificent. Many establishments sought to
draw customers inside with such gimmicks as floor-to-ceiling photos of
nude females, prize-fighting portraits and memorabilia, or draft beer to go,
a nickel a bucket. Other saloons sought to impress customers with ornate
finishes and opulent decorative details. In this category, none exceeded Tom
Anderson's district saloon, which he opened in 1901 and called the Arlington
Annex. He still maintained the original Arlington on Rampart, and he had
another establishment called the Stag, but the Annex became the new vice
district's unofficial headquarters. Its mahogany bar was thirty feet long, and
the ceiling in the main room was "studded with a hundred light bulbs," a
gesture of great showmanship in the early days of electricity. There was also
a "big electric sign outside showing Anderson's name in lights." Years later,
the saloon's long-time manager Billy Struve recalled that "the opening night
was a thing to marvel at. . . . Hundreds of people were there, representatives
of the big breweries and the wine companies from all over the country. . . .
Before the night was over, everyone was walking in champagne."[19]

Surely Josie and J. T. Brady were present to congratulate their friend and
business associate, to share in his reflected glory, and to quaff their share of
champagne. But the gleaming glassware and bright bulbs of Anderson's sa-

This well-known image of Storyville's main street with railroad sheds in the foreground was taken sometime after completion of the terminal station in 1908. *From the Louisiana Jazz Club Collection, courtesy Louisiana State Museum*

Interior of Tom Anderson's Arlington Annex saloon (ca. 1903). The saloon opened for business with a dazzling party in 1901. *Courtesy Louisiana State Museum*

loon could not disguise the fact that, even as technology made inroads into Storyville, indoor plumbing and closed sewers were a rarity in the district's first decade. Horse and carriage remained the primary means of transport for practically all of Storyville's existence. Dirt, dust, dung, and foul odors must have pervaded the so-called splendor of the district, especially in warmer months or in the rainy season. Then as now, whenever it rained the swampy, poorly drained streets of the area collected water and worse in deep, pervasive puddles. For those who arrived on Basin Street in style, massive carriage stones, like the half-ton embossed limestone slab in front of Lulu White's Mahogany Hall, kept well-heeled passengers out of the mud and the muck.[20]

Shallow pools of stagnant water and strong smells were accompanied by a plethora of sounds, most of them nocturnal, that included the discharge of pellet guns in the district's multiple shooting galleries. Music from the dance halls and the voices of barkers trying to lure customers into their establishments also spilled into the streets and populated the night with noise. Carriage vendors' cries filled the air as they rolled through the streets advertising food, drink, and sundries for sale. Their voices were joined by those of crib prostitutes who called to customers from the doorways of dank, narrow rooms that often resembled horse stalls in dimension and decorative detail.

By 1908 the sounds of the district included the screech and whistle of trains arriving at the newly constructed terminal station. In exchange for the right to bring extensive rail lines and support facilities into the heart of the city, the New Orleans and San Francisco Railroad Company agreed to construct "a passenger depot on the neutral ground of Basin Street" where it intersected with Canal. Although the extraordinarily detailed agreement was adopted February 10, 1903, more than a year elapsed before a design for the terminal building was accepted, and it was four more years before the building itself was completed.[21]

The editors of New Orleans's own architectural digest commented in 1905 that "the New Orleans Terminal Company's enterprises will practically change the face of the city in some respects." They could not have been more correct. Not only did the city's modern railway terminal rival those in other New South cities in size and architectural grandeur, but multiline railway access into the heart of the city made it easier for people from all across the country to visit the city with speed and convenience. Completion of the terminal also meant that, in geographic terms at least, the so-called back o'

A section of Storyville cribs, narrow rooms dedicated solely to sexual commerce.
Courtesy Louisiana State Museum

town area that was home to Storyville became more integrated into the heart of the city than it had been when the Mississippi River was the main point of arrival and departure for visitors. In significant ways, the back o' town was transformed by the decision to place one of the city's central rail stations along its edge. And as the back o' town became a vital part of the city's center, so did Storyville.[22]

After the New Orleans Terminal station opened in 1908, several railroad lines took passengers into the city on a route that directly abutted Anderson's bar, Josie's new brothel, and other Basin Street bordellos. The day the station opened, the *Times-Democrat* reported that trains would now arrive "in the heart of the city" and celebrated the fact that "the depot is so near to all the leading hotels that it will not be necessary for passengers to take either cars or cabs to reach them." Nor would it be necessary for anyone to look very hard to find the district reformers had worked so hard to hide away.[23]

As passengers rolled into the station, they could gaze out their windows at the glitzy, gaudy Basin Street brothels that were the district's showplaces. The exteriors of these houses varied significantly, but several of them featured outlandish architectural details embedded in respectable stone finishes or placed on top of bright paint jobs. Many of the fancier brothels also fea-

Ornate Basin Street brothels like these (including Josie Arlington's in the center) had
balconies from which prostitutes could solicit customers. *Courtesy Louisiana State Museum*

tured intricate wrought-iron balconies from which their inmates could see,
be seen, and solicit business from the street or the train below. Some of the
brothels also offered piano music, fine wines, thick walls, heavy doors, numerous bedrooms, and self-conscious decorum, all of which muffled the
sounds of sexual commerce. None of them exceeded the surfeit of decorative
and architectural detail in the brothel Josie had custom built within the
boundaries of the new district.

In 1898 Josie moved into the district and set up shop a few doors down
from Anderson's Arlington Annex. She called her own brothel simply the
Arlington. For a while she did business out of 227 Basin Street while Brady
oversaw construction of a sprawling building on property she had bought
next door. Once it was completed, 225 Basin Street became one of the district's show places. Its exterior, including its domed cupola, had many of the
Victorian architectural details common to the Hot Springs bathhouses and
hotels she had admired on her 1891 sojourn. A 1903 guide to Storyville noted
that the Arlington's interior made it "absolutely and unquestionably the

most decorative and costly fitted out sporting palace ever placed before the American public anywhere. The wonderful originality of everything that goes to fit out a Mansion makes it the most attractive ever seen." Indeed, the public rooms were richly furnished, heavily draped, and so elaborately "fitted out" that Josie had to hire professional decorators to gather and assemble the great variety of materials used in the numerous parlors.[24]

This same guide featured advertisements for fifteen other brothels, seven brands of liquor and champagne, three restaurant-saloon combinations, two brewing companies, and one attorney—but the visual focus throughout was on Josie's newly completed resort. Of the eleven photographs in the guide, ten were interiors of the Arlington. One showed the dining room and another a corner of Josie's personal apartment. Curiously, however, given the nature of her business, only one photograph featured a boudoir, although there were at least sixteen in the house. The rest of the images were of parlors and the elaborate "Mirror and Music Hall" that served as a ballroom.[25]

It might seem curious that a vice-district guide would offer peeks at Arlington's Viennese, Japanese, American, and Turkish parlors instead of tempting patrons with images of scantily clad women, but pervasive ideas about respectability help explain why this was the case. Josie's campaign to transform herself and her brothel's reputation after the death of her brother in the early 1890s was not just an individual response to tragic circumstances. Surely she was also responding to society's preoccupation with respectability. Although still in the business of selling sex, she had begun to exercise a certain amount of self-conscious propriety and élan even before she moved to Basin Street. In the process she appealed to Victorian rituals like visiting in the parlor; by decorating with classical images and sculpture, she attempted to convey a sense of refinement, worldliness, wealth, and sophistication. Whether she succeeded is another question, but the idea of respectability animated her design schemes.[26]

Ideas about respectability also influenced the listings of individual prostitutes in district guidebooks. The 1903 version, for example, was titled the *Storyville 400*. The title was probably a sarcastic reference to the list of four hundred socially acceptable people created for New York socialite Lina Astor, whose ballroom was said to comfortably hold that many people. In 1892, her close friend and frequent escort, a sycophantic southerner named Ward McAllister, obligingly created a list of the members of New York society deemed respectable enough by him and Mrs. Astor to be invited to her posh but stilted soirees. McAllister and Astor were so exclusive that only 319

The Vienna Parlor was one of four parlors with national themes used to entertain patrons of the Arlington. *Courtesy Louisiana State Museum*

The Mirror and Music Hall in Josie Arlington's Basin Street brothel provided a space for prostitutes to entertain and perform for prospective customers.
Courtesy Louisiana State Museum

people made it on to their initial list of 400. In contrast, the 1903 Storyville guide listed 651 prostitutes as part of the "Storyville 400." Obviously the actual number mattered less than the idea of respectability and exclusivity that led to the creation of such lists in the first place. Just like Mrs. Astor, Storyville's inhabitants and promoters sought to project an exclusive, upscale image for the district. Thus, just as ideas about respectability had driven the creation of the vice district, they also conditioned the publicity schemes of some of its influential promoters and prostitutes.[27]

As a tourist attraction dedicated to the pursuit of illicit sexual behavior in a legally recognized district, Storyville became an important but contested center of economic activity for the city, and the numerous extant guides to the district bear this out. Generically known as Blue Books, the guides were typically published in December or January in anticipation of the winter tourist season. The small-format, soft-cover booklets listed the names and addresses of some of the district's brothels and selected prostitutes along with advertisements for a staggering variety of products and services. Blue Books could be found in some of the district's restaurants and bars, especially Anderson's establishments, and were also offered to men leaving the Basin Street train depot. The introductions written for several versions of the Blue Book make clear that they were produced for tourists unfamiliar with the vice district. In one version, the book claims it will put "the stranger on a proper grade or path as to where to go and be secure from hold-ups, brace games, and other illegal practices usually worked on the unwise in Red Light Districts."[28]

According to Pamela Arceneaux, these directories were produced "on a more regular basis" in New Orleans than in "any other city with a sizable red-light district." Existing copies of the Blue Book, as well as business cards and advertisements generated by madams and other entrepreneurs, provide ample evidence of how the district's denizens promoted themselves and their businesses to tourists. They also demonstrate how these promotional schemes mimicked those employed by respectable businesses in the city at large. In fact, Joseph Roach argues that through "the normalizing courtesies of business cards and consumer guides," Storyville was "subsumed into the 'legitimate' economy of the city."[29]

Although the organization and categorization of Blue Book listings of prostitutes changed several times over the years, many can be dated conclusively by their advertisements for French balls. Organizers advertised French balls in many ways, including ads in mainstream newspapers and intricate invitations that aped the high-style versions created by elite, old-line Mardi Gras krewes. Although similar "sporting people's balls" had been held since the 1850s, Storyville's French balls reached a level of regularity and notoriety that qualified them as a central tourist attraction. In fact, Anderson was a sponsor of the Ball of the Two-Well Known Gentlemen, "the most notorious" of all the French balls. His saloons and restaurants sold tickets and handed out invitations to his ball and to the other significant event known as the C.C.C. Ball. Typically one was held the Saturday prior to Mardi Gras and the other on Mardi Gras night.[30]

Although they were sponsored by a number of different organizations and individuals over the years, French balls had significant common features. First, they were intended for the entertainment of white men, who could mingle with the city's prostitutes and fast women far from the restraints of Victorian sexual morés. Local men and visitors alike could revel "in explicit displays of female sexuality for male enjoyment." Second, although some respectable women were probably able to sneak into the balls, the women who attended were mainly prostitutes and other women of questionable reputation who received invitations from the Storyville establishments they frequented.[31]

According to Mardi Gras historian Karen Leathem, "the French ball was a more festive version of a visit to a brothel." Although they were wild and wooly affairs, eventually accessible to any white man willing to pay a significant admission price, French balls mimicked the exclusive Carnival rituals created by the city's elite. All-male clubs, called krewes, originated the private and secretive masked balls that have become the hallmark of the city's Carnival season. Like the private society balls they both mimicked and mocked, French balls sometimes featured intricately designed invitations and the selection of a queen. But while society krewes selected a queen from among elite debutantes, French balls crowned the prostitutes and entertainers of Storyville.[32]

French balls and the advertisements for them provide an explicit example of how entrepreneurs like Anderson simultaneously replicated and ridiculed the ideas about respectability that shaped the culture beyond the boundaries of the vice district. But if respectability was a theme in the advertisements, other marketing schemes appealed to tourists' taste for the exotic. The names of Storyville brothels such as the Cairo or Emma Johnson's House of All Nations were meant to entice tourists with their exotic aura. Other names, like Mahogany Hall or The Star Mansion, evoked the mystique of

Tom Anderson was one of the "Two Well-Known Gentlemen" who
sponsored an annual French ball that took place on Mardi Gras night.
This ornate invitation predates the opening of Storyville by two years.
Courtesy Louisiana State Museum, loan of the Louisiana Historical Society

the Old South plantation house and promoted quality of construction,
sumptuous furnishings, and decorative detail. Inside these and other Basin
Street brothels customers could play out their sexual fantasies in multi-
themed Victorian pleasure palaces. Josie's customers could imagine that they
were courtly lovers or sheiks in a harem rather than clients paying prostitutes for their time and the madam for the substantial overhead and over-
priced liquor.[33]

Some names were meant to evoke a sense of familiarity for tourists. Josie's use of the name Arlington is only one example of using well-known
regional landmarks to lure tourists. Cafés like the Monte Carlo and the
Waldorf, and bars like the Milwaukee Saloon sought to give their customers
a sense of familiarity and convey refined or, in the case of the Milwaukee,
casual hospitality. This kind of name recognition directed at tourists was the
case with the New World Hotel as well. This sprawling hotel on Robertson
Street in the "Negro section" of the district occupied a building that had
housed a "colored" school before the adoption of the Story Ordinance. Al-

though the exact number of guests the hotel could accommodate is not recorded, 830 children attended the school in 1897. Fire-insurance maps
indicate that the developers of the New World Hotel made only minor
changes to the building's footprint, expanding it slightly when they renovated the school into a hotel. Thus we can deduce that the building's capacity for guests ran into the hundreds.[34]

While the significance of the hotel's name is not readily apparent, it probably took its name from the most famous turn-of-the-century brothel in
Clarksdale, Mississippi. For tourists coming into New Orleans from the
Delta, advertisements for the New World Hotel would have struck a familiar
chord. W. C. Handy described the Clarksdale brothel as a place where "lush
octoroons and quadroons from Louisiana, [and] soft cream-colored fancy
gals from Mississippi towns" plied their trade. "While the Baptist and Methodist black families living nearby clearly disapproved of the events inside,
especially the overt interracial sex," white officials turned a blind eye to the
brothel, probably induced by graft and other favors from the New World's
owners and resident prostitutes. Handy recalled that the "rouge-tinted girls,
wearing silk stockings and short skirts, bobbing their soft hair and smoking
cigarets . . . were wonderful clients, especially when important white men
were their guests."[35]

This migration of a brothel name from Clarksdale to New Orleans mirrors the way that individual prostitutes used regional identification to draw
customers to their doors as well. For instance, the Carnival edition of the
Sunday Sun, dated February 25, 1906, included this advertisement: "Two
sweet girls from Hattiesburg Miss. have come here and have embarked in
business at No. 1418 Conti Street. . . . visit these girls and they will entertain
you in true Mississippi style." Although Mississippi certainly had its own
brothels, and apparently its own erotic "style," the "two sweet girls" knew
that the most lucrative place to market their wanton wares, at least during
Carnival season, was in Storyville.[36]

In the same issue, Lulu White, described as "the Queen of Diamonds and
the proprietress of Mahogany Hall," assured prospective customers that she
was "always surrounded by the finest and prettiest lot of Octoroons to be
found in the country." In one version of the Blue Book, she claimed her
house was "the most noted pleasure resort in the South." Whether her own
brothel had "a national reputation," the city clearly did. As far north as Louisville and as early as 1885, southern madam Sallie Scott bragged about the
"famous Creole beauties" she could offer her clients.[37]

With dozens of city blocks largely dedicated to vice and male leisure establishments, Storyville constituted a veritable sexual amusement park. As with most other amusement parks, the district experienced seasonal fluctuations, both in its customer base and in its population of prostitutes. According to the mayor and chief of police, in 1900 there were "about 1500 prostitutes" working in the district. They noted, however, that the number of prostitutes "largely increased in the winter, say by 500 more." Obviously the population of prostitutes would not have risen so significantly had there not been a customer base in place to support them. Why did so many tourists come to New Orleans in the winter, and what, if anything, did Storyville have to do with their visits?[38]

Writing in *Harper's* in 1899, Julian Ralph opined that New Orleans was well on its way to becoming "the chief winter resort of those who journey southward to escape the winters in the North." The author was no doubt correct that the city's temperate winters helped to account for its seasonal appeal, but Ralph, like Charles Dudley Warner a dozen years before, gave short shrift to the city's more sensual attractions. In addition to balmy days, the winter tourist season featured horse racing and other forms of legalized gambling, Mardi Gras festivities, few restrictions on the sale of alcohol, and access to Storyville. While many tourists, especially those from the North, were escaping the cold, they were also indulging in the pleasures of the flesh. The city offered its winter sojourners a constellation of sensual delights and, for many of them, particularly single male travelers, Storyville was the star attraction. While it was not the focus of articles in genteel magazines or "booster" publications, over the next two decades the vice district would become one of the city's, and the South's, most prominent and infamous tourist destinations.[39]

There is substantial evidence to suggest that the region's and perhaps the nation's largest vice district was a site where male visitors could engage in activities and behaviors that elsewhere were taboo. Thousands of men from the immediate region joined the "two sweet girls from Hattiesburg" on sybaritic pilgrimages to the Great Southern Babylon. For residents of north Louisiana and the more conservative, largely Protestant region that surrounds the state, New Orleans was a place where male visitors could let down their hair with little fear of censure for activities that would have been out of the question at home. Historian Ted Ownby suggests that even the most rural and conservative southern cities and towns generally set aside an area, either geographically or temporally, for "exclusively male professions, services, and

recreations." But in the prevailing Protestant evangelical culture that dominated life in the South, these spaces were frowned upon by most people in
the community. Questionable "masculine recreations could take place
largely unchallenged as long as those who disapproved rarely had reason to
see them."[40]

While small towns provided their male residents with occasional and limited outlets for rowdy behavior, New Orleans, and Storyville in particular,
acted as a multidimensional regional safety valve. According to nineteenth-
century sexual ideology, prostitutes provided the physical safety valve that
uncontrollable male sexuality required. In significant respects, Storyville was
a geographic expression of this ideological belief. The district was a year-
round erotic space, inside the boundaries of which men of all descriptions
and convictions could indulge in a variety of sensual, even sinful, pleasures
for days and nights on end, free from the moral restraints that their home
communities imposed on them.

There is evidence that even men who were in the business of subduing
Satan in their own communities came to New Orleans to revel with his min-
ions, if only for a few days during Carnival each year. Historian Reid Mitchell notes the Reverend Charles L. Collins's visit to New Orleans for the 1908
Carnival season. Apparently Collins's work for the Kentucky Anti-Saloon
League required him to make at least two visits to Storyville. In another case,
a man from Hazelhurst, Mississippi, reported that he had seen the pastor of
his church at "a sporting people's ball," and that the reverend was in the
company of a woman wearing "a dress that was simply awful in its short
skirts and worse in low neck." W. W. Hamilton, an itinerant Baptist
preacher, actually held revival services in the heart of the vice district. He set
up a group of Gospel Wagons at the intersection of Franklin and Customhouse Streets, but his decision to bring his wife and children along to provide musical accompaniment got him booted out. Anonymous ministers on
brief forays were welcome in Storyville, but the Reverend Hamilton's revival
services were not.[41]

The presence of Hamilton's wife and children in the district, like the advertisement taken out by the "two sweet girls from Hattiesburg," reminds us
that men were not the only ones who made pilgrimages to Storyville. Over
the course of two decades, thousands of women traveled to New Orleans
from the surrounding region or even farther afield. Whether they came seeking work or adventure, many of them worked in the brothels and cribs of
Storyville until they got established or made enough money to get back

home. If Storyville acted as a safety valve, it did not do so simply as a place for men to blow off steam. City ordinances required that any woman who engaged in sex work do so within the boundaries of the district. Thus, for most of the women who worked there, Storyville was not a resort but a restricted reservation—although not a very effective one.

Traffic in and out of the district was brisk, especially during the winter tourist season, and Josie Arlington's experiences suggest that it was common for women to come and go as they chose. They might do so on a daily basis to shop or go on excursions to outlying places, such as the West End or Spanish Fort amusement parks. Some women left for weeks or even months at a time when business was slow. In Josie's case, the district's scarcest commodities seemed to be peace, quiet, and the guise of respectability. Her cousin Margaret Mclafflen and an African American maid named Harriet Dumas both recalled that in the district's early years Josie and her paramour Brady spent many nights outside the district at Mclafflen's house on nearby St. Claude Street. While they were there, the neighbors referred to them not as Josie and Tom but as "Mr. and Mrs. Brady." Dumas later testified that Josie and Tom generally left the district at 2:30 in the morning and took a cab to her cousin's house. Dumas recalled that she often transported meals for Josie and Tom from the brothel to St. Claude Street around noon the same day. Depending on what needed to be done at the Basin Street house, Josie would either go back to the district in the early afternoon or wait until just before the Arlington opened for the evening at 8:00 or 8:30.[42]

Josie and Brady also traveled outside the city fairly often in the district's first decade. For three summers near the turn of the century Josie rented a house at Pass Christian, a nearby Mississippi town that overlooked the Gulf of Mexico. In doing so, she may have been following the example of the respectable and socially prominent citizens she sought to emulate. With its cool breezes and warm waters, Pass Christian was a fashionable resort for those who could afford to leave the city during the hottest months when business was slow and yellow fever was at its height. Josie called her Mississippi house "Cooley Cottage" and invited many members of her family to visit during the three seasons she leased it. In addition to a young girl named Evelyn, the daughter of one of her brothel employees, Josie hosted Margaret Mclafflen and her children. The maid Harriet Dumas, who also went along, testified that Tommie Mclafflen, who had been born in the Customhouse Street brothel, had a special relationship with Josie and called her his "Nanan." While Brady visited for several days at a time, frequently returning to New Orleans to tend to business, Josie shared the house continuously with her brother Henry, his wife Mary, and their five children. Four of the children were boys, one of whom had been named John Thomas at Josie's request. His mother recalled that "Miss Mary A. Deubler asked me to let [Brady] stand" as godfather at the child's christening, while Josie acted as godmother. Serving as godmother to her nephews is yet another example of Josie's interest in being "respectable" in spite of being a prostitute.[43]

Josie may have been fond of her nephews, but the apple of her eye was her niece and namesake Anna Mary Deubler, who was born in 1884. There is overwhelming evidence that Josie favored Anna over all her other relatives and even over Brady. According to court testimony, Josie was "in love with Anna," and "the girl was all that she was living for." While Anna's name mirrored her aunt's, Josie made certain that her niece's life experiences were far different from her own. About the time Storyville was established, Josie (whom Anna knew as "Aunt Mary") began to pay for Anna's education, initially at the Dominican Convent in New Orleans. In 1901, when Anna finished her studies at Dominican, Josie and Brady took her to Emmitsburg, Maryland, and enrolled her in another convent school, St. Joseph's Academy, which was run by the Sisters of Charity. Anna spent the school year at Emmitsburg and returned to spend the summer with her Aunt Mary, her "Uncle" Tom, and the rest of her family on the Mississippi coast. As Anna recalled in court testimony, she had always believed her aunt and Tom Brady were married since everyone referred to her aunt as Mrs. Brady. According to Anna, "That is all I ever heard her called . . . and I supposed it was the same as my mother and papa."[44]

In the autumn of 1902 "Mr. and Mrs. Brady" took Anna back to Maryland but were unable to reenroll her in the convent school at Emmitsburg. Although Anna was ignorant of the source of her aunt's largesse and the nature of Josie's relationship with Brady, the mother superior at the academy had discovered the facts of "Mrs. Brady's" life and the source of her wealth. In a telephone call, the mother superior told Josie flatly that she was not to return Anna to the school. Anna returned to Cooley Cottage in Mississippi while Josie proceeded to New Orleans, where she contacted a well-connected friend for help. James G. Schwabrick had been Josie's grocer for many years. He noted that "Josie Arlington—that was the name I knew her by—told me that her niece wasn't allowed to go back in the convent, for the reason that a certain gentleman in town—she didn't mention the name—

objected to her going back there, stating that if [Anna] came back to the convent he wouldn't allow his daughter to return."[45]

Josie asked Schwabrick to intercede with Cardinal Gibbons of Baltimore, to whom he was related. Schwabrick agreed, and the cardinal's secretary "wrote to the Mother Superior of the convent" asking to have Anna reinstated. Schwabrick's effort failed, but Josie was undaunted. Shortly afterward, "Mr. and Mrs. Brady" arranged to take Anna to Europe. If Emmitsburg, Maryland, was not far enough away to guarantee Josie's anonymity and protect Anna's future as a respectable woman, perhaps Europe would be.[46]

Josie had secured a letter of introduction from a local priest and planned to enroll Anna at a convent in Ireland or England, but Anna had ideas of her own. She testified, "I didn't think it was any use to go there, because we had English institutions at home and instead of entering the convent there, I asked Auntie whether it would be just the same to go to either Germany or France or Italy." The threesome embarked on a grand tour of Europe, visiting convent schools along the way. They made stops in Germany, Switzerland, Austria, Italy, and France and managed, according to Anna, to see all the continent's principal points of interest. After all the traveling, Anna and her aunt settled on the Sacred Heart Convent in Paris, where Anna remained for the next two years.[47]

With Anna safely tucked away in Paris, Josie was free to focus on business and was rewarded handsomely for her efforts. During this period she opened the newly constructed Arlington and began her ascendancy to the social and economic heights of the vice district. Although precise figures are hard to come by, Josie must have been making astounding amounts of money. In addition to financing Anna's education and their European sojourn, she began enlisting Brady to buy and sell residential and commercial properties on her behalf. Eventually she owned commercial properties on Canal Street and in the business district and residential properties scattered around the city, including at least one other house in the district. She also bought a house and some land in Covington, Louisiana, just across Lake Pontchartrain from the city. This small town was near Abita Springs, where Joseph Mathis had gone to recuperate during one of his final illnesses. Covington was pleasantly rural, wooded, and isolated enough that, upon her return to Louisiana, Anna would not be likely to meet other city folks or to discover her aunt's false identity and true occupation. According to one witness, Josie told him she bought the property "because she didn't want her niece to know what life [she] was leading" in New Orleans.[48]

When Anna completed her studies in 1904, she traveled from Paris to New York and from there "as far as a place called Pearl River, and from Pearl River . . . directly to Covington," noting that she never "came to New Orleans at all." Her Aunt Mary, it seemed, was taking no chances. She met her beloved niece in Pearl River and rode with her by carriage to Covington. When they arrived, Anna met her mother, father, and four brothers at the country house her aunt had purchased and had named "Anna's Villa." Anna spent the next several months in Covington with her family, but in 1905 she left for a year of postgraduate training in music at the convent of the Sacred Heart in Clifton, Ohio.[49]

While Anna was away Josie's business continued to thrive, but in 1905 her brothel was so damaged in a fire that Josie had to relocate for a time. While the house was being renovated, Josie's girls moved to the floors above Anderson's Arlington Annex and continued with business as usual. While she and Brady oversaw the renovation of the Basin Street property, Josie also began looking for a house in the city. Ultimately she settled on a house and grounds that encompassed twelve lots on upper Esplanade Avenue. The site was ideal in many respects. It was still rural enough that Josie was able to keep chickens, horses, and cattle on the property and employed one of Anna's brothers to care for the animals. Like the house in Covington, its semi-rural location provided a buffer from the heart of the city. She also bought more modest houses nearby, where she allowed close relatives like Mrs. Mclafflen and Anna's grown brothers and their families to live. Josie's generosity was remarkable, but it was also a way to keep Anna encircled with family and in the dark about the realities of her aunt's other life.

The central advantage of the property was that it was grand and proper enough to house her upright, well-educated, and extremely sheltered niece. Josie went to great expense to furnish the house in the extravagant style she believed a woman of Anna's respectability deserved. According to court documents, the home's furnishings included significant collections of "valuable cut glass, silverware, [antique] furniture, statues, and paintings." The other grand houses along Esplanade Avenue included Sidney Story's family home. It was ironic that Josie Arlington, who was required by law to ply her trade within the boundaries of the vice district Story had helped to create, was able to purchase and occupy a house on the thoroughfare once occupied by his parents. But Josie's wealth, ill gotten though it may have been, allowed

Mary Deubler in evening wear at the height of her success as a Storyville madam (ca. 1900). *From the Josie Arlington Collection, courtesy Earl K. Long Library, University of New Orleans*

Mary Deubler bought this house on Esplanade Avenue and furnished it in grand
style for her beloved niece Anna. *From the Josie Arlington Collection,
courtesy Earl K. Long Library, University of New Orleans*

her to buy the accouterments of elevated class status, even if her reputation
would never follow.[50]

Josie did make a significant attempt to appear respectable by asking
Brady to move into the Esplanade house and live with her as man and wife.
He had played this role for many years, especially in Anna's presence. But
now that her niece was moving back to the city full time, Josie needed
Brady's explicit cooperation if Anna was to continue to believe that the two
were husband and wife. (In court testimony, Brady recalled that he had proposed marriage to Josie as early as 1904 but she had refused, saying "we went
along this far" without being married and "we might as well go along the
balance.")[51]

The location of the new house no doubt pleased Brady, since it was
within walking distance of the Fairgrounds racetrack. During the racing season, which ran from Thanksgiving through early spring, he had only to walk
a short distance to the track to bet on the ponies. But there were other con-
cessions that he desired as well. Brady recalled that Josie had told him that
she wanted him to move into the house on Esplanade primarily to "protect"
Anna. In early-twentieth-century culture, of course, protecting a woman

Anna Deubler, ca. 1910. *From the Josie Arlington Collection,
courtesy Earl K. Long Library, University of New Orleans*

meant protecting her reputation; although Josie was not willing to marry
Brady, she understood the role marriage played in defining a household as
respectable. Yet she was no fan of the institution. Her corset maker recalled
that Josie once told her "she regretted the day that Anna would ever marry."
When the woman asked why Josie replied, "because men are such dirty
dogs."[52]

Regardless of her opinion of men in general, Josie convinced Brady to
move in and act the part of her husband. She also asked for and received
similar cooperation from a variety of friends and business associates. In the
dispute over her estate more than a dozen witnesses testified that the woman
they had known as Josie Arlington had asked them to call her Mrs. Brady in
the presence of her niece. Tradesmen, retailers, dressmakers, tailors, and
even three doctors took the stand and recounted conversations in which

Josie had impressed upon them the importance of referring to her only as "Mrs. Brady" in Anna's presence. One of them was Una Dill, the niece and assistant of Josie's dressmaker. Apparently Josie took a shine to the girl and considered her respectable enough to serve as a companion for Anna. According to Dill's recollection, Josie gave her "instructions before she introduced me to her niece, she impressed me not to let her niece know her other name."[53]

Over the next several years the woman born Mary Deubler, who became wealthy as a prostitute and madam called Josie Arlington, began to live her day-to-day life as Mrs. J. T. Brady. Just as Joseph Mathis had two decades before, Josie attempted to live two completely separate lives. In her case, the reasons had nothing to do with changing racial morés but were an attempt to protect the reputation of her niece by participating in the social forms demanded by the arbiters of civilized morality.

Anna, along with her father, mother, and two youngest brothers moved into the grand house on Esplanade with her Aunt Mary and "Uncle" Tom in October 1906. Although Josie maintained ownership and control of the Arlington during these years, she entrusted the day-to-day management of the brothel to her friend and business associate Anna Casey. The Arlington, like most other establishments within the district, continued to be a profitable enterprise for many years after 1906, but the forces of reform were slowly but surely making inroads into Louisiana.[54]

Local women were among the first to act. A loosely affiliated group of female reformers had acted in the early 1890s to protest a police ordinance that required the medical inspection of prostitutes. By 1892, local women had also established at least two institutions intended to provide an alternative to prostitution by offering girls and women free housing and vocational training. Yet the rhetoric of respectability, and the promise that respectable women would no longer have to share physical space with prostitutes and brothels, convinced many New Orleans women to support the Storyville solution at its outset. A decade or so into the district's existence, however, it had become apparent to many of those same women that Storyville was a segregated district in the heart of the city that only marginally served its stated purposes. By the time the terminal station was completed in 1908, it was difficult not to notice the sprawling, raucous vice district located along its edge.

That same year a group of local women formed a Travelers' Aid Society. One history of the organization explains that the Association was "instituted for the purpose of fighting the White Slave traffic, an exceptionally flagrant case of which had come to the attention of the women of New Orleans." In response, the women called a mass meeting, after which a consortium of white, Protestant church groups and women's social clubs joined together to "consider ways and means of legally fighting the conditions which, though always existent, had become more heinous than usual." In their estimation, Storyville had not solved the city's prostitution problem, it had only concentrated commercial sex and confined it to a location that was increasingly visible.[55]

One of the society's members "called attention to the danger of having the Frisco depot so near the Red-light District. She said that the boundaries of this district should be removed from this location and should be so clearly outlined" and that the new boundaries selected "should be far removed from the shopping district." Storyville's prostitutes and their customers did business within eyeshot of the virtuous white women who shopped in the major department stores on Canal Street, while the city's increasingly diverse and numerous tourists were treated to a panoramic view of the district on their way into the new depot.[56]

Local women were not the only ones to raise their voices in opposition to the district and its excesses. For example, in the February 29, 1908, issue of *Collier's,* New Orleans received a stern reprimand in an article titled "The American Saloon." While many other cities came in for criticism as well, author Will Irwin focused on the close connections among the politicians, the liquor interests, and the leaders of the vice district. Irwin complained particularly about Tom Anderson, whom he called the restricted district's "law-giver and its king," and he described Storyville's "unblushing" evils in detail, including its "saloons with wide-open poker and crap games," and its "dives where negroes buy for fifty cents five cents' worth of cocaine." Referring to the district as "Anderson County," Irwin asserted that "no other city of the country runs vice of every kind so wide open." He also pointed out a fact he considered astounding—that, in addition to serving as unofficial boss of the district, Anderson was repeatedly elected to the state legislature, where he won important committee appointments and wielded enormous influence. Irwin concluded that Anderson "does not believe in sumptuary laws; he thinks that it degrades the citizen to take away from him the privilege of choosing for himself between right and wrong."[57]

Irwin clearly suggested that Anderson's position on sumptuary laws was objectionable. But most New Orleanians seemed to agree with Anderson

that individuals were free to choose between "right and wrong," especially
when it came to indulgence in their favorite vices. But the laissez-faire morality for which New Orleans was so well known had also come under fire
from the northern, heavily Protestant areas of the state, where arguments
like Irwin's about temperance and vice reform had begun to find a receptive
audience by 1908.[58]

In this era, most Americans understood vice to include several objectionable activities, including prostitution, gambling, and the intemperate use of
alcohol. In fact, during the late nineteenth century "vice connoted a range
of frowned-upon activities, but it especially meant prostitution and alcohol." The conceptual relationship between alcohol and prostitution created
problems for Storyville's many alcohol-oriented businesses once Prohibition
forces began to gain ground in the state. Anderson was perhaps the most
notorious figure who was openly associated with Storyville; but many other
less visible and flamboyant businessmen were also heavily invested in the
city's reputation for tolerating "vice of every kind." Unfortunately, for Josie
Arlington, Tom Anderson, and others who made money selling the potent
combination of wine, women, and song, many people in the state, particularly outside New Orleans, agreed that the time had come for more restrictive liquor laws.[59]

Throughout 1908, the debate over Prohibition in Louisiana exploded
onto front pages across the state. In response, a group of New Orleans businessmen organized to fight it and "to educate the public on the evils of prohibition." They chose Sidney Story as their spokesman. Story's leadership of
the anti-Prohibition forces reveals yet another connection between those
who profited from the twin evils of prostitution and alcohol, since he had
authored the ordinances that created the vice district in the first place. Just
as he had with prostitution a decade earlier, Story argued that, with proper
regulation, the alcohol industry could be run in a responsible manner for
the economic and moral benefit of the entire state.

He focused his efforts on the northern, heavily Protestant part of the state
where Prohibition sentiment was strongest. In commenting on that demographic difference, Mayor Behrman remarked that "people from the country
were for prohibition at home but when they came to New Orleans they were
wet and wanted New Orleans to be saturated." In his own colorful way,
Behrman confirmed the belief that the city functioned as a safety valve, providing opportunities for regional tourists to indulge in activities that would
be considered vices at home.[60]

The state legislature adopted a solution that seemed to reflect this attitude when it passed the Gay-Shattuck Law. This statute was "designed to forestall prohibition through liquor regulation and to remove women from all places where liquor was sold and consumed." It also stipulated, among other things, that blacks and whites could no longer be served in the same establishments, and it banned musical instruments and musical performances from saloons. The only exceptions to these rules were restaurants and hotels that served meals. This exception meant that respectable men and women could be served alcohol with their meals in fancy restaurants; but in lower-class establishments without food service—namely saloons—women were barred, as was cross-racial socialization.[61]

Of course, the extensive, complicated stipulations of the Gay-Shattuck Law indicated how central the saloon had become to entertainment and leisure pursuits for all colors and classes of people in New Orleans and throughout the state. But the law was most likely to have a dramatic effect in Storyville, whose activities were fueled by alcohol combined with the potent mixture of men and women, black and white, and song and dance. The initial enforcement of Gay-Shattuck in New Orleans was swift and surprisingly thorough. In early January 1909, the *Daily Picayune* reported that the "police put the lid down in the Tenderloin district last night, and saloon men and dive keepers raised a howl which vibrated from one end of the district to the other." The paper also noted that musical instruments were no longer "among the attractions to lure the slummer into the saloons and dance halls." In addition to policing saloons for females and musical instruments, the police also enforced racial segregation in the saloons, suggesting that the race mixing the *Mascot* had complained about two decades earlier was still characteristic of the neighborhood. One saloon proprietor known for serving "refreshments indiscriminately to whites and blacks" was forced to choose one clientele during the early Gay-Shattuck raids. He posted a sign that read "For Colored Patrons Only," once again suggesting how integral African Americans were to the district's economy.[62]

Of course, many Storyville proprietors sought ways around the law, ostensibly by turning their establishments into restaurants. "The notorious Ada Hayes" for example, installed "a weinerwurst and tamale stand" in the courtyard of her establishment, the New Waldorf Café, which had "a saloon in the front and a dance dive in the rear." Similar "restaurants" popped up all around the district, so that boarded-up dance halls and ladies' entrances to saloon-restaurant combinations were soon back in business. "Minor ad-

justments, combined with minimal enforcement, left dance hall life relatively untouched" in the long run. Though reformers had intermittent
success at enforcing the newly adopted statutes, Storyville limped along. It
may not have been respectable, but the vice district was durable—and so
profitable that few owners and operators seemed willing to dispose of their
interests.[63]

Even Josie Arlington, who for all intents and purposes had changed her
identity to Mrs. Tom Brady and moved out of the district altogether, retained ownership of her brothel and maintained a liquor license under the
name Josie Arlington. By this time, however, she was leasing the property
with all of its furniture and fixtures to Anna Casey on a yearly basis. In fun-
damental ways, Josie was engaged in the kind of absentee profiteering in
which many respectable New Orleanians participated. She continued to receive monies from the sex trade, but she no longer had to dirty her hands
with the day-to-day details. As "Mrs. Tom Brady," she settled into a routine
existence with Anna and other members of her extended family, who
crowded the Esplanade house and relied on her for support. Anna and her
aunt gardened, shopped for jewelry and hats, threw each other lavish birthday parties, had clothes custom made for themselves, and, when they tired
of the city, spent time at Anna's Villa in Covington.[64]

Despite Josie's deception, the relationship between the two women was
extremely close. According to one witness Josie was "perfectly devoted" to
her niece. And in 1913, when her Aunt Mary fell ill, Anna returned the love
and care that had been lavished upon her with an equal measure of "absolute devotion." By that autumn, Josie's health worsened, and her niece knew
this illness would be her last. Anna personally took on the physically demanding tasks of caring for her aunt, who had grown quite heavy. One doctor even testified that Anna had injured herself by the repeated "lifting of
her aunt who had lost control of her bladder and bowels" in the months
before her death.[65]

Anna was forced to deal with the revolting physical realities of caring for
her invalid aunt; perhaps just as distressing for someone of Anna's piety, she
also learned about her aunt's other life as Josie Arlington. Some court records contend that Mary Deubler "was insane for about six months preceding
her death." In contrast, Anna's testimony suggests that Deubler experienced
intermittent periods of delirium but was often lucid. During her episodes of
dementia, Mary Deubler told her niece that she and J. T. Brady were not

At a dinner party to celebrate Mary Deubler's forty-eighth birthday, in February 1912, John T. Brady, Deubler's long-time paramour, is shown here seated between Mary and Anna Deubler, whom he married two years later. *Courtesy Historic New Orleans Collection, acc. no. 1993.55*

married, and she revealed the source of her great wealth. Anna testified further:

> I think auntie was not herself. She was delirious, and she would say, "Little Girl, how I have been fooling you!" and I would say, "You were fooling me very badly, very painfully indeed." . . . [A]nd she would come out at times and would ask me what she had said. . . . At times I would tell her and at other times I wouldn't; the things were too awful to repeat. . . . I was very much astounded to hear auntie's life was such; and she told me she wasn't married, and told me the life she had been leading.[66]

Anna also learned of her Aunt Margaret Mclafflen's foray into prostitution and her cousin Thomas Mclafflen's conception and birth in the Customhouse Street brothel. For twenty-nine-year-old Anna, a sheltered, convent-educated woman who had never married, her aunt's revelations must have been shocking. During periods of lucidity, and perhaps to help mollify the niece she so loved, Mary Deubler told Anna that she wanted her "to write a book for the protection of young women." According to Anna, her aunt planned for each year of her life to be a chapter in the book; in recalling her experiences she would ask, "Have you chapter 5th, or chapter 4th, or chapter 3rd if you would recall it?"[67]

Mary Deubler had always been a demanding and determined person; dealing with her in those final weeks was a challenge for everyone in the household. Anna recalled one conversation in which she had confronted her "Uncle" Tom and asked if her aunt's recollections were the truth. He confirmed the facts with an apology. Anna recalled that she was angry and "I demanded my jewelry, because I didn't intend to live under the roof where such things existed." During the course of that argument, she recalled, Mary Deubler "got out of bed and came into the room and . . . insisted on sleeping in the same room, in the same bed with Mr. Brady." Anna objected and was "very indignant about it"; she did not reveal whether her aunt had prevailed.[68]

Mary Deubler had overcome extraordinary odds in her life. She survived a tumultuous and impoverished childhood, became one of the city's most prosperous madams and brothel owners, and, in her final years, even attained a prosperous, quaint, and quiet retirement with her concubine, her favored niece, and members of her extended family. One marvels at her survival instincts, business acumen, financial success, devotion to her niece, and generosity to her family while simultaneously lamenting the circumscribed social circumstances that left her few options besides prostitution in the late 1870s. Her relatively brief life encompassed an extraordinary range of peaks and pitfalls; it ended on February 14, 1914, eight days after her fiftieth birthday. A few days later the *New Orleans Item* ran a story that began: "Josie Arlington, so-called 'Queen of the Demi-Monde' is dead." The paper recounted the details of her funeral and interment in Metairie Cemetery where several years earlier she had purchased a plot and had an impressive and costly monument constructed. The newspaper described the tomb as "a magnificent affair of brown marble. It shows the single figure of a woman standing with her hand outstretched toward the door of the sepulchre, a wreath of flowers just laid down. . . . Only one word, 'Deubler,' is carved upon the shaft. It was her maiden name."[69]

Even the newspaper writers believed that Mary Deubler had married Tom Brady many years before her death. But Deubler had refused to marry

Brady. Although most of those close to Deubler assumed that the bulk of her estate would go to Anna, none of the parties involved had actually seen her will. Court records reveal that, even before Deubler died, Brady and members of her family had begun scheming about how to guarantee their portions of the estate. Many witnesses testified that Deubler had told them she intended to leave the majority of her estate to Anna, but in 1913 Deubler made a bequest to Brady that raised questions about precisely what portion of the estate Anna would control. Exactly a year and a day before her death, Deubler signed a document in which she transferred ownership of the Esplanade house and its contents to Brady. The document of transfer suggested that the "sale" of the house to Brady was made in return for "$25,000 in cash" which Deubler had received from him "at various times during the last twenty years." Later court testimony, even by Brady, suggests that this figure was exaggerated, but the balance of the terms seems to have been better grounded in reality. The agreement detailed the many tasks Brady had performed for Deubler over the years, including giving her "advice and information" that enabled her "to purchase and sell at great profit . . . various pieces of real estate." The agreement also specified that Brady had acted as Deubler's agent "without compensation" and had "given his personal attention to the management of all her financial and business affairs" for more than twenty years. He had collected her rents, arranged leases for her properties, paid the taxes and insurance premiums, and arranged for repairs whenever they were necessary.[70]

Why Deubler agreed to transfer the house to Brady in 1913 remains a mystery. Although it was signed by Brady and Deubler and witnessed by Anna and by Brady's lawyer, Brady chose to keep the agreement a secret. Anna contended that she was ignorant of its details until much later. According to her, her aunt had asked her to accompany her to a lawyer's office and sign a document, and she had agreed without inquiring about its contents. If Brady had filed the transfer in 1913, any court would have later ruled it null and void since, as Deubler's concubine, he was by law incapable of receiving such a valuable bequest of personal property, or any donation of real estate, from her. Perhaps Brady knew this, for he kept the document to himself and played his cards close to his chest as any good gambler would.[71]

In the months leading up to Deubler's death, Anna's parents also began to consider how best to guarantee themselves a portion of the estate once the family matriarch died. In the battle over the succession, many witnesses testified that in the fall of 1913 Anna's mother had come up with an auda-

cious plan to accomplish this goal. Anna testified that her mother was the
first to suggest that Anna should marry J. T. Brady as soon as her aunt died.
Although her mother later denied that she had encouraged such a union,
several other witnesses contradicted her. Mrs. David Jackson, who had
served as a masseuse to Mary Deubler in the final weeks of her life, recalled
that Anna had looked particularly troubled on one of her visits. According
to Jackson, Anna had said, "Mrs. Jackson, isn't it awful, they are talking
about me marrying Mr. Brady as soon as aunty dies?" According to Jackson,
Anna's mother, who was also present, "said that she felt it would keep the
family together and it was for the best." Anna testified that her mother had
told her not to be "a silly goose; marry Tom, for if Tom has it, you will get
it just the same as if it was left to you."[72]

According to Anna's testimony, she was initially troubled by the suggestion that she marry her "Uncle" Tom. She recalled that she "thought it was
simply horrible for [her family] to have lived there as they had lived. My
father knew it; my brothers and my mother knew of the existing circumstances and they countenanced it, but I didn't." The "existing circumstances" of her aunt's prostitution and concubinage with Brady were
troubling, but Anna sought to come to terms with the situation once she
understood it. She also sought counsel from two local priests. According to
their testimony, both advised her that marriage to Brady was, perhaps, the
best course to take under the circumstances. Father Anselm Maenner admitted that he was aware of Deubler's occupation and her cohabitation with
Brady but advised Anna to go ahead with the marriage. He recalled, "I
thought it would be the best thing for her to do . . . so she wouldn't be
slandered in any way at all."[73]

According to Anna, there was a consensus among her spiritual and secu-
lar advisers that a marriage was for the best. Mrs. Jackson purportedly told
her, "Mr. Brady can do you no good, but you can do him a world of good."
Perhaps, in the eyes of respectable society this was the case, but Anna also
admitted that she "needed a protector; someone who would guide me, and
since Mr. Brady, all during my childhood had shielded me and protected
me, I thought he was the one most capable of doing it." Anna's father, who
was at first ambivalent and later angry about the marriage and its outcome,
put it differently. When Anna and Brady asked his permission to marry,
Anna testified that her father had replied, "Take her Tom; you helped to
spoil her; now take your own medicine." According to him, his daughter
"was so terribly spoiled no one could stand" her.[74]

Although Anna was initially troubled by the suggestion that she marry her "uncle," several weeks before her aunt's death she did agree to marry J. T. Brady. Her aunt died on a Saturday evening, February 14; the funeral services and interment took place the very next day. The following week was a busy one at the house on Esplanade Avenue. Because Mary Deubler had entrusted the combination of her safe to no one, Brady applied to the court for permission to have a locksmith open it. Once he gained approval, the safe was opened and Brady found a handwritten will dated June 29, 1903. The will was read on Friday afternoon, February 20. In it, Deubler had named Brady executor of her estate. She had provided monetary bequests to her brother, her cousin, and their children. But the majority of the estate, including the brothel at 225 Basin Street, all of her personal effects, and any other property she owned at the time of her death was to go to Anna.

On February 21, the day after the reading of the will and one week after Mary Deubler's death, Anna Deubler and Tom Brady were married in the house on Esplanade Avenue, which had been purchased for her in 1906 and transferred to him in 1913. Not wishing to leave this legacy to chance, Brady escorted Anna to her lawyer's office hours before the wedding and had her sign papers reconfirming his ownership of the house and its contents. They then returned to the house, where close family and friends attended the wedding. It must have been a surreal occasion, especially considering the fact that exactly one week before, in the same house, the woman who was the bride's aunt and the groom's concubine had died. Anna, who was thirty years old to Brady's fifty-one, seemed content to go ahead with the match, but her father, who gave her away, was beside himself. According to his own testimony, he had been drinking heavily before the ceremony and was crying when he told another man, "I have been done up. . . . I was done up in this deal."[75]

The "deal" between Anna and Brady was sealed by the sacrament of holy matrimony on February 21, 1914. With that act, Mary Deubler's favored niece, to whom she had left a fortune in real estate and personal property, shared that bequest with her aunt's long-time lover, business partner, and companion. One can only guess at how Mary Deubler would have viewed this turn of events; it was probably fortuitous that she had been buried in such a large tomb, leaving plenty of space for rolling over in her grave. Whatever Deubler's feelings might have been, her only surviving brother, Anna's father Henry, was infuriated. Three weeks after the wedding, he filed suit to nullify both the will and the transfer of the Esplanade house and its contents to Brady.

His petition to the court was lengthy, but his objections boiled down to two complaints. First, because Mary Deubler and Tom Brady had "lived together in open concubinage" for many years, Brady was incapable of receiving more than "one tenth of the whole value of the movable property belonging to her estate." Second, Henry argued, his daughter Anna "was a mere intermediary interposed and selected by said Mary A. Deubler, for the express purpose of illegally and fraudulently transmitting her property" through her niece to her concubine Brady. Not surprisingly, Henry argued that the will should be nullified and that the entire estate should go to him as his sister's closest living relative.[76]

Like *Stringer v. Mathis,* this case revolved around charges of concubinage and remained in the courts for several years. The lower court initially dismissed Henry's suit, but he appealed and the state supreme court sent the case back to the lower court for reconsideration. (It was during this rehearing that the testimony quoted in this chapter was given.) Although the defendants in the case clearly slanted answers to their own advantage, their testimony was given privately in the judge's chambers, lending some credibility to the candor of their responses. Still, given Brady's history with Mary Deubler and his new wife's religious piety, many of the questions must have been painful for Anna. Even her premarital virginity was called into question as her father's lawyer sought to substantiate the charge that Anna, Brady, and her aunt had acted in league to position Anna as an intermediary who would illegally transfer the estate to Brady.[77]

In deciding the case, the judge based his decision largely on Anna's respectability. According to him, "The evidence shows that Anna M. Deubler is a well educated but unsophisticated young woman, who was the favorite relative of Mary A. Deubler, known as Josie Arlington, the proprietress of a house of ill fame in this city. The Aunt, however, was particularly careful to prevent the taint of that occupation [from] reaching her favorite niece." The judge concluded, "I feel satisfied from the evidence that Anna M. Deubler was not a person interposed to defraud the law. She was inexperienced in the ways of the world and only acted as [she] did upon the advice of those qualified to advise and like any other well educated and unsophisticated woman would do."[78]

Mary Deubler's worldly experiences and disreputable activities earned her a fortune. Ironically, her niece's inexperience "in the ways of the world," which her aunt had guaranteed by providing her with convent education and a closely monitored adulthood, led the judge to rule in her favor. Perhaps this part of the saga would have given Deubler some satisfaction. She had used her ill-gotten gains to purchase the trappings of respectability and to keep Anna naïve enough to make her acceptable to condescending judges and other arbiters of civilized morality. Even given the unsavory circumstances of her marriage to Brady, Anna's respectability was critical to ensuring her legal victory and her continued control over the estate her aunt had left her.

Anna may have been respectable, but her reputation did not blind her to the economic rewards to be reaped from her aunt's brothel. Although she sold the Arlington's contents, she and Brady kept the brothel and continued to lease it to Anna Casey on an annual basis. As pious as Anna was, the practical advantages of lucrative rents from a Storyville brothel outweighed moral misgivings about the business that had, after all, provided her with a convent education, a fortune, and a fine home. Even during the turmoil of her father's lawsuit, Anna continued to support several members of her extended family, some of whom continued to live in the Esplanade house with her and Tom Brady. And, although she experienced two miscarriages in the interim, two years after her aunt died Anna gave birth to Brady's child. (They ultimately had two children.) Though hers was not an ideal life or storybook romance, Mary Deubler's hardscrabble life and financial success had guaranteed her niece a fine home, ample economic resources, and a respectable if somewhat unorthodox marriage.[79]

Yet Anna surely suffered irreparable harm, even if only to her reputation. As he closed his brief to the state supreme court, one of her lawyers noted that "in this case we are dealing with unusual situations and remarkable people." He directed particular disdain at Anna's father who, he reminded the court, "for years was a suppliant of his unfortunate sister's gains, permitting himself and his family to be supported by her and ultimately closing his career by this vicious and unwarranted attack which will reflect upon his daughter and upon his two grandchildren, the issue of John T. Brady and Anna M. Deubler, until their closing days." He was probably right.[80]

Throughout the four years and eight months that Deubler's succession was being considered by the courts, local reformers were agitating against Storyville, trying to chip away at the political support and the widespread public apathy that had allowed it to continue for so long. On the very day that Deubler died, for instance, the *Item* ran an editorial titled "No Necessary Evil." The lengthy column questioned the sexual double standard that had countenanced the presence of a vice district by portraying it as a "safety valve" that protected respectable women from the virulent sexuality of men. The column also promoted a newly published pamphlet by the social hygiene committee of the City's Federation of Clubs. Titled "Segregation and Morality," the pamphlet railed against the vice district and called for the adoption of state statutes to end or inhibit the operation of Storyville. The authors outlined an exhaustive case against segregating women within the boundaries of a vice district when its male patrons could come and go as they pleased. These reformers were preoccupied with respectability and critical of the sexual double standard, but, as the final chapter will make clear, race was also a critically important element in Storyville's spectacular success and its ultimate demise.[81]

5

"As Rare as White Blackbirds"

WILLIE PIAZZA, RACE, AND
REFORM IN STORYVILLE

Local, regional, and even national reformers railed against Storyville throughout its existence. Before 1917, they won mostly token victories and only marginal, intermittent support from municipal authorities. In that year, however—with the moralistic Woodrow Wilson beginning his second presidential term and the nation caught up in the patriotic fervor of war preparations—local reformers seized on the national mood to press for meaningful change in New Orleans. Formerly reluctant city leaders conceded that the time had come to reorganize Storyville, but their original aim was to cleanse rather than to close the district. Commissioner of Public Safety Harold Newman initiated a "clean up campaign" in January, and he quickly zeroed in on what local reformers deemed the most dangerous, disgusting and disorderly aspect of the district. In short order, the "clean up" became a campaign to segregate the district's prostitutes and customers by race.[1]

From the beginning, ideas about race, prostitution, and segregation had been critical in the creation and passage of the Story Ordinances. City leaders had hoped to deal with the related problems of prostitution and sex across the color line by segregating prostitutes within two sets of boundaries and by turning a blind eye to the continuing prevalence of interracial sex and socialization within those areas. But in the district's final decade, as reformers gained ground, they began to focus on the scandalous and troubling visibility and popularity of the district's social and sexual integration of the races. In casting about for a solution that would both appease reformers and save Storyville, city leaders focused on segregation—this time, racial segregation.

Accordingly, in early February 1917 the city council passed Ordinance 4118 C.C.S., which called for the immediate racial segregation of Storyville. If, as the *Times-Picayune* claimed in 1917, racial segregation of the district's two sections had been the original objective of the 1897 Story Ordinances, the very existence of the new ordinance confirms that segregation had not been put into practice. In fact, Storyville had become notorious largely because of its well-known toleration of interracial intimacy and socializing. Now, in early March 1917, "the negro inmates of the district were ordered to move into that part of the district originally set aside by the Story law as the place for their habitat," while white prostitutes were to remain in the area below Canal Street.[2]

City officials did not anticipate that the district's women of color would fight back. But in an unusual and virtually unknown legal challenge, a group of African American and mixed-race prostitutes prevailed. Although their legal victory did not save the district, their actions constitute an extremely important if little-known episode in the history of Storyville—and, indeed, in the ongoing quest for African American civil rights in the Jim Crow South. In exploring the roles that race and reform played in the district's final decade and ultimate downfall, we will be guided by the experiences of a remarkable mixed-race woman, a prostitute and madam named Willie Vincent Piazza. It is indicative of the direct way she approached her life that Piazza, unlike many women who worked as prostitutes in New Orleans, never adopted an alias. Like Mary Deubler, who was best known as Josie Arlington, Piazza became a successful brothel owner and madam who accumulated a small fortune between 1897 and 1917. But beyond her success and the notoriety of her profession, Piazza is a compelling subject for scholarly attention. Because she challenged city officials who sought to evict her from her own property and deny her the privilege of doing business in downtown Storyville in 1917, parts of Piazza's story have been preserved in court records. Although she never took the stand in any of these cases, they still provide compelling glimpses of a proud, practical woman who fashioned herself into a sexual icon and stubbornly fought to maintain the property, privileges, and prosperity she had attained.[3]

Her relevance to the history of New Orleans and the South extends far beyond the walls of her brothel and the boundaries of Storyville. In fact, her imprint on the historical record has much to teach us about the intricate

intersections of gender, racial identity, and commercial sexuality in a particular time and place. Ideas about respectability, particularly as they applied
to African American and mixed-race women, help to explain why Piazza's
story and the significance of her legal victory have not been adequately ana-
lyzed before. In exploring Piazza's life and experiences, we come to understand more about how and when a black and white South was created, what
role New Orleans played in this regional drama, and the complex and sometimes contradictory roles sexuality and desire played in the process.

At the beginning of the twentieth century, tolerated prostitution and sex
across the color line remained the two most characteristic elements of New
Orleans's culture of commercial sexuality. Self-described "octoroon" prostitutes like Willie Piazza combined both elements of the city's remarkable culture of commercial sexuality in their sexual personae. As prostitutes and as
products of the city's long and often romanticized legacy of sex across the
color line, light-skinned, mixed-race women occupied a contingent but
profitable position in Storyville throughout its existence. In fact, the significance of octoroon prostitutes far exceeded their numbers, which were always
relatively small in comparison to the majority of women, who identified
themselves as either black or white. From their tenuous position between the
hardening racial categories of black and white, the experiences of octoroon
prostitutes like Piazza provide important guides to understanding the wide
variety of roles people of color played in Storyville. Their experiences also
reveal how ideas about race contributed to the reform movements that ultimately closed the district.

The ordinance that aimed to segregate Storyville by race stipulated in its
first section that "any prostitute or woman notoriously abandoned to lewdness, of the colored or black race," had to move into the uptown district by
March 1, 1917. Although the ordinance nominally affected every prostitute of
color in the city, those who had the most to lose were mixed-race women
like Piazza, who had accumulated substantial wealth and bought real estate
inside Storyville; the ordinance's third section forbade them to lease, do
business in, or even live in their own properties. The city defended its ordinance, and section three in particular, by claiming that cases of successful,
property-owning madams of color like Piazza were exceedingly rare—in
their words "as rare as white blackbirds"—and thus could not be considered
as the basis for legislation. City attorneys concluded that such a "distribution
of the district would be quite appropriate, as there is everywhere manifest

the exceedingly strong tendency of the members of each race to separately congregate."[4]

This assertion ignored two critical issues. First, despite officials' statement that the separation of the races was "everywhere manifest" in New Orleans by 1917, the city had been most remarkable historically for its racial and ethnic integration. This was particularly true inside the boundaries of Storyville. Residential segregation, like segregation in education and other areas of social interaction, was actually the result of a long-term process that began in postbellum New Orleans and was not fully accomplished until well after Storyville officially closed in 1917. The city's assertion also ignored the fact that women like Piazza had been able to accumulate wealth and property inside Storyville precisely because they were favorites among the district's elite white male clientele. If, in fact, there was a strong "natural" tendency for the races "to separately congregate," the realm of sex, especially in Storyville, was an important, if often ignored, exception to this rule.

Sex across the color line had been a characteristic of the city's sexual culture since its founding. In 1917, however, a constellation of events led city officials to take a hard, explicit stand against this long-tolerated practice. City leaders were convinced to act by the accumulated weight of Jim Crow legislation, state-court rulings, the demands of local reformers, and the influence of federal officials who threatened to withhold lucrative military contracts and encampments on the eve of World War I.

Storyville in Black and White

Women and men of all classes, colors, and descriptions worked in, patronized, or went slumming in the two neighborhoods deemed vice districts by Ordinance 13,485 C.S. The geographic separation of these two sections has led many to speculate that one area was intended for white patrons and the other for African American men. One local historian has even suggested that the uptown portion of the vice district "had no actual legal recognition" and was "held in abeyance" until many years later, but events as early as 1900 call such claims into question.

Following the United States Supreme Court ruling in the *L'Hote* case, for example, Mayor Paul Capdeville ordered city officials to enforce the final Story Ordinance, Ordinance 13,485 C.S., to the letter, and actively opposed efforts to alter the ordinance in any way. It was his belief that "an amended ordinance would not be the measure the Supreme Court passed upon, and if changed in one particular, would be susceptible to change in other partic-

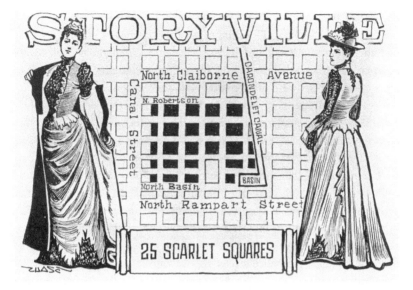

This drawing by political cartoonist John Chase reflects the mistaken belief that the city's final vice district was limited to the area below Canal Street. Storyville was the common nickname for this set of vice-district boundaries, but four additional blocks above Canal were also specified by Ordinance 13,485 C.S. *Courtesy Historic New Orleans Collection, acc. no. 1979.167.21a, a gift of John C. Chase and John W. Wilds*

ulars." In light of Capdeville's instructions to city officials and his stubborn refusal to revise the ordinance, the claim that the upper portion of the vice district existed in some sort of legal limbo between 1900 and 1917 seems dubious.[5]

Even if, as jazz historian Donald Marquis argues, the upper section of the vice district was "never officially enfranchised as 'black Storyville,'" it is also true that the area was both a de jure and a de facto vice district and acted in that capacity throughout Storyville's existence. Although both sections were heavily populated by brothels and other vice establishments, significant numbers of working-class families—black, white, and recent immigrants—continued to live in and on the margins of these two areas. There is substantial evidence that only the area below Canal Street was considered Storyville proper, but there's also no question that the area above Canal Street also functioned as a prostitution district frequented and inhabited by people of all races, classes, and colors.[6]

Louis Armstrong, who grew up along the edge of the uptown portion of the vice district, made a clear distinction between the two sections of the district. He recalled that life in the neighborhood above Canal Street "was just about the same as it was in Storyville except that the chippies were cheaper." Armstrong's recollection supports the contention that the two areas of the district were distinct from, although not much different from, one another. In fact, both neighborhoods were most remarkable for their racial and ethnic heterogeneity—not for their racial segregation. Although Storyville's Blue Books, the local press, and respectable persons tended to ignore the existence of the area above Canal Street, most New Orleanians were keenly aware that rampant prostitution and sex across the color line could be found in both sections of the district.[7]

Racial segregation was observed intermittently in the vice district, often in response to periods of intense reform agitation and its attendant temporarily heightened police scrutiny. After passage of the Gay-Shattuck Law in 1908, for example, the police forced saloons with reputations for interracial socialization to specify one clientele or the other. The level of segregation also seems to have increased over time. By the time Storyville closed, for example, even liquor licenses specified the race of the patrons to be served. Some establishments observed racial segregation throughout the district's existence. Many of the Basin Street brothels, including the octoroon houses run by women like Piazza, actually guaranteed racial segregation as a marketing device to attract a white male clientele. Jazz musician Johnny St. Cyr recalled that there were rules, spoken and unspoken, designed to keep African American men out of the upscale brothels frequented by white men. St. Cyr told music historian Alan Lomax that "colored men couldn't go to the white houses." But, he noted, segregation "was only forced on one way though. White men could go to Negro houses." St. Cyr concluded by expressing his personal frustration with the hypocrisies of sexual segregation in the district and the region. "That's the bad part about the South! Should be, if going to be segregation, be complete segregation." But, as the testimony of St. Cyr and many other early jazz musicians makes clear, segregation was far from complete within the boundaries of New Orleans's two tolerated vice sections.[8]

Even in the expensive and allegedly whites-only parlor houses and entertainment establishments on Basin Street, men of color were present, if only to provide service and entertainment. Consider, for example, the testimony of Ferdinand La Menthe, who later called himself Jelly Roll Morton and claimed to have invented jazz. La Menthe, who was sometimes hired to play the piano in Basin Street brothels, recalled that a screen was placed between him and the white male audience as they watched white and mixed-race women strip or perform sex acts. Not surprisingly, La Menthe managed to see through the flimsy divide between him and the action. At Emma Johnson's house, for instance, he recalled, "a screen was put up between me and the trick they were doing for the guests, but I cut a slit in the screen. I had become a sport now, myself, and wanted to see what everybody else was seeing."[9]

Just as La Menthe could surreptitiously view Basin Street sex shows as an entertainer, other African American men, even former slaves, gained access to establishments where whites and people of color mixed with shocking familiarity. Frank Moss, who was born a slave in Alabama in 1860, became an itinerant worker as an emancipated adult. He recalled that after months of hard work "trucking cotton, loading boats, [and] cuttin' cane," he and his friends "looked forward to when our job would end 'cause then we knowed we was goin' to have a good time. With all our money, most of the time we'd high-tail it to New Orleans." According to Moss, in the early twentieth century prostitutes could be found in a wide area that exceeded both sets of officially established boundaries.[10]

Moss recalled visiting two dance halls on the corners of Iberville and Franklin Streets. The Twenty-Eight was across the street from the official boundaries of Storyville, while the Pig Ankle was just inside the Iberville Street boundary. Moss called the Pig Ankle "'the' place" to be and noted that "seven nights out the week niggers and white folks used to crowd in there" together. But Moss also recalled that the "white folks like to died laughin'" at the spectacle put on by drunken prostitutes. His assertion that whites came to the Pig Ankle "just to throw nickels and dimes" suggests that slumming rather than socializing as equals was the reason for these encounters. Yet even this level of interracial mixing was extraordinary for the time.[11]

Regardless of claims to the contrary, race mixing and people of color were central to the history of the city's last official vice district—both above and below Canal Street. While Jim Crow laws had begun to affect the city's broad social morés by the 1890s, there was still a great deal more ambiguity about racial classifications in New Orleans, especially in Storyville, than in most other places in the region. This ambiguity, an artifact of the city's antebellum system of three-tiered racial classification, had both positive and negative repercussions for people of color during Storyville's existence. On one hand, racial complexity—and the resulting confusion it engendered—

meant that passing and enforcing strict segregation statutes, especially those related to intimate contact, took longer in New Orleans and Louisiana than in other places in the South. Yet even as debate raged about the necessity and practicality of racial segregation, whites from all over the region and the nation descended on Storyville in droves.

In significant respects, Storyville's function as a regional safety valve for sinful behavior was mirrored in the role it played in the region's racial politics. The district was, after all, one of the few places in the turn-of-the-century South where men and women of all classes, races, and ethnicities mingled so intimately, casually, and continuously in the pursuit of sex and leisure activities. Just as the district provided a place for people to break free from the constraints of civilized morality, it also allowed them to take a vacation from the requirements of Jim Crow while maintaining the pretense that white supremacy and racial segregation were absolute necessities in their home communities.

For some white visitors, the district's three-tiered system of racial classification was a quaint curiosity, an opportunity to see the exotic excesses for which New Orleans was so well known embodied in its still-significant population of mixed-race women and men. For others, especially white men, Storyville's African American and mixed-race prostitutes allowed them to indulge sexual fantasies of racial submission, domination, and desire in a variety of settings with women whose physical descriptions were as varied as their skin tones. But, as the recollections of Frank Moss remind us, white men were not the only ones attracted by the city's tolerated vice districts and raucous reputation.[12]

While some people of color came in search of "temporary pleasure," others took "up residence in hopes of achieving a better life." For Mississippians in particular, "New Orleans had special allure. White people from the stern, puritanical society of the Magnolia State viewed it as an exotic oasis of romance and forbidden delights," but for many "rural blacks, the city held a reputation for racial liberality and job opportunities—relatively speaking." For African American men, job opportunities could be found on the riverfront or in other venues for manual labor around the city.[13]

For African American women, the slim occupational pickings were even thinner. Domestic work was among the best options for women of color in New Orleans. But even in those jobs African American women often became the targets of sexual advances or abuse by white males. Such situations, and the widely held assumption that "black women's innate promiscuity" was to blame, make the choice to engage in sex work all the more understandable. As was the case with white women in Storyville, the financial rewards for African American and mixed-race women willing to engage in prostitution, although often fleeting, far exceeded what they could earn at "honest labor."[14]

During the 1890s alone more than two thousand African Americans migrated to New Orleans from Mississippi. Willie Piazza was one of them. She was born around 1865 to a woman of color named Celia Caldwell. Both her mother and her father, Vincent Piazza, were natives of the state. Willie's father was the offspring of Italian immigrants who had settled in the rich agricultural region of southwestern Mississippi, probably in Copiah County, during the antebellum period. Willie's parents were not married, and census data provides little information about her background or childhood, except that her father was "white" and her mother was "black." Celia was around fifteen and Vincent a few years older when Willie was born.[15]

By the time Willie reached her teens, her parents had migrated to separate Mississippi towns. In the 1880 census, Celia Caldwell was living in Jackson, and her occupation was "keeping house." The census taker noted that she was unable to read and write, possible evidence that she had been a slave before the war. Willie, her older sister, and younger brother were listed as "in school." By that time, Vincent Piazza was living about sixty miles away in Vicksburg and had married an Irish immigrant named Kate. She was ten years his junior, and they had a one-year-old son. Celia Caldwell disappeared from census records after 1880, but Vincent Piazza was still in Vicksburg in 1900, described as a "hotel proprietor" and the father of eight children.[16]

It is unclear what, if any, relationship Willie Piazza had with her father, but it is possible she passed through Vicksburg in the 1880s or 1890s, if only to board a boat to New Orleans. "To some extent," Vicksburg was "a miniature version of New Orleans, complete with rows of saloons and bawdyhouses." Baptists there referred to it as the "Sodom of Mississippi," much as other Protestants in the region referred to New Orleans as the "Sodom of the South." It is impossible to say whether Piazza engaged in prostitution in Mississippi, but some time in the 1890s she migrated to New Orleans. She first appeared in a city directory there in 1898, when she was listed as head of household at 315 N. Basin Street. Her position as madam of her own house suggests that she had been engaged in prostitution, both successfully and profitably, prior to the establishment of Storyville.[17]

Robert Charles was another Mississippi native who migrated to the city in the same decade as Piazza. In general terms, he had a significant amount in common with her. He was born about the same time and in the same region of the state. But both of Charles's parents were former slaves. Jasper and Mariah Charles raised their four sons by working "as sharecroppers on one of the cotton plantations along Bayou Pierre in the northwestern section of Copiah County." Later "descriptions and drawings of Robert Charles indicate some admixture of races in his background," and he was "referred to variously as a 'mulatto' and 'a Cuban-looking negro.'" Although Piazza and Charles probably both had mixed-race backgrounds, this fact resulted in strikingly different outcomes for the two.[18]

Charles was the central figure in events that led to "one of the bloodiest, most anarchic weeks in New Orleans' history." On a steamy Monday night in July 1900, just a month after Mayor Capdeville had declared that the city would begin to enforce the Story Ordinances, Charles was sitting on a stoop with a friend. The men were waiting to meet two women who worked as domestic servants in a nearby residence. Around 11:00 P.M., the men were approached by three white police officers who had received a report that "two suspicious looking negroes" were in the area. Although exactly what happened next remains a mystery, a fracas ensued in which Charles and one of the officers fired their guns.[19]

Charles, like one of the officers, was injured, but he managed to escape the scene. He was bleeding badly enough, however, that he had little choice but to return to his nearby apartment to tend his wound. It took four hours for police to track him there. In the exchange of gunfire that followed, Charles killed two police officers and wounded another. With the murder of two white policemen, what had begun a few hours earlier as a fairly common minor incident blossomed into a major race riot. Charles had managed to escape the police twice, which only further inflamed angry white citizens.[20]

Over the next three days, while the manhunt for Charles was on, hundreds and sometimes thousands of armed white men gathered in different parts of the city looking for revenge. Already simmering racial tensions boiled over. According to Hair, "hostility between whites and blacks had been mounting for some time" and "any trifling episode . . . could have provided the spark for an explosion." Robert Charles's actions "furnished not a spark but a flame." On Tuesday night, with Charles still missing and tension mounting, "several black men and two women were severely beaten by roving packs of young white men." The following day, inflammatory newspaper stories, combined with the news that rumors of Charles's capture had proved false, ratcheted tensions higher. On Wednesday night, more than three thousand angry white men spilled into the streets intent on vengeance.[21]

Although the *Times-Democrat* led the next morning's coverage with the headline "Mob Anger Is Vented at Random," a closer look at the path the rioters took through the city on the night of Wednesday, July 25, reveals a pattern that was anything but arbitrary. First, the group went to the parish prison with the hope of having Charles's accomplice handed over to them for lynching. They were frustrated in the attempt by the Orleans Parish sheriff and his deputies. According to press accounts, hundreds of men then headed to Storyville. "The mob's apparent objective now was the black area of cabarets and saloons along Franklin and Customhouse Streets"—the same ones Frank Moss had described. Although most of the dance halls and honky-tonks were closed by the time they arrived, the mob spotted an African American man at the corner of Canal and Villere. The mob pursued him on foot and caught up with him on Customhouse Street, a block away from the Union Chapel. Several rioters took shots at him and one finally hit his mark. Then the crowd embarked upon a horrifying lynching that included several bouts of violent beating and kicking. According to the *Times-Democrat*, "every few moments the [rioters] would stop" beating the man and "to better see if he was dead, they would stick lighted matches to his eyes." After this sequence had been repeated several times, someone emerged from the crowd and shot the anonymous black man at point-blank range, finally ending his life.[22]

The violence did not stop there. As the rioters moved farther into the vice district "many places of ill-fame closed their doors," especially those inhabited by "colored women [who] pulled their doors shut and put on every fastening." Later, however, some of the white prostitutes emerged from their brothels and joined the melee—according to one account, "inciting the [men] to murder." The rioters eventually left the vice district and continued their rampage in the French Quarter. The next day Charles was finally located by police in an uptown apartment where friends had given him refuge. Once discovered, he did not go quietly. Before he was killed, Charles fatally wounded another two policemen and three white civilians. Police finally managed to smoke him out of the second-story apartment in which he had barricaded himself, but not before he injured nearly thirty officers and armed vigilantes with his amazing marksmanship.[23]

Charles was killed instantly by a single gunshot as he descended the stairs to escape the rising smoke. His lifeless body was dumped into the street in front of the house where he had been hiding, and his corpse received a beating similar to the one the mob had delivered the previous night in Storyville. Bystanders who could get close enough kicked and stomped the corpse until it "became almost indistinguishable from the trodden mud" of the street. The virulence may have been inspired by the fact that Charles had done the one thing no African American or mixed-race man could afford to do if he valued his life—he had successfully challenged white supremacy. He had not only challenged it, he had single-handedly killed nine and injured more than thirty white people in the process.[24]

Sporadic violence continued for several more days, but by the end of the week relative calm had returned to the city. Although the "Robert Charles Riot" would provide fodder for the press and keep race relations raw for some time, Storyville, like the rest of the city, regained a wary racial equilibrium over the next several months. One can only imagine how Willie Piazza and other women of color in the district felt about Robert Charles and his actions. But her gender and her mixed-race background gave her an option that mixed-race men like Robert Charles did not have. Piazza could have sex with white men and profit handsomely in the exchange. Although she and hundreds of other black and mixed-race prostitutes and madams weathered the temporary storm of mob violence that rained down on the district on the night of July 25, 1900, they probably never forgot it.

The white mob's furious foray into the district surely provided a powerful reminder of how prostitutes—black, white, and those whose racial designations fell somewhere in the middle—understood and navigated the racial terrain of Storyville in 1900. The murder of the anonymous black man by the angry white mob, the fear exhibited by prostitutes of color, and the encouragement white prostitutes offered the white mob, present a chilling snapshot of the extreme social, racial, and gender hierarchies embodied in the organization of the vice district. The Story Ordinances codified the social, sexual, and racial privileges of white men. Their enforcement created a space where white manhood could be expressed through unfettered sexual access to women of all descriptions. Men of color were also present in Storyville as tenants in the neighborhood, members of the Union Chapel, visitors to the dance halls, and even customers at some of its cribs and brothels. But, as the lynching of the unidentified black man reminds us, access to Storyville was limited and controlled, sometimes brutally, by rules and conventions established by and for white men. The creation of Storyville grafted white male social and sexual dominance on to the city's geographic grid, bestowing sexual privilege on white males and, in the process, giving institutional status to an outrageous sexual and racial double standard in the city for the next two decades.

The Appalling Appeal of Octoroon Prostitutes

The sheer existence of commercial sex across the color line was not a distinctive aspect of Storyville per se. Virtually all of the sex districts in the nation offered their male clientele the opportunity to traverse racial or ethnic boundaries in the pursuit of sexual satisfaction. Certainly the most expensive brothels in any city were more selective in their clientele, and some brothels—even some run by women of color like Piazza—had a firm "whites-only" policy for patrons. But oral histories and promotional materials confirm that sex across the color line was a central attraction in Storyville, just as it was in many of the region's and the nation's other red-light districts.[25]

But two related factors set Storyville apart from most other vice districts in the South. First, New Orleans's institutionalized history of sex between white men and women of color provided an enduring precedent for commercialized sex across the color line in the city; that precedent did not disappear, even in the face of rising racial animosity throughout the region. While the brothels of colored and mixed-race prostitutes wisely closed during the Robert Charles riots, they were soon back in business, and some of them were among the district's premier establishments. Second, the presence of mixed-race prostitutes was one of Storyville's chief selling points. This small but savvy population of self-identified octoroon prostitutes and madams was intensively marketed and wildly successful. And when they relocated to other southern vice districts, light-skinned, mixed-race women marketed themselves as octoroons with Louisiana, New Orleans, or "Creole" heritage; this heritage was the source of their appeal.[26]

The women who identified themselves as octoroons for the purpose of sexual commerce in Storyville sagely exploited the city's romanticized history of sex across the color line to forge sexual personas that set them apart from their white competitors. This racial categorization also placed them above darker-skinned prostitutes of color in Storyville's complex caste system. In effect, they replicated in miniature the tripartite racial system that had dominated the city's culture and made it so distinct in the antebellum period. Although Charles Dudley Warner had assured his readers in 1887 that "the peculiar prestige of the quadroon and the octoroon" was "a thing of the past," their heyday as a sexual attraction in New Orleans was reinvigorated by Storyville, and they became an important feature of the district's appeal and notoriety. Of course, the district's attractions were numerous, limited only by the amount of money and imagination a patron could muster. Still, white males flocked to the brothels of self-proclaimed octoroon madams like Piazza and Lulu White, eagerly crossing the color line that they defended so vigorously in other areas of their lives and of the region.[27]

Women's historians, including Evelyn Brooks Higginbotham and Glenda Gilmore, have demonstrated conclusively that research into the lives of African American women can deepen and revise our understanding of political conditions—and the meaning of politics itself—in the turn-of-the-century South. Gilmore, for instance, focuses on middle-class African American women in North Carolina who were involved in religious groups, educational institutions, benevolent organizations, and reform movements. She argues that during the Jim Crow era, "as black men were forced from the political, the political underwent a redefinition, opening new space for black women." Certainly Gilmore's subjects would have considered themselves to have very little in common with women like Piazza. But both groups of women share at least two critical characteristics as historical subjects. First, historians largely ignored the lives of women of color until the 1970s, no matter what their social status, class, or occupation. Second, like the African American women reformers studied by Gilmore, Storyville's octoroon prostitutes managed to maintain a modicum of political influence and social efficacy during the consolidation of segregation. Both groups enhanced their political efficacy by maintaining contact with elite, powerful whites, although they did so through very different channels.[28]

Even after the bitter and sometimes violent period of Reconstruction and redemption—when blacks and whites occasionally engaged in armed combat in the streets and white men cavalierly took the lives of black men and women for a variety of trumped-up offenses against white supremacy—light-skinned, mixed-race women maintained a powerful erotic appeal among Storyville's white male patrons. Women who identified themselves as octoroon for the purpose of selling sex weathered the storms of intermittent protest and the rising tide of institutional racism. And, as with plaçage and the quadroon ball in the first half of the nineteenth century, that appeal was not only openly acknowledged and tolerated but achieved institutional status inside Storyville.

Eroticized octoroons in turn-of-the-century New Orleans, like their ante-bellum quadroon counterparts, were as much myth as reality, but there were real women behind those myths. Piecing together the story of even one of those lives gives us the opportunity to see the city and its vice district from an important new angle. A few hundred light-skinned, mixed-race women translated the myth of the erotic octoroon into temporary material prosperity between 1897 and 1917. A much smaller number was able to turn that myth into significant accumulations of wealth and property. Willie Piazza was one of them.

The technical definition of an octoroon was a person who was one-eighth black, or the offspring of a quadroon and a white person. However, in the same way that the term quadroon became a feminized and eroticized descriptor in antebellum New Orleans, the term octoroon was less a designation of exact "blood" proportions and more an identification predicated upon appearance, skin color, and the myth of light-skinned, mixed-race women as erotic types. The myth suggested that these women were beautiful, cultured, refined, deeply passionate, and skilled in the erotic arts. In the imprecise erotic milieu of Storyville, if a woman looked and acted as an octoroon was supposed to, she could claim and promote that identity and capitalize upon the power of the myth, no matter what her actual ancestry.

Another designation used to describe prostitutes in Storyville's Blue Books provides an interesting point of comparison. Over the years, the Blue Books used a variety of designations to describe women, including White, Colored, Octoroon, Jewish, and French. While one might assume that the word "French" referred to women of French nationality, it did not. It referred to women who were willing to engage in oral sex because, in the sexual vernacular of the day, this activity was referred to as French. Thus, a national designation was transformed into an erotic descriptor. The same transformation occurred with the term octoroon.[29]

As the nineteenth century came to a close, the sexual stereotypes that had predominated throughout those hundred years still had cultural currency. The dominant sexual ideology of that century assumed a virulent, voracious, and dangerous male sexuality, which had to be controlled around wives and other respectable women and was best and properly indulged with prostitutes. The terms used to describe those prostitutes, and other inappropriately sexual women, speak precisely to society's view of them. They were "women notoriously abandoned to lewdness" or "fallen women." They were considered degenerate in contrast to respectable women, who transcended their sexuality and achieved a state one historian has called "passionless-ness." These stereotypes, especially the antebellum tendency to place women on a pedestal of passionlessness, applied almost exclusively to white American women. If African Americans or other women of color were considered at all, it was assumed that their sexuality was beyond their conscious control—animal-like and depraved.[30]

The cultural power and appeal of the octoroon as an erotic type came partly from her ability to integrate strands of all the nineteenth-century sexual stereotypes of women. Octoroons were supposedly refined and cultured, sophisticated and cosmopolitan, but their physiological make-up also promised something of the rapacious sexuality attributed to those with colored skin. Their sexuality was constrained, but not overridden, by their whiteness. Further, they could relate to white men in many of the same ways that refined white women could without the burden of passionlessness to regulate those encounters. Octoroons stood astride the breaches in nineteenth-century sexual ideologies, a feat that could only be managed by those who could claim to be two kinds of women inside one body. Octoroons were simultaneously white and "colored," and they promoted themselves as the best of both worlds.

Of course, the erotic appeal of light-skinned, mixed-race women also owed something to the glamorized mythology of antebellum New Orleans and its population of free quadroons and enslaved "fancy girls." Sex with an octoroon prostitute offered the curious white male customer the ability to transgress the color line in pursuit of sexual pleasure, yet he could do so with a woman he believed superior in beauty, grace, intelligence, and erotic skill. She also claimed to be one generation "whiter" than her antebellum quadroon predecessor. For white men who were embarrassed by or ashamed of their sexual desire for women of African descent, the almost-white octoroon offered an alternative that was, perhaps, more psychically comfortable in a virulently racist society.

Willie Piazza was one of Storyville's most successful octoroon madams, partly because she played the role of the glamorous, refined octoroon to the hilt. She was said to have been so light-skinned she could have passed for white. According to local historian Al Rose, she spoke four languages fluently, referred to herself as "the Countess," "wore a monocle, smoked Russian cigarettes in a two foot ivory, gold, and diamond holder, and favored a

The only known image of Willie Piazza, which appeared in
one of Storyville's Blue Books. *Courtesy Williams Research Center,*
Historic New Orleans Collection, acc. no. 1969.19.3

diamond choker." Local lore also suggests that Piazza was a New Orleans
fashion plate, and that society women took their seamstresses to the races
with them so they that could copy the clothes that Piazza and her girls were
wearing. Piazza was also reputed to have had a music box installed in her
mattress and an impressive library in her brothel that included titles by Robert Burton and Alphonse Daudet.[31]

According to local legend, Piazza was both sophisticated and salty, well-
read and randy, a woman who transcended the boundaries of nineteenth-
century sexual ideology and exhibited characteristics that supposedly existed
at opposite ends of the Victorian sexual spectrum. It is impossible to verify
local legends about Piazza; and with the existing census data, it is impossible
to substantiate her claim that she was one-eighth black. But in some ways
this makes her an even more interesting and typical example of an eroticized
octoroon. Even if all we ever know about her is limited to her appearance
on the scene in New Orleans in the 1890s, and her accumulation of wealth
and notoriety inside Storyville, we know enough to certify that Piazza excelled at her chosen profession. While her legend owes more to fantasy than
to fact, she herself helped create the myth.

Her advertisements in Storyville's promotional Blue Books demonstrate
this point. In one, Piazza was referred to as "the most charming young landlady on Basin Street," and her house was said to be full of "cultivated enter-

tainers" who could sing "all of the latest jubilee songs." Another
advertisement suggested that Piazza's house was "the place to visit, especially
when 'one' is out hopping with friends—the women in particular." Clearly
Piazza prided herself on running one of Storyville's most respectable and
orderly disorderly houses. Her advertisements promoted the octoroon
image for her boarders as well. One read, "she has, without doubt, the most
handsome and intelligent octoroons in the United States. You should see
them; they are all cultivated entertainers and are numerous. . . . The Countess wishes it to be known that while her Maison Joie is peerless in every
respect, she serves only the 'amber fluid.' "[32]

Advertisements for other octoroon madams struck a similar note. An-
tonia Gonzalez, whose surname suggests Hispanic heritage, ran a Blue Book
advertisement that read:

> The above party has always been a head-line among those who keep first-class
> Octoroons. She also has the distinction of being the only singer of opera and
> female cornetist in the Tenderloin. She has had offers to leave her present vo-
> cation and take to the stage, but her vast business has kept her among friends.
> Any person out for fun among a lot of pretty Creole damsels, here is the place
> to have it. For ragtime, singing, and clever dancing . . . Antonia stands in a
> class all alone.[33]

Lulu White was probably the most well-known and financially successful
octoroon madam in Storyville, not only because she relentlessly promoted
herself but also because she built and ran one of the nation's most famous
brothels. She called it Mahogany Hall, and its over-the-top grandeur, including a parlor with a mirrored ceiling and walls, rivaled that of Mary Deubler's Arlington two doors down. To promote Mahogany Hall and certify
her claims of superiority, White oversaw the production of an entire Blue
Book devoted solely to the charms of her house and its inhabitants. In addition to rich and sumptuous furnishings, the brothel had five parlors, fifteen
bedrooms (each of which had a private bath with hot and cold water), and
an elevator built for two.[34]

White's personal style was as excessive as her decorating schemes. She
reportedly wore diamonds on every finger and was said to shine as brightly
as the "lights of the St. Louis Exposition." She was so widely known in early-
twentieth-century America that Mae West is said to have used her as a model
in the 1934 film *Belle of the Nineties.* Like West, White had a significant
amount of entrepreneurial substance to go along with her gaudy style. Lulu,

as she was commonly known, told a variety of tales over the years about her background and heritage, but she did one thing consistently—she eagerly and creatively marketed herself and her girls as sexual objects.[35]

The Blue Book advertisements by and about Storyville's octoroon prostitutes and madams reveal just the sort of juxtaposition octoroons were able to negotiate so well. While they unabashedly hawked sexual services and promised uninhibited fun, the advertisements also stressed the respectability and sophistication of the octoroon landladies and their tenants and bragged that their houses were ornate showplaces, respectable enough that even women from outside the district could be entertained in them. But while octoroons could transcend the female stereotypes of nineteenth-century sexual ideology, their position was always a tenuous one. To maintain the delicate balance that underlay their appeal, they had to tread the increasingly troubled waters of racial politics in early-twentieth-century Louisiana. As the storms of racial divisiveness raged, city and state officials crafted laws and made judgments that closed in more and more specifically on those who sought to engage in sex across the color line.

From 1908 on, state laws focused directly on keeping black and white persons from sharing each other's beds and bodies. With increasing precision, these laws sought to separate the races socially and sexually. As early as 1894, the right to marry across the color line, which had been legalized by a state statute in 1870, was revoked. In 1908, the same year the state passed the Gay-Shattuck Law, legislators prohibited interracial concubinage; two years later, they made the penalties for engaging in long-term interracial liaisons even more severe. The state also adopted a variety of other laws that sought to limit social contact between white and "colored" in schools, bars, restaurants, and public conveyances—in short, wherever the races interacted on the basis of equality. But the state legislature was loath to place too precise a definition on what exactly it meant by the term "colored" and who, precisely, fell under the restrictions enunciated in such laws. The state's long history and toleration of sex across the color line made the enforcement of such statutes inherently problematic.[36]

It was left up to the state supreme court to push the legislature to adopt more precise definitions. In *State v. Treadway* (1910), for example, the court argued that under the terms of Legislative Act 87 of 1908, which sought to prevent interracial sexual unions outside of marriage, a "negro [was] necessarily a person of color, but a person of color [was] not necessarily a negro." Such complicated legal postulations were made possible by the legislature's reluctance to define precisely what it meant by "colored," even as it tried to zero in on and penalize those who fell under that description. The court encouraged the legislature to address this problem by tightening the restrictions on cross-racial concubinage at its next session, making a trenchant observation about why members of the legislature may have failed to make the law clear in the first place:

> If conjectures are admissible . . . as to what considerations may have prompted the Legislature to enact separate car statutes, while leaving the concubinage and illicit commerce of the race untrammeled, one consideration which readily suggests itself is that without separate car statutes the whites could be brought into contact with the colored no matter how objectionable the proximity might be to them, whilst their concubinage or illicit commerce with them could only be voluntary.[37]

Although the legislature followed the court's advice and further tightened restrictions on cross-racial concubinage during its 1910 session, the law's enactment had no real or immediate impact on conditions for colored or mixed-race prostitutes working inside Storyville. In fact, as reformers continually pointed out, the voluntary "concubinage" and "illicit commerce" across the color line, about which the supreme court had complained, continued to be commonplace in the culture of white male sexual permissiveness and privilege for which New Orleans was so well known.

Although sex across the color line continued in the district despite adoption of these laws, local reformers became increasingly critical of its existence. In 1910 Phillip Werlein, a local reformer and president of the city's Progressive Union, contended that "the open association of white men and [N]egro women on Basin [S]treet, which is now permitted by our authorities, should fill us with shame as it fills the visitor from the North with amazement." Werlein and other reformers were troubled by the district's visibility on the city's landscape and in nationally circulated newspaper and magazine stories. In response, they declared war on Basin Street in the winter of 1910. In pressing for meaningful change, reformers focused their complaints on the availability and apparent popularity of sex across the color line, conflating prostitution in general with sex across the color line in particular. According to Werlein and members of the local Laymen's Missionary Association, for example, "relations between the races in the district" ought to be "punished by the same penalty as violation of the concubinage law—a term in the penitentiary." If the city did not act, they argued, conditions in the district were "calculated to prejudice the casual visitor against the sacred tenet of the Southern people—racial purity."[38]

The district attorney responded to these criticisms in a letter to Werlein. He argued that the recently adopted state concubinage law, which defined the act as the "unlawful co-habitation of persons of the Caucasian and of the [N]egro races whether open or secret," did not "prohibit the conditions on Basin [S]treet." Responding with great vituperation, Werlein declared it was "a shame and a disgrace and it is wrong, law or no law, that negro dives like those of Emma Johnson, Willie Piazza, and Lulu White, whose infamy is linked abroad with the fair name of New Orleans, should be allowed to exist and to boldly stare respectable people in the face."[39]

Apparently Werlein and his reform allies were bothered less by the existence of the district per se than they were by the profitable and well-known establishments like White's and Piazza's where patrons could cross the color line sexually with ease. On several occasions during his 1910 campaign Werlein reiterated this argument, in one case stating that "the real cancer of the district is the congregation of the whites and [N]egroes under practically the same conditions." He even suggested that if women of color were removed from the area, it would be much easier, "after getting rid of the [N]egroes to concentrate the [white prostitutes] in the district."[40]

The district's opponents argued that the district in general was a disgrace, but they focused on the visibility of cross-racial sexual liaisons, charging that this aspect of Storyville was primarily responsible for smearing the city's reputation. Yet even this explosive charge barely caused a ripple in the larger body politic, nor did it make city officials waver in their support for the district's continued existence. Although it certainly was not respectable, the district was apparently so profitable that city leaders, those who owned the district's real-estate and entertainment venues, and those who sold alcoholic beverages to its patrons turned a deaf ear to Werlein's charges of interracial sex and a blind eye to the fact that the city was synonymous with sin and sex "across the color line" in the minds of many outsiders.[41]

Reformers criticized Storyville from the outside, but evidence suggests that there were racial tensions inside the district as well. Although octoroons and "colored" women did a thriving business within the district through most of its existence, a closer look reveals that conditions there mirrored the racial prejudices of the larger community. The contents and organizational schemes of the Blue Books, for instance, suggest that racial designations were open to interpretation. Although the earliest Blue Books contained ad-

vertisements and listings for women of all races and colors, racial designations were rather arbitrary and were joined by a number of other
categorizations. One of the earliest guides had a cover that read *Blue Book:
Tenderloin 400,* and was organized rather schizophrenically. The guide had
some women's names and addresses organized racially under the headings
"Jewish" and "Octoroon," but it also organized women under the rubric of
a variety of establishments and specialties including "Beer Houses," "Speak
Easy Houses," and "French 69." "Mahogany Hall" had its own category as
well, although Lulu White and her boarders were listed without being formally identified as octoroons.[42]

In a guide produced the following year, *The Red Book: A Complete Directory of the Tenderloin,* all of the women were organized by street address.
And although a full-page photograph of Lulu White was captioned "Queen
of the Octoroons," none of the Basin Street octoroons was designated as
such in individual listings. Nor did Willie Piazza's earliest advertisements in
the Blue Books mention the fact that she and her boarders were octoroon.
By the 1905 edition, however, although the names of women were organized
by street address, they were also classified under three racial designations,
"White," "Colored" and "Octoroon." In 1906, although the women were still
listed in street order, the list of racial designations now included "Jewish."
In the 1907 and 1908 issues, only two racial designations remained—"White"
and "Colored." Thus, in these issues, for the first time Willie Piazza and her
boarders were classified as "Colored." Yet her advertisements in the same
issues stressed that she and her boarders were octoroons. In the *Blue Book*
of 1912, the listings of "White" and "Colored" women themselves had been
segregated, but Willie Piazza and the other octoroons had regained a distinct
listing between those two categories. This might be explained by the fact that
these later editions were produced in an office above a saloon owned by Lulu
White.[43]

It is difficult to establish chronological causality for the shifts in racial
designations in the Blue Books, but the disappearance of a separate category
for octoroons in 1907 does suggest that there was an unsuccessful attempt to
create a bifurcated system of racial classification inside the district around
that time. Furthermore, the fluctuation in racial classifications suggests that
these issues were in dispute inside Storyville and that they ebbed and flowed
in response to the vicissitudes of racial politics and reform drives outside the
district.

While Piazza and other octoroons were beginning to have their preferred

Willie Piazza purchased the property at 317 North Basin Street (foreground) in 1906 and
continued to live there until her death in 1932. *Courtesy Louisiana State Museum*

identity called into question inside Storyville by 1907, such controversies
were not powerful enough to keep white patrons out of their brothels. In
fact, Piazza was doing such a thriving business that she was able to purchase
the house in which she ran her establishment. She paid a total of twelve
thousand dollars between June 1906 and June 1907 to acquire the house at
317 N. Basin Street, furnished it in "an elaborate and expensive manner and
expended approximately twenty thousand dollars" in the process. Court records also reveal that Piazza "derived an annual net revenue from the said
property and business of over two thousand dollars."[44]

Obviously Piazza prospered inside the district in spite of racial tensions,
but she was no doubt aware of and alarmed by the racial focus of the 1910
War on Basin Street. Phillip Werlein's contention that Storyville would be
more acceptable if the "negro" and "French" women were removed from it
posed a direct threat to Piazza, even as she continued to cling to the octoroon middle ground. When Werlein said that "the negro woman must be
stamped out of the district," he surely meant Piazza and the octoroons as

well. It is clear that the drive toward a bifurcated system of racial classification, predicated upon the categories white and black or "colored," presented a real danger to Piazza and her livelihood. Werlein was unable to achieve the goal of segregating the vice district racially in 1910. Over time, in fact, city officials resisted changes that would substantially alter the vice district. This all changed in early 1917, however, when city leaders made a dramatic break with their previously unwavering support for the Storyville status quo.[45]

City of New Orleans v. Willie Piazza

In early 1917, life in New Orleans went on as usual. Carnival season had begun, elaborate plans were being made for Mardi Gras, and many in the city were flocking to see D. W. Griffith's spectacular new film, *Birth of a Nation*, which was beginning its seventh week of playing to sold-out crowds at the Tulane Theater. The film's negative portrayal of mixed-race people and celebration of white supremacy foreshadowed events that would affect Willie Piazza and the vice district's other prostitutes of color in the weeks to come. There were indications that this was going to be an unusual year in the life of the city. For one thing, the temperature had dropped below freezing and refused to budge as the region was caught in the grip of an unusually long-lasting cold spell that drove all its residents, even its criminals, indoors. And a citywide "clean up campaign" further dampened the city's already chilly atmosphere.

Led by Commissioner of Public Safety Harold Newman, city officials began to wage an aggressive cleanup campaign in the vice district in mid-January. In response, at least one reformer suggested that their activities amounted to too little, too late. Jean Gordon, one of the city's most consistent, tenacious, and acerbic reform activists, suggested that city leaders were themselves responsible for the current state of lawlessness, especially when it came to the nonenforcement of liquor laws and the lax enforcement of the Story Ordinances. On January 15, she reminded the audience at a mass meeting that she "had been keeping tabs on the political and moral conditions in" the city "for the last twenty-five years." She had never "seen such open, flagrant violation of all moral laws as have been permitted to gradually develop under the present commissioner of police and public safety." Gordon suggested that Commissioner Newman's recent embrace of reform was less than completely sincere.[46]

Sincere or not, Newman's campaign was aggressive and began to bear fruit almost immediately. The *Times-Picayune* reported on January 15 that "the moral wave, the cold wave, and Saturday night's rain apparently had some effect . . . as records from the various police precincts show the smallest number of arrests in years during a Saturday and Sunday." While Newman's cleanup campaign had contributed to a quiet weekend for the municipal court's night shift, it was about to generate a great deal of noise, fuss, and bother for a variety of working-class New Orleanians. Newman's first action was to have police enforce the state's Sunday closing laws, which had been all but ignored after an initial burst of enforcement following their passage in late 1908. His next target was the city's many cabarets, which were clustered along Rampart Street at the edge of the French Quarter and separated by one block from Basin Street.

The Tango Belt, as this area was known, was a growing entertainment district that even respectable men, women, and young people from around the city frequented on occasion. Newspapers reported that Newman's decision to ban live music from the cabarets, which had been allowed by special permits issued by the mayor in defiance of the Gay-Shattuck Law, led to the immediate unemployment of hundreds of musicians, entertainers, waiters, and "cabaret girls" who had made their livings in these establishments. The closing of the cabarets also led to the layoff of "more than forty policemen," many of whom depended on well-paid "detail" assignments at the bars and cabarets within and surrounding the vice district.[47]

Although many citizens complained about Newman's reforms, he was undaunted, and his efforts even gained the approval of some members of the now invigorated and increasingly vocal Louisiana Citizen's Council. Newman's campaign proceeded with lightning speed in a city never known for quick, decisive, or effective metropolitan government and included elements that directly answered the complaints lodged by the Citizens' League. Thus, his early actions focused specifically on liquor-law violations and forcing prostitutes who lived outside Storyville to move within its boundaries. Newspaper stories listed dozens of women, black and white, who were served with notices to move into the district within five days or face fines or jail time. Several saloon proprietors, who by this time had licenses that specified the race of the people they were allowed to serve, were also charged for serving mixed-race clientele.[48]

On January 24, however, there were some "unexpected developments" in Newman's campaign. According to the *Times-Picayune* these developments were "not brought about by the Citizens' League crusade." The first of these was a promise by Commissioner Newman to do away with "Jackal Land-

lordism" in the district. This charge related to the issue of cribs and Newman's "ruling that the women must actually live in the houses they occupy
instead of renting them at exorbitant rentals from night to night." Newman
claimed that inflated rental rates drove these women to engage in theft and
other petty crimes, and he explained that under his "new order the parti-
tions of the 'cribs' will be knocked out. The houses will be utilized as living
houses, and in these [houses] the women who have been living outside the
district, and who have been given five days vacate notices . . . will find shel-
ter." Whatever Newman's intention, his actions resulted in the displacement
of large numbers of prostitutes from the district who then took to soliciting
business in the city's deserted streets and dark alleyways.[49]

Newman's second surprise order "was for the separation of the races" in
the district. If the city council agreed to the ordinance he planned to introduce, Newman claimed that segregation of the races in the two separate vice-
district sections would be "rigidly enforced" and would apply to both men
and women. According to him, "the appearance of a white man in the negro
district will cause his arrest," and "should a negro woman even stroll in the
white district she will be jailed." Newman's plan represented a sharp departure from how business had been done in the district previously. It also provides additional evidence that sex across the color line had been an ongoing
activity throughout the district's existence and in both of its existing sections. The city council agreed with Newman that the time had come to segregate the vice district and unanimously adopted Ordinance 4118 C.C.S. in
early February.[50]

Passage of Ordinance 4118 cut right to the heart of Willie Piazza's livelihood. First because it only made provisions for white and "colored" prostitutes, women whose identities fell outside those categories were literally
forced into one or the other. Because she had openly identified as an octoroon, there was no question about which category she would be assigned.
According to the ordinance, her presence and that of her octoroon boarders
would become illegal inside Storyville effective March 1. It also meant that
Piazza would be forced to abandon her own property and place of business
inside the district. It is little wonder, then, that she balked when police officers came to her house on the morning of March 1. The policemen demanded that she and her boarders immediately abandon the premises at 317
N. Basin Street and move into the new segregated vice district set aside for
Negroes.[51]

Piazza's initial reaction was to plead not guilty to the charge of being a

Carrie Gross, one of more than two dozen African American
women who joined Willie Piazza in filing suit against the city of
New Orleans in 1917. *Courtesy New Orleans Public Library*

"colored" prostitute operating illegally in Storyville, which had become a
vice district for whites only as of March 1. Ten days later, however, she
signed a notarized affidavit in which she gave legal sanction to the city's contention that she was, in fact, a "member of the colored or negro race." While
her decision seems curious under the circumstances, this action gave her the
ability to wage a legal challenge against the city's first residential segregation
ordinance based primarily on racial criteria. Lulu White was able to secure
an injunction that barred immediate enforcement of the ordinance. But in
spite of it, city officials continued pressuring Storyville's women of color to
move. Over the next several weeks, policemen hauled dozens of dark- and
light-skinned women of color into recorder's court in an attempt to force
them to move immediately into the district limits above Canal.

Piazza and four of her boarders had a hearing on March 13, during which
Piazza's attorney Nathan H. Feitel was all but silenced by an aggressive pros-
ecution and a compliant recorder. Before her case was decided, however,
Feitel did manage to insert a bill of exception into the lower-court record.
In it he proposed to show that the "defendant Piazza runs an orderly house

of prostitution and that the order of her house compares favorably with the order maintained in the immediate neighborhood by the white houses presently run in said restricted district." To the degree that he could, Feitel stressed Piazza's respectability and the orderly way in which she ran her brothel. Police Captain Louis H. Leroy, the only person who testified in the lower-court case, agreed, noting that the reputation of Piazza's house "has been very good." In fact, there had been "no complaint of any kind" lodged against her as far as he knew. The lower court noted Feitel's exceptions but remained unimpressed. Piazza was found guilty and ordered to pay a twenty-five-dollar fine for each count or be jailed for sixty days.[52]

She immediately filed an appeal with the state supreme court, and her stubborn refusal to go quietly seems to have inspired others to follow her example. Although Lulu White and Willie Piazza were the first to file suit against the city, over the next four months nearly twenty other prostitutes of color filed suit as well. Some of them were, like White and Piazza, light-skinned, mixed-race women who had identified themselves as octoroons. Others, however, were African American women with very dark complexions who worked in cribs or brothels in some of the district's seediest sections. These women of color were joined by one African American male, a white woman, and a white male who also filed suits claiming that they would lose their African American prostitute-tenants and suffer significant economic loss as a result.[53]

The brief Feitel wrote to the state's high court on Piazza's behalf reflected the economic dimensions of his client's case. He began by noting that the "discussion of this question affects most essentially the value of a vast amount of private property." While playing down arguments that focused on race, he did not avoid them altogether, noting explicitly that "the discrimination in this case . . . is not due to any act or vice, but solely to defendant's color—the color constituting the misdemeanor under this ordinance." If white prostitutes could do business in Storyville, "colored" prostitutes must be able to as well, or the ordinance was overtly racially discriminatory and therefore unconstitutional.[54]

Feitel furthered his argument by speaking to the case of Mamie Christina, another self-identified octoroon prostitute and acquaintance of Piazza's, who had also been charged under the disputed ordinance. Christina had avoided prosecution by proving to the court's satisfaction that, "although she had been reared from an infant by colored foster parents, she in fact was of Indian extraction." This "thin line of demarcation," which had saved

Christina, demonstrated Feitel's point that the law was not aimed at behavior but was a punitive measure that sought to define racial categories and then assign punishment, and in this case residential boundaries, based on those new racial definitions.[55]

Feitel suggested that Piazza and her boarders—Sweetie Miller, Minnie Williams, and Lucille White—were not "common colored criminals" as the city alleged, but were, in fact, above-average members of the "colored or negro race." To this end, he argued that the "ordinance would operate to confine certain members of the colored race . . . to undesirable quarters of the city, in which section they will be constantly thrown in close touch with and contaminated by the degraded and criminal class of negroes, which element will necessarily predominate in this restricted area." He concluded that the enforcement of Ordinance 4118 would "lower the women in question, instead of benefiting them and correcting the evil existing."[56]

Thus, even though Piazza and her boarders had signed affidavits in which they had conceded that they were "member[s] of the colored or negro race," Feitel's arguments suggested that they were unwilling to identify with all "colored" people. Piazza's attempt to separate and distinguish herself from other African Americans based on class distinctions was only one of many such efforts among light-skinned, elite people of color in the city, although whites often failed to recognize the difference. But the terms of the debate did not allow for the privileged middle ground that Piazza and her boarders had occupied as octoroons. In fact, the term never appeared in any of the records in the case, suggesting that it was no longer a meaningful legal term. While Piazza's lawyer argued that she and her boarders were a step above the "colored" people with whom the city was trying to segregate them, the city compared them not only to "common colored criminals" but to every other social evil imaginable. Piazza and her boarders—and by extension all prostitutes of color in the city—were compared to "lepers," "victims of the white plague," "the unsound in mind," "vagrants," "beggars," and all other "undesirables of various sorts." The attorneys asked, by way of conclusion, if the city had the right to segregate these "moral lepers (who are often physically such), whose vice or evil, if not yet in this community authoritatively stigmatized as crime, makes them total outcasts, unclean, [and] infamous."[57]

In this astounding passage, the city's attorneys argued in no uncertain terms that there was an equivalency among disease, crime, prostitution generally, and African American prostitutes specifically, who were the only targets of the ordinance they sought to defend. It is particularly interesting that even Piazza's lawyer spoke of cross-racial interaction in terms of contagion, including a nod to current cultural cant when he stated that the legislature absolutely had the right to "prohibit whites and blacks from intermarrying . . . based on the sound principle that intermarriage between whites and blacks tends to weaken the vitality of the white citizens." There was no longer any question that social contact, especially intimate contact, between white and "colored" was problematic. That much seems to have been predetermined. Thus the arguments offered in the case of *City of New Orleans v. Willie Piazza* demonstrate how city officials sought to define the negative aspects of prostitution in racial terms on the eve of World War I.[58]

Surprisingly, however, the Louisiana Supreme Court sided with Piazza because, in its opinion, Ordinance 4118 went too far in specifying where individuals could and could not live, even if they were known prostitutes. In other words, the rigid residential segregation prescribed by the ordinance trumped the city's attempt to further segregate the vice district on the basis of race. The court's opinion read, in part, that the "city of New Orleans has the right to regulate or abolish houses of prostitution there can be no doubt. . . . But . . . the ordinance under consideration does not attempt to regulate houses of prostitution in any way. . . . It directs that prostitutes shall not live outside of certain named localities. In so ordaining, the council has exceeded its authority."[59]

The city responded by passing a revised ordinance in July, this one numbered 4485 C.C.S. The only significant difference between the two lay in the addition of a section specifying that white prostitutes had to live in the existing boundaries below Canal Street. Perhaps city leaders hoped that this strategy would undercut arguments aimed at the obvious racial discrimination of the first version. In any case, they applied to the state supreme court for a rehearing. In the meantime, several of the district's prostitutes of color amended their original petitions to enhance their defense against the revised ordinance. The contents of some of their petitions demonstrate just how hard it was for the city of New Orleans to enforce an ordinance that operated only on the blunt categories of black and white in a city with such a long and pervasive history of sex across the color line. The petition of Bessie Christmas, for example, began by noting that she was "reputed to be and believes that she is of the negro race, being of black complexion, but not as black as some white persons, but that, for the purpose of this suit . . . admits that she is of the negro race."[60]

Other plaintiffs were equally ambivalent on the question of their racial identity. Lulu White—who, like Piazza, had signed an affidavit in March admitting she was a member of the colored or negro race—apparently had a change of heart. In August she filed an amended petition in which she averred that she was "not of the negro, colored or black race, although" she admitted "that she held herself out for the purpose of her business . . . as an octoroon." To hedge her bets, Lulu claimed that even if the revised ordinance was found to be constitutional, it would not apply to her because "her father and her mother were both Spanish people of the Caucasian race . . . and were duly married in Havana, Cuba," where White claimed to have been born.[61]

In spite of the city's new ordinance and the individual plaintiffs' maneuvering, the Louisiana Supreme Court's ruling in Piazza's case stood. The logic of their ruling undercut the whole concept on which Storyville had been based in the first place, a point which lawyers for the city repeatedly and hysterically pointed out in their request for a rehearing. That request was tabled, and the point became moot a few months later at the time of Storyville's formal prohibition.

Piazza's victory made it impossible for the city to enforce its race-based cleanup of the vice district in 1917, but her case was meaningful in other ways as well. The timing of Piazza's victory was extraordinary, considering that she challenged the city and racial segregation at a time when such actions could have lethal consequences for persons of color. Her victory was all the more remarkable in light of her gender and the fact that she was a known prostitute. While she may have lost her privileged racial and erotic status as an octoroon, she pressed a legal challenge that had ramifications far beyond the walls of her brothel and the boundaries of Storyville. Until now, the critical role she played in defeating the city's first racially specific residential-segregation ordinance has languished in the State Supreme Court records, obscured by her racial identity, her gender, and her occupation.

While all historians of the South and many citizens of the region recognize the importance of the decision handed down by the U.S. Supreme Court in the *Plessy v. Ferguson* case, the connections between that case and Piazza's have not been recognized until now. The outcome in *Plessy* gave legal sanction to the "separate but equal doctrine" in railroad travel, yet this single ruling literally changed the course of southern history over the next half-century. Twenty-one years later, in Piazza's case, New Orleans's city attorneys included extensive quotations and arguments from the *Plessy* decision in their brief to the State Supreme Court. Like Homer Plessy, Willie

Piazza identified herself as an octoroon, but her profession as a prostitute and madam, and the erotic connotations that surrounded that racial identity when it was attached to a woman, have obscured the importance of the legal battle she waged and won against the city in 1917.

Even though Piazza won her case, and arguably delayed the passage of ordinances that required residential segregation based on race in New Orleans for many years, the arguments made by attorneys for both sides made it clear not only that the octoroon had disappeared as a viable legal category, but that the idea of the octoroon as an erotic type was losing its cultural viability. City attorneys, for example, opined that "the real reason for [Piazza's] opposition and objection" to Ordinance 4118 "is the fear of the loss of trade of those debased white men on whose indulgence of their appetites in sexual intercourse with colored prostitutes the keepers of negro bawdy-houses hope to thrive and prosper."[62]

The history of sexual contact between white men and light-skinned, mixed-race courtesans and prostitutes had a long and varied history in New Orleans. It had gone from being a matter of perceived necessity and later preference in the colonial period, to an elite prerogative in the antebellum period, to a legally sanctioned and highly remunerative activity inside Storyville. In 1917, however, even long-tolerant city officials finally condemned sex across the color line as "debased" and sought to use that issue to cleanse the city's vice district and protect it from its critics. In the process, women like Piazza, who for two decades had skillfully manipulated white men's desire for light-skinned, mixed-race women were relegated to the category "colored."

Piazza made the money to buy her property inside Storyville by selling her flesh, and that of other "octoroons," to white men who had a taste for this erotic type. Yet in the course of her two trials, it became clear that the very identification that had made her a wealthy woman could no longer offer her the protection and privileges that it had for the previous twenty years. The disappearance of the octoroon as a viable legal category offers an interesting counterpoint to the experiences of free black elites in New Orleans following Emancipation. The quadroon and the octoroon lost their privileged place in the sexual culture of the city in much the same way that the class of free black elites lost social privileges following Emancipation, but it took decades longer for it to happen to women who identified themselves as quadroon and octoroon for commercial sexual purposes. This was the case because white men protected their own sexual privilege and preferences, in this case for octoroon women, for decades beyond Emancipation. During the cold winter of 1917, as part of the drive toward a bifurcated racial system in Louisiana, in which everyone was either white or "colored," official toleration of the erotic taste for octoroon women ultimately had to be sacrificed to what were perceived as more pressing social imperatives. In the process, mixed-race prostitutes like Willie Piazza were forced into an ill-fitting but surprisingly powerful system that froze racial categorizations in Louisiana for the next several decades.

So the octoroon disappeared from the officially sanctioned commercial sexual culture in New Orleans. But what happened to Willie Piazza in real life? One local historian propagated the myth that Piazza had "retired to France, where she changed her name, wed a genuine Gallic nobleman, and lived out her life in a villa on the Riviera, an honored and respected dowager." As with so much that has been written about the women of Storyville, the story is colorful but completely without foundation. In fact, Piazza continued to live in her house at 317 N. Basin Street until her death in 1932 at the age of 67. Her death certificate notes that she died from complications of rectal cancer and that she also suffered from chronic heart and kidney ailments.[63]

Her succession and other records in the city's notarial archives yield a wealth of information about her life after Storyville. Piazza continued to buy and sell property in New Orleans and its environs until very late in her life. In 1927, for instance, she sold "Constance," a thirty-eight-foot luxury yacht that she had acquired some years earlier in Florida. Her speculation in real estate allowed her to bequeath twenty-nine parcels of land in Slidell, a city just east of New Orleans, to one James Richardson. In addition to her two properties on Basin Street, she left behind a luxurious 1926 Chrysler touring car and a safe-deposit box that held several pieces of impressively sized diamond and gemstone jewelry.[64]

In piecing Piazza's life together, we discover that, in addition to having been a prostitute and a madam, she was a savvy business woman, a real-estate speculator, an entrepreneur, a wheeler-dealer, a bon vivant, and an all-around gutsy person. Knowing about her life enables us to question many other stereotypical qualities attributed to women of color, especially those who played a role in the city's culture of commercial sexuality at the turn of the twentieth century. We can applaud Piazza's grit and gusto, yet bemoan the culture that left so few economic options open to women a hundred years ago, especially talented and resourceful African American and mixed-race women like Piazza.

Piazza's power and individual agency were severely constrained and always predicated upon her cleverly marketed sexual appeal. She called the shots in her brothel inside Storyville, but even though she owned it, the physical space had been allotted to her by white male politicians, and they attempted to take it away from her in 1917. For all practical purposes, outside that space she was as powerless as most other African Americans of the time. Piazza's ability to choose and exploit the identity "octoroon" was a luxury that light skin afforded her, but that identity was always contingent on the whims of white elites. While Piazza spun white men's sexual fantasies about African American and mixed-race women into gold, she could not translate her material prosperity into political power when it came to determining legal definitions of race.

In arguing its case against her, the city of New Orleans asserted that "[l]egislation is powerless to eradicate racial instincts or to abolish distinctions based upon physical differences." But the case of Willie Piazza, and the endurance of the octoroon as a privileged racial category as long as it was attached to white male sexual privilege, rebuts such assertions. Legislation allowed Piazza and other octoroons to make their fortunes inside Storyville. Once the presence of these mixed-race prostitutes became inconvenient in an increasingly bifurcated racial system, legislation attempted to usher them—and the erotic appetite they served—off the historical stage. Prosperous and powerful octoroons like Willie Piazza became, in the words of the city's attorney's, "as rare as white blackbirds"—not by chance, as the city argued, but by design, thanks to another even heartier and increasingly powerful breed of bird known as Jim Crow.

Epilogue

The story of Willie Piazza and her counterparts filing suit against the city is a compelling and important episode in the final year of Storyville's existence, but it was not the only drama in the vice district in 1917. City fathers were working hard to protect segregated prostitution and commercial vice from the encroaching power of reform forces in other, more direct ways as well. Attempting to segregate the vice district on the basis of race was one way they chose to curry favor with reformers. But local reformers were in no mood to compromise, especially since the actions of federal authorities strengthened their own position immeasurably.

The country's preparation for and involvement in World War I was a boon to the city's overall economy. The Association of Commerce, for instance, reported in 1917 that "in normal times New Orleans is a most attractive city in which to hold conventions. In war times, with overseas travel impossible, New Orleans has become the mecca of an ever increasing number of tourists." City officials also worked aggressively to enlarge the presence of military encampments, soldiers, and sailors as the country prepared to enter the war in Europe. "With the cooperation of Mayor Behrman," city boosters "succeeded in having a naval training station established" in the city. The Association of Commerce also lobbied military authorities to make the city an official quartermaster depot, which would enhance the volume and importance of cargo handled by the Port of New Orleans. Apparently, war was good for business on many fronts.[1]

Soldiers and sailors were a welcome addition to the city's economy, but, according to reformers, their presence also created problems and revealed, once again, why the city's reputation as the Great Southern Babylon endured. For the women of the Travelers' Aid Society, "problems and difficulties [increased] . . . a thousand fold" as the society went about its mission of "protecting women and girls arriving in the city, who, through ignorance or inexperience, are in danger of being exposed to the influence of the representatives of organized vice." According to the society's records the "soldiers encamped in . . . City Park and the students enrolled at Camp Martin, on the campus of Tulane University" made their task all the more difficult.[2]

Local reformers were not the only ones who were troubled. Men and women from rural Louisiana also raised concerns during 1917 about the dangers that New Orleans and its vice district posed to young military men. For example, M. E. Dodd, pastor of the First Baptist Church in Shreveport, wrote to the federal Commission on Training Camp Activities (CTCA) in June. He expressed interest in the "moral and spiritual welfare" of the fifteen boys from his church who had "volunteered for service in the defense of our national honor." He was particularly worried about the young men who had been stationed near New Orleans, and concluded his letter by noting, "It is well known that New Orleans is the sodom of the South and if our boys cannot be protected there, I earnestly request your consideration in moving them."[3]

Mrs. A. C. McKinney of Ruston, Louisiana, wrote a long, impassioned letter to the national office of the Woman's Christian Temperance Union that was forwarded to the CTCA. She reported that officials from New Orleans and Alexandria were in Baton Rouge "doing all in their power to defeat the bill . . . for the protection of the boys that are to be encamped in Louisiana." Why, she asked, "is it that the government makes an exception of New Orleans? They have made other places clean up, or failing in that, have moved the boys. Must the Louisiana boys be sacrificed?" She concluded that "conditions in New Orleans are indescribable and if the Government does not do something to close those saloons and brothels, many of the boys will be rendered unfit for service."[4]

Members of the city's Travelers' Aid Society may have been concerned about protecting young women from seduction, but the military establishment and some in northern Louisiana were more interested in protecting soldiers from venereal disease. Reflecting this attitude, the War Department often focused on penalizing and controlling women, especially prostitutes, to limit venereal infection. Under the auspices of the CTCA, the military services implemented a "rigorous policy of vice suppression" and offered the thousands of soldiers stationed in training camps "wholesome recreational and social opportunities" instead.[5]

"The CTCA's authority to suppress prostitution in the communities surrounding military training camps was based on Section 13 of the Selective Service Act, which outlawed any form of prostitution within five to ten mile-zones around each camp." To entice military authorities to place camps in their locales, many cities closed their districts as quickly as possible. Reformers in other cities had eradicated red-light districts a few years earlier. But in cities that were reluctant to do so "the threat of moving the training camp to another location was often sufficient to make local officials comply." According to Mark Thomas Connelly, "this was often the tactic used in the South, most notably in Louisiana."[6]

Mayor Behrman, however, remained convinced that a well-policed segregated district, closely monitored by both civilian and military personnel, was the best way to protect soldiers stationed in New Orleans from venereal disease. In fact, he went to Washington and made this case before Secretary of War Newton Baker in August 1917. Apparently Behrman was convincing; Baker agreed to allow Storyville to remain open until the effectiveness of the proposed patrols could be ascertained. Approximately two months later, however, Behrman received another set of direct orders to close the district, this time from Secretary of the Navy Josephus Daniels. Behrman introduced an ordinance a few days later, and Storyville was officially closed on November 12, 1917.[7]

To maintain military camps in New Orleans, local officials were forced to concede to the demands of federal authorities. They did so grudgingly, and some local citizens feared that reform of the vice district would interfere with the city's reputation for good times—and thus its special character and allure. For example, a writer identified only as R. W. C. expressed the following reservations in a telling letter to the editor early in 1917. "Are we not," he wrote, "in danger of violating the particular 'atmosphere' of our unique city, of dulling the local color, and impairing the individuality of our town, by the institution of 'radical reforms'?"[8]

With the benefit of hindsight we know that R. W. C. need not have worried. Even though Storyville officially ended in late 1917, its demise was much more apparent than real. In the short term and in classic New Orleans style, in fact, many of Storyville's brothels continued to operate, turning away only sailors and soldiers in uniform. This turn of events reportedly gave rise to a new cottage industry in which civilian clothes were rented by the hour to soldiers and sailors on leave. Although local authorities agreed to end the Storyville experiment, they did so with little enthusiasm, and enforcement was spotty. In short, the city's formal collusion in the promotion of prostitution and commercial sexuality had to be traded away, at least temporarily, in order to gain as much patriotic pork as possible in the months leading up to the United States' entry into the war. But, just as Charles Dudley Warner had noted thirty years before, there were still "more than enough of the resorts upon which the police are supposed to keep one blind eye."[9]

Three years after R. W. C. expressed his concern about the effects of radical reform in New Orleans, reformers seemed to have triumphed on all fronts, at least temporarily. According to the *Times-Picayune,* New Orleanians welcomed the year 1920 with unusual, perhaps unique, solemnity and circumspection. It was, the paper noted, "quite accurate to say that January 1, 1920 was the quietest New Year's Day in the history of New Orleans. . . . There was a new primness in the air, a prudery of address, a startling punctilio that surcharged the very atmosphere with an enveloping restraint." The story went on to paint a picture of bewildered New Orleanians taking part in the traditional New Year's Day promenades on Canal and Royal Streets, navigating social situations with a sort of shell-shocked sobriety and sheepishness unusual on such usually festive occasions. The story concluded that most citizens "betook themselves to church, where they listened to much sound advice and perfunctorily agreed that it was just as well that things were as they were." The way "things were" was that the city was dry due to the adoption of the Eighteenth Amendment, was without legalized gambling, and had just marked the second anniversary of Storyville's official closing. In significant ways, reform had turn the city upside down.[10]

But the downturn in good times, if it existed at all, was remarkably brief. During its 1920 election-year coverage, the *Picayune* blazed a trail for its readers into the heart of the city's now more obscure but apparently no less numerous vice establishments. Pointing out that Mayor Behrman had in the past supported and protected vice and that he continued to do so, the paper named names, gave addresses, and dared local authorities to do something about the brothels and gambling dens it had exposed. The *Picayune*'s charge that Behrman was "King of the Tenderloin" contributed in no small part to his loss of the mayor's office after sixteen consecutive years in the job. "Reform" candidate Andrew McShane won the election, but the city's vice interests would ultimately emerge victorious from the ongoing war over the city's reputation. This outcome was foreshadowed the year following the election when the United States Interdepartmental Social Hygiene Board issued a scathing report on vice in New Orleans in 1921. The report concluded that "immoral houses are operating openly . . . and that the city harbors numbers of women, especially negroes, who openly ply their trade."[11]

Newspaper exposés and the government report made it clear that brothels and other less visible forms of prostitution that used nightclubs, restaurants, hotels, taxi drivers, and boardinghouses as fronts, were thriving in the city in the 1920s. By the end of that decade one guidebook author assured his readers that visitors to New Orleans, a group he referred to as "hell-bound people," would find "plenty of liquor . . . gambling dens, cabarets, roadhouses, nightclubs, and a total lack of reformers." The writer did not mention prostitutes, but perhaps that was because the business had taken on new, more surreptitious forms.[12]

But prostitution did not go away. By the 1930s, in fact, the city's reputation for openly operating cribs and brothels was back in the national news, this time because political juggernaut and damn-near dictator Huey Long had launched a "clean up campaign" of his own. In response, national magazines featured stories that described the city in terms similar to those employed by James Davidson and Rachel Jackson a century before. *Vanity Fair,* for instance, proclaimed New Orleans "a Wicked City" and in particular focused on its history of "quadroon prostitution." The writers at *Real Detective* referred to the city as a "Vice Cesspool" and described in detail the "nightly saturnalia within the New Orleans red light district." According to author Edward Anderson, that district occupied the same boundaries Storyville had. Although Anderson claimed that women of all sizes, ages, races, and skin tones worked in the district, he noted that one of the "most notorious" places was called "Uncle Tom's Cabin," a venue where "sex circuses" were "arranged for those interested."[13]

In the end, it became clear that Long's cleanup campaign had as much to do with his bid for complete control of the state's politics as it did with a sincere effort to reform the city's stubbornly sinful mores. Whatever his intentions, the result was the same as it had been when reformers won a victory and created a vice district that came to be known as Storyville in 1897. As the history of the city's last, smallest, but most notorious vice district makes clear, the city's legendary reputation for sexual immorality grew stronger every time reformers sought to erase or control it.

More than a century after Storyville was established, and more than eighty years after it was abolished, the city's reputation for sexual liberality, sensual tourism, and laissez-faire morality remains intact. It also remains indebted, at least in part, to the romanticized mythology that has developed about Storyville. By now, of course, prostitution and sex across the color line are no longer the most characteristic elements of the city's culture of commercial sexuality. Yet the city remains one of the nation's principal sites of sybaritic pilgrimage, a place where people come to eat and drink to excess and to let down their hair. Many are also willing to pull up their shirts or drop their pants or, perhaps more commonly, to photograph or film the surreal spectacle. Today those aspects of the city's commercial sexual culture have moved to Bourbon Street, where throngs gather to watch one another flash body parts and exchange tokens in an economy based on flashy beads, bawdy abandon, and bravado.

Some New Orleanians eagerly embrace and try to profit from this reputation, much as Otto Schoenhausen did more than a century ago. Others are still troubled by the lack of respectability inherent in the city's reputation. *Playboy* magazine's decision to feature a story called "Mardi Gras 2000, Wild Party Heaven" on the cover of its March 2000 issue brought this enduring debate back into sharp relief. The eight-page photo spread, which featured both amateur and professional models willing to bare it all on Bourbon Street, sparked a controversy that led local police to warn visitors that they should "refrain from obscenity in general and the display of breasts and genitals in particular" while celebrating the first Mardi Gras of the new millennium.[14]

Police officers even posted broadsides explaining that it was unlawful to "manage, produce, sponsor, present or exhibit obscene live conduct" during Mardi Gras celebrations. When the *Playboy* issue hit newsstands, the local papers and their editorial pages were filled with opinions about whether the story and images presented "a good image for Carnival tourism." After much debate, and just days before Mardi Gras, the mayor called a press conference in which he and the police superintendent assured prospective revelers that they weren't "treating nudity any differently" than they had in previous years. The so-called crackdown on flashing during Carnival 2000 was short-lived. It was soon shoved aside in favor of making sure that the billion-dollar business of Carnival was not threatened by the perceived Puritanism of the city or its law-enforcement officers.[15]

While the breast-flashing debate dominated newspaper coverage of Mardi Gras in the first year of the new century, a smaller but no less telling story had appeared in the local newspaper on December 31, 1999. Society columnist Nell Nolan chronicled the "Concert Bal" given for five debutantes at Storyville District, the most recent music club and restaurant to use the name and reputation of the prostitution district as a marketing device. Coverage of the coming-out party dominated the "Social Scene" society column that Sunday; Nolan was too polite to note the irony inherent in well-scrubbed, boa-draped debutantes posing for the camera in rooms decorated to resemble turn-of-the-century brothels.[16]

This party provides a surreal example of how Storyville's reputation has evolved into a benign, romanticized, and cherished piece of the city's history. A hundred years earlier, city fathers had rationalized their establishment of a vice district as a way to separate such respectable, upper-class women from their fallen sisters. But as sexual culture changed and the flapper emerged in the 1920s, such distinctions were already well on their way to becoming meaningless. (Willie Piazza was reputed to have said, "The country club girls are ruining my business!") At the debutante party in Storyville District, no one seemed to distinguish between country-club girls and fallen women or to notice the paradox inherent in staging a coming-out party in a venue that celebrated legalized prostitution and the mandatory segregation of its female practitioners.[17]

Like the rest of the South and the nation, New Orleans's culture of commercial sexuality has changed remarkably over the course of the twentieth century, but the local pride in and promotion of Storyville is sometimes jarring. Many people seem to have forgotten that Storyville was first and foremost a prostitution district where women who lacked educational or economic opportunities were forced to live and work in order to reap the economic benefits of selling their bodies to the men who visited the district.

New Orleans's reputation as an exotic, erotic hot spot grew out of the demographic, social, and economic conditions that prevailed in the city in the colonial and antebellum periods. After the Civil War, profoundly altered social and economic conditions reshaped the meaning and import of prostitution and relationships across the color line, particularly when they were sexual. Economic and social crises also raised questions about the desirability of the city's erotic reputation in general. Although reformers sought to control vice by segregating its practitioners and their places of business between 1897 and 1917, this political victory had unforeseen outcomes. Ironically, the creation of Storyville guaranteed that the city's sexual mythology would remain a powerful part of its appeal throughout the twentieth century.

Storyville as a physical reality is long gone. Most of the district's buildings were razed in the mid-1940s to make way for a sprawling public-housing development called the Iberville Housing Project. Today most tourists and many locals assiduously avoid the area where the vice district once flourished, but the soft-focus romantic myth that has grown up around Storyville is alive and well. People still come to New Orleans in search of the permissive atmosphere that made the city a "notorious attraction" in the early twentieth century. Contemporary New Orleans enjoys and endures a reputation that began to take shape in the nineteenth century and crystallized in the national imagination between 1865 and 1920.

Prostitution and sex across the color line are no longer the principal attractions in the city's sexual culture, and respectability—at least among most Americans—is no longer the great national obsession it was a century ago. Nor does anyone now refer to New Orleans as the Great Southern Babylon. Yet the city's contemporary appeal springs from the same sources that nourished its nascent tourist economy between 1865 and 1920. Compared to the region that surrounds it, New Orleans retains an alluring and lurid reputation. The city still serves as a safety valve, a place where visitors from near and far come to cut loose for brief periods of time. These days, the city's nickname—the Big Easy—is much less glamorous. But, as the preceding chapters attest, its history is more complex than this moniker suggests.

As for *Brise Légère,* the statue that once stood atop a newel post in Storyville, she now resides in a tranquil uptown house where she is a cherished family heirloom. Her storied past is behind her, and what she witnessed in the vice district remains her secret.

But even scratching the surface of Storyville's history reveals significant new information about New Orleans and its relationship to the rest of the South and the nation. From a historian's perspective, there are many questions that remain unanswered and much work still to be done, especially regarding the personal histories of the vice district's mostly female inhabitants. But as Mary Deubler and Willie Piazza knew very well, a woman's work, no matter what her profession, is never really done.

Notes

PREFACE

1. The statue is now the property of Timothy G. Schafer, the great-grandson of Thomas C. Anderson. He and his wife Judith Schafer have graciously granted permission for a photograph of it to be used in this book.

INTRODUCTION

1. On the city's position as the nation's largest slave market see Walter Johnson, *Soul by Soul: Life inside the Antebellum Slave Market* (Cambridge: Harvard University Press, 2000). For further analysis of the city's importance as a sexually oriented tourist destination, see Alecia Long, "A Notorious Attraction: Sex and Tourism in New Orleans, 1897–1917," in Richard D. Starnes, ed., *Southern Journeys: Tourism, History and Culture in the Modern South* (Tuscaloosa: University of Alabama Press, 2003). On the reasons for using the phrase "sex across the color line" rather than "interracial sex" or "miscegenation," see Martha Hodes, *White Women, Black Men: Illicit Sex in the Nineteenth-Century South* (New Haven: Yale University Press, 1997), 9.

2. Carl Brasseaux, "The Moral Climate of French Colonial Louisiana, 1699–1763," *Louisiana History* 27 (1986): 27–41. For an example of work that disputes the city's reputation for widespread sexual immorality in the colonial era, see Thomas Ingersoll, *Mammon and Manon in Early New Orleans* (Knoxville: University of Tennessee Press, 1999), 35–36, 54; Kimberly Hanger, *A Medley of Cultures: Louisiana History at the Cabildo* (New Orleans: Louisiana Museum Foundation, 1996), 149. Hanger is citing Christian Schultz, a traveler who came to New Orleans in 1808 and published his observations two years later. See Schultz, *Travels on an Inland Voyage,* 2 vols. (New York: Isaac Riley, 1810). Other travel accounts that focus on similar themes include Karl Bernhard Duke of Saxe-Weimar Eisenach, *Travels through North America, during the Years 1825 and 1826,* vol. 2 (Philadelphia: Carey, Lea & Carey, 1828), 61–3; Harriet Martineau, *Society in America,* ed. Seymour Martin Lipset (1837; reprint, New Brunswick, N.J.: Transaction Books, 1981), 225; Frederick Law Olmsted, *The Cotton Kingdom: A Traveller's Observations on Cotton and Slavery in the American Slave States,* ed. Arthur M. Schlesinger Sr. (1861; reprint, New York: Modern Library, 1984), 237; Frances Trollope, *Do-*

mestic Manners of the Americans (1832; reprint, New York: Dodd, Mead, 1894), 15–6; John Fanning Watson, "*Notitia* of Incidents at New Orleans in 1804 and 1805," *American Pioneer* II (May 1843): 233–6. For numerous other examples focused on sex across the color line, see Jennifer M. Spear, "'Whiteness and Purity of Blood': Race, Sexuality, and Cultural Identity in Colonial Louisiana, 1699–1795" (Ph.D. diss., University of Minnesota, 1999), 1–10.

3. James Davidson, "A Journey through the South in 1836: Diary of James D. Davidson," ed. Herbert A. Kellar, *Journal of Southern History* 1 (August 1935): 357–62; Rachel Jackson to Mrs. Eliza Kingsley, 27 April 1821, cited in Robert V. Remini, *The Battle of New Orleans* (New York: Viking Press, 1999), 31.

4. Davidson, "A Journey through the South," 358.

5. On the relationship between slavery and sexuality in general, see Ronald G. Walters, *The Antislavery Appeal: American Abolitionism after 1830* (Baltimore: Johns Hopkins University Press, 1976), 70–87, and Eugene D. Genovese, *Roll, Jordan, Roll: The World the Slaves Made* (New York: Pantheon Books, 1974). On the relationship between sexuality and the commodification of slave bodies, see Edward E. Baptist, "'Cuffy,' 'Fancy Maids,' and 'One-Eyed Men': Rape, Commodification, and the Domestic Slave Trade in the United States," *American Historical Review* 106 (December 2001): 1619–1650; and Johnson, *Soul by Soul*. For a literary perspective on sex across the color line in New Orleans, see Monique Guillory, "Some Enchanted Evening on the Auction Block: The Cultural Legacy of the New Orleans Quadroon Balls" (Ph.D. diss., New York University, 1999).

6. Long, "A Notorious Attraction."

7. I am indebted to Dr. Judith Kelleher Schafer for the information that "lorette" is one of many French slang terms for prostitute. See also Richard Tansey, "Prostitution and Politics in Antebellum New Orleans," *Southern Studies* 19 (Winter 1980): 455–70; Al Rose, *Storyville: Being an Authentic, Illustrated Account of the Notorious Red-Light District* (Tuscaloosa: University of Alabama Press, 1974), 8–9.

8. For an extended discussion of this issue see Gaines Foster, *Moral Reconstruction: Christian Lobbyists and the Federal Legislation of Morality, 1865–1920* (Chapel Hill: University of North Carolina Press, 2002). On the tension between sincerity and disreputability in the nation's rapidly growing cities, see Karen Halttunen, *Confidence Men and Painted Women: A Study of Middle-Class Culture in America, 1830–1870* (New Haven: Yale University Press, 1982).

9. John D'Emilio and Estelle B. Freedman, *Intimate Matters: A History of Sexuality in America* (New York: Harper & Row, 1988), 172. See also John C. Fout and Maura Shaw Tantillo, eds., *American Sexual Politics: Sex, Gender, and Race since the Civil War* (Chicago: University of Chicago Press, 1993), and Laura F. Edwards, *Gendered Strife and Confusion: The Political Culture of Reconstruction* (Champaign: University of Illinois Press, 1997).

10. Two historians who include New Orleans in comparative studies are Ruth Rosen and Mary Ryan. See Ruth Rosen, *The Lost Sisterhood: Prostitution in America, 1900–1918* (New York: Basic Books, 1983); Mary Ryan, *Civic Wars: Democracy and Public Life in the American City during the Nineteenth Century* (Los Angeles: University of California Press, 1997); Ryan, *Women in Public: Between Banners and Ballots, 1825–1880* (Baltimore: Johns Hopkins University Press, 1990).

11. Nancy Hewitt, *Southern Discomfort: Women's Activism in Tampa, Florida, 1880s–1920s* (Champaign: University of Illinois Press, 2001), 15.

12. Hodes, *White Women, Black Men,* 12.

13. Ibid., 9.

14. Catherine Clinton, *Public Women and the Confederacy* (Milwaukee: Marquette University Press, 1999); Barbara Meil Hobson, *Uneasy Virtue: The Politics of Prostitution and the American Reform Tradition* (New York: Basic Books, 1987); Rosen, *The Lost Sisterhood;* Rosen, *The Maimie Papers* (1977; reprint, Bloomington: Indiana University Press; Old Westbury, N.Y.: Feminist Press, 1985); Judith Walkowitz, *Prostitution in Victorian Society: Women, Class, and State* (New York: Cambridge University Press, 1980).

15. George Chauncey, *Gay New York: Gender, Urban Culture, and the Making of the Gay Male World, 1890–1940* (New York: Basic Books, 1994); Timothy J. Gilfoyle, *City of Eros: New York City, Prostitution, and the Commercialization of Sex, 1790–1920* (New York: W. W. Norton, 1992); Kathy Peiss, *Cheap Amusements: Working Women and Leisure in Turn-of-the-Century New York* (Philadelphia: Temple University Press, 1986); Christine Stansell, *City of Women: Sex and Class in New York, 1789–1860* (Champaign: University of Illinois Press, 1987).

16. For examples of other scholars who have used court cases and legal testimony in similar ways, see Peter Bardaglio, *Reconstruction of the Household: Families, Sex, and the Law in the Nineteenth-Century South* (Chapel Hill: University of North Carolina Press, 1995); Edwards, *Gendered Strife and Confusion;* Hodes, *White Women, Black Men;* and Suzanne Lebsock, *The Free Women of Petersburg: Status and Culture in a Southern Town, 1784–1860* (New York: W. W. Norton, 1984).

CHAPTER 1. "IT'S BECAUSE YOU ARE A COLORED WOMAN":
SEX, RACE, AND CONCUBINAGE AFTER THE CIVIL WAR

1. For the significance of sex across the color line in a variety of forms during Reconstruction see D'Emilio and Freedman, *Intimate Matters,* 104–8.

2. Judith K. Schafer, "'Open and Notorious Concubinage': The Emancipation of Slave Mistresses by Will and the Supreme Court in Antebellum Louisiana," *Louisiana History* 28 (Spring 1987): 165–82; *Adeline E. Stringer v. Louis Mathis (1889),* Supreme Court of Louisiana, Docket No. 10293, digested in 41 *Louisiana Annual:* 985. The lower-court case was *Adeline E. Stringer v. Louis Mathis (1888),* Docket No. 217888, Civil District Court for the Parish of Orleans, Division E, City Archives, New Orleans Public Library. Although the contents of the two court records vary slightly, their substantive content is the same, and the case will be cited hereafter as *Stringer v. Mathis.* Other concubinage cases include *Viens v. Brickle (1820),* Supreme Court of Louisiana, Docket No. 454, digested in 8 *Martin's Reports:* 11; *Succession of Pereuilhet (1871),* Supreme Court of Louisiana, Docket No. 2031, digested in 23 *Louisiana Annual:* 294; *Succession of Jahraus (1905),* Supreme Court of Louisiana, Docket No. 15,020, digested in 114 *Louisiana Reports:* 456.

3. Guillory, "Some Enchanted Evening on the Auction Block."

4. See *Viens v. Brickle; Succession of Pereuilhet; Succession of Jahraus.*

5. Hodes, *White Women, Black Men,* 1–2; *New Orleans Times,* Jun. 11, Aug. 14, 1874; *Mascot,* Mar. 26, 1887.

6. *Daily Picayune,* Apr. 3, 1887.

7. In the nineteenth century, the term *griffe* was usually used in reference to a person's skin color. A griffe could be the offspring of a Negro and a mulatto or of a Negro and a Native American. *Griffe* could also be used simply to refer to a darker-skinned mulatto.

8. In deciding how best to integrate Joseph Mathis's letters into the text I was guided by Helen Lefkowitz Horowitz and Kathy Peiss, eds., *Love across the Color Line: The Letters of Alice Hanley to Channing Lewis* (Amherst: University of Massachusetts Press, 1996).

9. *Stringer v. Mathis.*

10. Ibid.

11. Ibid.

12. On the mobility of slaves in urban areas see Genovese, *Roll, Jordan, Roll,* 415, and Howard Rabinowitz, *Race Relations in the Urban South: 1865–1890* (New York: Oxford University Press, 1978). Rabinowitz does not cover New Orleans in detail because he "felt that its pattern of race relations was likely to be atypical" (xv).

13. *Daily Picayune,* Dec. 7, 1867; *Succession of Joseph Mathis,* Orleans Parish Civil District Court, Division B, Docket No. 20866, Apr. 19, 1887, City Archives, New Orleans Public Library. The *True Delta* article is reprinted in Herbert Asbury, *The French Quarter: An Informal History of the New Orleans Underworld* (1936; reprint, Garden City, N. Y.: Garden City Publishing, 1938), 291–4.

14. *Gardner's New Orleans Directory for 1859* (New Orleans, 1858); *Cohen's New Orleans Directory for 1854* (New Orleans, 1854).

15. *Stringer v. Mathis.*

16. Master Rolls, Battalion Washington Artillery: 1861–1865. Special Collections, Howard-Tilton Library, Tulane University.

17. Powell Casey, *An Outline of the Civil War Campaigns and Engagements of the Washington Artillery of New Orleans* (Baton Rouge: Claitor's, 1986), 75; *Daily Picayune,* Aug. 21, 1864; Oct. 7, 1865.

18. *Graham's Crescent City Directory for 1867* (New Orleans: L. Graham, 1866); Orleans Parish Conveyance Records.

19. U.S. Bureau of the Census, *1870 Manuscript Census, Louisiana.*

20. *Stringer v. Mathis.*

21. *Graham's Crescent City Directory for 1867; Edwards's Annual Directory to the Inhabitants, Institutions, Incorporated Companies, Manufacturers, Establishments, Etc., in the City of New Orleans* (New Orleans, Southern Pub. Co., 1871); U.S. Bureau of the Census, *1870 Manuscript Census, Louisiana.*

22. John Blassingame, *Black New Orleans, 1860–1880* (Chicago: University of Chicago Press, 1973), 206–7; *Edwards's Annual Directory* (1872); U.S. Bureau of the Census, *1870 Manuscript Census, Louisiana.*

23. U.S. Bureau of the Census, *1880 Manuscript Census, Louisiana.*

24. U.S. Bureau of the Census, *1870 Manuscript Census, Louisiana.*

25. Mary Scott Duchein, "Research on Charles Etienne Arthur Gayerré" (master's thesis, Louisiana State University, 1934), 125; *Historical Sketch Book and Guide to New Orleans and Environs, 3rd Issue with Map,* ed. and comp. "Several Leading Writers of the New Orleans Press" (New York: Will H. Coleman, 1885), 88. A copy can be found in the Rare Books and Manuscripts Division, Howard-Tilton Library, Tulane University.

26. *Stringer v. Mathis.* See also Tera W. Hunter, *To 'Joy My Freedom: Southern Black Women's Lives and Labors after the Civil War* (Cambridge: Harvard University Press, 1997).

27. Asbury, *French Quarter,* 388. Also see, for example, *James A. Koehl et al. v. Otto H. Schoenhausen (1895),* Supreme Court of Louisiana, Docket No. 11616; *George L'Hote v. City of New Orleans et al. (1898),* Supreme Court of Louisiana, Docket No. 12753.

28. U.S. Bureau of the Census, *1870 Manuscript Census, Louisiana.*

29. Joe Gray Taylor, *Louisiana Reconstructed, 1863–1877* (Baton Rouge: Louisiana State University Press), 112.

30. Eric Arnesen, *Waterfront Workers of New Orleans: Race, Class, and Politics, 1863–1923* (New York: Oxford University Press, 1991), 26.

31. On the role of sexual violence in the reestablishment of white social control, see D'Emilio and Freedman, *Intimate Matters,* 104–8.

32. For a thorough account of the events surrounding the Battle of Liberty Place, see Taylor, *Louisiana Reconstructed,* 291–6; for information about the living arrangements of Joe and Adeline, see *Stringer v. Mathis.*

33. *Stringer v. Mathis.*

34. Ibid.

35. Kevin Fontenot, *A History of Lafayette Insurance Company* (New Orleans: Lafayette Insurance Co., 1994).

36. For the most thorough account of the riot in which Hahn was injured, see James G. Hollandsworth, *An Absolute Massacre: The New Orleans Race Riot of July 30, 1866* (Baton Rouge: Louisiana State University Press, 2001).

37. For more on Hahn, and this quotation specifically, see John Frederick Nau, *The German People of New Orleans, 1850–1900* (Leiden, The Netherlands: E. J. Brill, 1958), 34; *Stringer v. Mathis.*

38. *Stringer v. Mathis.*

39. Ibid.

40. Ibid.

41. Ibid.; Orleans Parish Conveyance Records.

42. *Stringer v. Mathis.*

43. Ibid.

44. Ibid.

45. Asbury, *French Quarter* 294; *Daily Picayune,* Jul. 29, Aug. 1, 13, 18, 1879.

46. *Daily Picayune,* Aug. 18, 1879; *Stringer v. Mathis.*

47. *Daily Picayune,* Sept. 12, 1903.

48. *Stringer v. Mathis.*

49. Ibid.

50. Ibid.

51. Ibid. See also Robert Taylor, "Crime and Race Relations in Jacksonville, 1884–1892," *Southern Studies* (Spring 1991): 17, 18.

52. Taylor, "Crime and Race Relations in Jacksonville," 18–37.

53. *Stringer v. Mathis; Soards' New Orleans City Directory for 1880* (New Orleans: L. Soards & Co., 1880).

54. *Stringer v. Mathis.*

55. Ibid.

56. Ibid.

57. Ibid.

58. Ibid.

59. Ibid.

60. U.S. Bureau of the Census, *1880 Manuscript Census, Louisiana.*

61. *Stringer v. Mathis.*

62. *Harper's Weekly,* Jan. 3, 1885: 13.

63. Ibid., Jan. 10, 1885: 27; *Historical Sketch Book and Guide to New Orleans,* 88.

64. *Stringer v. Mathis.*

65. Ibid.

66. Ibid.

67. Ibid.

68. Ibid.

69. Ibid.

70. Ibid.

71. Ibid.

72. Ibid.

73. Ibid.

74. Ibid.

75. Ibid.

76. Ibid.

77. Ibid.

78. Ibid.

79. Ibid. For a lengthy discussion of the history of concubinage, see the summary of *Succession of Jahraus,* 114 *Louisiana Reports:* 456.

80. *Stringer v. Mathis.*

81. Ibid.

82. Ibid.

83. Ibid.; *Succession of Joseph Mathis.*

84. *Stringer v. Mathis.*

85. Ibid.

86. *Compiled Edition of the Civil Codes of Louisiana: Louisiana Legal Archives,* vol. 3, Part 1 (Baton Rouge: Louisiana State Law Institute, 1940), Art. 1481, RCC 1870, 812.

87. Ibid., Art. 1483, RCC 1870, 813.

88. *Stringer v. Mathis.*

89. Ibid.

90. Glenn R. Conrad, ed., *A Dictionary of Louisiana Biography,* vol. 1 (Lafayette: Center for Louisiana Studies, 1988), 211–2.

91. *Stringer v. Mathis;* Orleans Parish Conveyance Records.

92. *Stringer v. Mathis.*

93. Ibid.

94. Ibid.

95. Ibid.

96. Ibid.

97. Ibid.

98. Ibid.

99. Ibid.

100. *Succession of Jahraus.*

101. Ibid.

102. Ibid.

103. *Stringer v. Mathis.*

104. Ibid.

105. For a description of Louis's house on St. Charles Avenue see Dorothy G. Schlesinger, Robert J. Cangelosi Jr., and Sally Kittredge Reeves, eds., *New Orleans Architecture*, vol. 7, *Jefferson City* (Gretna, La.: Pelican Publishing Co., 1989), 169; *Daily Picayune*, Sept. 12, 1903.

106. U.S. Bureau of the Census, *1900 Manuscript Census, Alabama.* Becoming white was not solely an issue of crossing the color line. On the social construction of "whiteness" in this same period see, for example, Grace Elizabeth Hale, *Making Whiteness: The Culture of Segregation in the South, 1890–1940* (New York: Pantheon, 1998); and Matthew Frye Jacobson, *Whiteness of a Different Color: European Immigrants and the Alchemy of Race* (Cambridge: Harvard University Press, 1998).

CHAPTER 2. THE BUSINESS OF PLEASURE: CONCERT SALOONS AND SEXUAL COMMERCE IN THE ECONOMIC MAINSTREAM

1. Charles Dudley Warner, "New Orleans," *Harper's New Monthly Magazine* (January 1887), 186–205.

2. Ibid.

3. Ibid.

4. *Mascot*, Jan. 22, 1887.

5. *Mascot*, Jan. 12, 1884.

6. For a close look at this process in another southern locale, see Thomas W. Hanchett, *Sorting Out the New South City: Race, Class, and Urban Development in Charlotte, 1875–1975* (Chapel Hill: University of North Carolina Press, 1998).

7. D'Emilio and Freedman, *Intimate Matters*, 111. On concert saloons generally, see Robert C. Allen, *Horrible Prettiness: Burlesque and American Culture* (Chapel Hill: University of North Carolina Press, 1991), 73–6; and Gilfoyle, *City of Eros*, 224–39.

8. *James A. Koehl et al. v. Otto H. Schoenhausen (1895),* Supreme Court of Louisiana, Docket No. 111616, digested in 47 *Louisiana Annual:* 1316. The lower-court case was *James A. Koehl et al. v. Otto H. Schoenhausen (1893),* Docket No. 40999, Civil District Court for the Parish of Orleans, Division B, City Archives, New Orleans Public Library. Although the contents of the two court records vary slightly, their substantive content is the same, and the case will be cited hereafter as *Koehl v. Schoenhausen.*

9. Ibid.

10. Ibid.

11. Ibid.

12. Connelly, *Response to Prostitution in the Progressive Era,* 8.

13. Gail Bederman, *Manliness and Civilization: A Cultural History of Gender and Race in the United States, 1880–1917* (Chicago: University of Chicago Press, 1995), 16–20.

14. See Ryan, *Women in Public,* 58–94.

15. Allen, *Horrible Prettiness,* 140. See also Gerilyn Tandberg, "Sinning for Silk: Dress-for-Success Fashions of the New Orleans Storyville Prostitute," *Women's Studies International Forum* 13 (1990): 229–48.

16. Lafcadio Hearn, *Lafcadio Hearn's America: Ethnographic Sketches and Editorials,* ed. Simon J. Bronner (Lexington: University Press of Kentucky, 2002), 170.

17. *The State of Louisiana v. Henry Wenger (1890),* Supreme Court of Louisiana, Docket No. 10580, digested in 42 *Louisiana Annual:* 556, hereafter cited as *State v. Wenger.*

18. *State v. Wenger.*

19. Ibid.

20. See Eric Lott, *Love and Theft: Blackface Minstrelsy and the American Working Class* (New York: Oxford University Press, 1993) and Robert Toll, *Blacking Up: The Minstrel Show in Nineteenth-Century America* (New York: Oxford University Press, 1974).

21. *State v. Wenger.* For a history of burlesque see Allen, *Horrible Prettiness.*

22. *Koehl v. Schoenhausen.*

23. Ibid.; *Times-Democrat,* Mar. 14, 1905.

24. Gilfoyle, *City of Eros,* 129.

25. Allen, *Horrible Prettiness,* 73.

26. *Mascot,* Sept. 18, 1886. See Allen, *Horrible Prettiness,* 51–72, for a detailed description of how "legitimate" theaters expunged elements in the mid-nineteenth century that were commonly reinstated in concert saloons by the 1860s.

27. *State v. Wenger.* For an abbreviated account of the controversy surrounding the premiere of the can-can in New Orleans, see John Magill, "That Disgraceful French Dance—Cancan in the Crescent City," *The Historic New Orleans Collection Quarterly* (Autumn 1998): 8–9.

28. *Koehl v. Schoenhausen; New York Evening Post,* Jan. 2, 1862, cited in Allen, *Horrible Prettiness,* 75.

29. Ibid. The "beer brothels" appellation comes from the *Daily Picayune,* Oct. 13, 1873. See also the *New Orleans Republican,* Oct. 23, 1873.

30. I am indebted to Emily Landau for directing me to the story of Jennie Reckwig that appeared in the *Daily Picayune,* Feb. 16–22, 1891. Also see the *Daily Picayune,* Dec. 9, 1893.

31. *Daily Picayune,* Oct. 13, 1873. See the *Republican* and the *Daily Picayune,* Oct. 9–Nov. 14, 1873, for details of the trial that led to Schoenhausen's conviction on a charge of larceny. As a result of this conviction, Schoenhausen was incarcerated from 1873 through 1882.

32. *New Orleans Bee,* May 1, 1869; *Daily Picayune,* May 1, 1869.

33. Ibid. The records from the coroner's inquest held the night of the murder were not present in *Coroner's Office, Record of Inquests and Views,* vol. 19, *1868–1870,* Districts 4, 5, and 6, or vol. 20, *1868–1870,* Districts 2 and 3. Also see Taylor, *Louisiana Reconstructed,* 238.

34. Asbury, *French Quarter,* 323.

35. In May 1873, Schoenhausen was the defendant in three cases. In the first, dated May 26, 1873, *State v. Otto Henry Schoenhausen and E. E. Duffy,* Civil District Court, Docket No.

5439, he was charged with robbery and larceny. In the second, also called *State v. Otto Henry Schoenhausen and E. E. Duffy*, Civil District Court, Docket No. 5440, he was charged with keeping a disorderly ale and tippling house. Both of these cases were ultimately disposed of as *nolle pros* in January 1874. The final time Schoenhausen appeared in court records in May was in the matter of *State v. Otto Henry Schoenhausen and E. E. Duffy*, Civil District Court, Docket No. 5441, also dated May 26, 1873. This trial was for forgery and counterfeiting. Schoenhausen was found not guilty in this matter on June 21, 1873. All available records relating to these cases can be found in the Louisiana Division, New Orleans Public Library.

36. *Daily Picayune*, Oct. 9, 1873.

37. Ibid., Oct. 10, 1873; *Republican*, Oct. 11, 1873.

38. Ibid.

39. *Daily Picayune*, Nov. 14, 1873.

40. Ibid., Nov. 6, 1873.

41. *Republican*, Oct. 23, 1873.

42. *Times*, Jun. 18, 1869.

43. *Koehl v. Schoenhausen.*

44. *Times-Picayune*, May 10, 1964.

45. Joseph R. Roach, "Slave Spectacles and Tragic Octoroons," *Theatre Survey* 33 (November 1992): 173. See Johnson, *Soul by Soul*, 162–72, for details about the slave markets in this vicinity.

46. John Chase, *Frenchmen, Desire, Good Children, and Other Streets of New Orleans* 2nd ed. (New Orleans: Robert L. Crager, 1960), 210; *Koehl v. Schoenhausen.*

47. Tulane University, *Vieux Carre Survey of 108 Municipal Squares* (New Orleans: unpublished manuscript, 1961–66), orig. housed at Historic New Orleans Collection, Williams Research Center (WRC), Squares 34, 35, 65, 66. For details of the fire, see the *Daily Picayune*, Feb. 18, 1892.

48. On the Globe and Louisiana ballrooms, see Tansey, "Prostitution and Politics in Antebellum New Orleans," 473. On the Gallatin Street dance halls see Asbury, *French Quarter*, 336–7; Rose, *Storyville*, 9; and Gilfoyle, *City of Eros*, 225.

49. Ordinance 416 of 1870 placed two restrictive clauses on concert saloons, but they were nonfiduciary, and the licensing fee remained the same until December 1878. See list of "City Taxes on Trades, Professions, &c." in *Cohen's New Orleans and Southern Directory for 1856* (New Orleans: Daily Delta Print, 1856), 319. See also *City of New Orleans v. John P. Becker (1879)*, Supreme Court of Louisiana, Docket No. 7486, digested in 31 *Louisiana Annual*: 644; *G. S. Goldsmith v. City of New Orleans (1879)*, Supreme Court of Louisiana, Docket No. 7494, digested in 31 *Louisiana Annual*: 646.

50. See *State v. Michael J. O'Hara (1884)*, Supreme Court of Louisiana, Docket No. 8990, digested in 36 *Louisiana Annual*: 93 and *State v. O. H. Schoenhausen et al. (1885)*, Supreme Court of Louisiana, Docket No. 9286, digested in 37 *Louisiana Annual*: 42.

51. *G. S. Goldsmith v. City of New Orleans (1879)*.

52. Ibid.

53. For details about gambling on Royal Street in this era see Joy Jackson, *New Orleans in the Gilded Age: Politics and Urban Progress, 1880–1896* (Baton Rouge: Louisiana State Univer-

sity Press, 1969), 63–5. Schoenhausen's connection to prize fighting is discussed in the *Daily Picayune,* Mar. 14, 1905, and the *Times-Democrat,* Feb. 29, 1904.

54. *Koehl v. Schoenhausen; Daily Picayune,* Dec. 28, 1893.

55. Taylor, *Louisiana Reconstructed,* 436.

56. *State v. Wenger; Daily Picayune,* Feb. 18, 1892.

57. Ibid., Apr. 7, 1892.

58. *Koehl v. Schoenhausen; State v. Wenger.*

59. *Koehl v. Schoenhausen.*

60. *The Daily States,* May 5, 1891; *Koehl v. Schoenhausen.*

61. *The City of New Orleans: The Book of the Chamber of Commerce and Industry of Louisiana and Other Public Bodies of the "Crescent City"* (New Orleans: George W. Engelbardt, 1894), 41–2.

62. *Koehl v. Schoenhausen.*

63. *City of New Orleans, 1894,* 43; *Koehl v. Schoenhausen.*

64. Ibid.

65. Ibid.

66. *Daily Picayune,* Dec. 10, 1893; *Koehl v. Schoenhausen.*

67. *Koehl v. Schoenhausen.*

68. Ibid.; *State v. Wenger.*

69. *Koehl v. Schoenhausen.*

70. *City of New Orleans, 1894;* Koehl was so pleased with this directory (and presumably his portrayal in it), that his business gave copies of it to Solari's customers and vendors for Christmas that year along with an insert that read, "In appreciation of your patronage and of the very cordial relations existing between us, we take pleasure in presenting you with this Souvenir and Exposition of New Orleans To-Day. Wishing you continued prosperity and the compliments of the season, we are respectfully yours, A. M. & J. Solari, Ltd., Est. 1864."

71. Ibid.

72. Ibid.

73. Ibid.

74. Ibid.

75. *Times-Democrat,* Mar. 14, 1905; *Daily Picayune,* Mar. 14, 1905.

76. *Times-Democrat,* Mar. 14, 1905.

77. *Times-Picayune,* Aug. 13, 2000.

78. *Times-Picayune,* Aug. 16, 1923; Robert J. Cangelosi Jr., and Dorothy G. Schlesinger, eds., *New Orleans Architecture,* vol. 8, *The University Section* (Gretna, La.: Pelican Publishing Co., 1997).

79. *Koehl v. Schoenhausen.*

CHAPTER 3. "WHERE THE LEAST HARM CAN RESULT": SEX, RACE, AND RESPECTABILITY IN A SINGLE NEIGHBORHOOD

1. *Daily Picayune,* Mar. 18, 1896.

2. Recent scholarship that explores the interconnectedness of race and sexuality in other

southern locales includes Catherine Clinton and Michele Gillespie, eds., *The Devil's Lane: Sex and Race in the Early South* (New York: Oxford University Press, 1997); Glenda Gilmore, *Gender and Jim Crow: Women and the Politics of White Supremacy in North Carolina, 1896–1920* (Chapel Hill: University of North Carolina Press, 1996); and Hodes, *White Women, Black Men.* For an account contemporary with events covered in this chapter see "A Colored Woman, However Respectable, Is Lower than the White Prostitute," *The Independent,* Sept. 18, 1902, reprinted in Gerda Lerner, ed., *Black Women in White America: A Documentary History* (New York: Pantheon Books, 1972). For a similar argument about New York and Chicago, see Kevin J. Mumford, *Interzones: Black and White Sex Districts in Chicago and New York in the Early Twentieth Century* (New York: Columbia University Press, 1997).

3. *George L'Hote v. City of New Orleans et al. (1898),* Supreme Court of Louisiana, Docket No. 12753, digested in 51 *Louisiana Annual:* 94. The lower-court case was *George L'Hote v. City of New Orleans et al. (1897),* Docket No. 54533, Civil District Court for the Parish of Orleans, Division B, City Archives, New Orleans Public Library. Although the content of the two court records varies slightly, their substantive content is the same, and the case will be cited hereafter as *L'Hote v. City of New Orleans.* The United States Supreme Court decision is digested in 20 *Supreme Court Reporter:* 788.

4. David Pivar, *Purity Crusade: Sexual Morality and Social Control, 1868–1900* (Westport, Conn.: Greenwood Press, 1973), 52, 62.

5. Connelly, *Response to Prostitution in the Progressive Era,* 3; Joel Best, "Careers in Brothel Prostitution: St. Paul, 1865–1883," *Journal of Interdisciplinary History* 7 (1982): 601; Marion M. Jackson, "The Atlanta Campaign against Commercialized Vice," *Social Hygiene* 3 (1916–1917): 180.

6. Ted Ownby, *Subduing Satan: Religion, Recreation, and Manhood in the Rural South, 1865–1920* (Chapel Hill: University of North Carolina Press, 1990).

7. Eric J. Brock and Jim Montgomery, "Shreveport's Legalized Red-Light District," *Louisiana Cultural Vistas* (Spring 1997): 50–1; Barbara Smith Corrales, "Prurience, Prostitution, and Progressive Improvements: The Crowley Connection" (paper presented at the annual meeting of the Louisiana Historical Association, Hammond, La., March 2001); Thomas Mackey, "Red Lights Out: A Legal History of Prostitution, Disorderly Houses, and Vice Districts, 1870–1917" (Ph.D. diss., Rice University, 1984), 193–5. For the "plague of prostitutes" reference, see the *Mascot,* Jun. 11, 1892, which is reproduced in Rose, *Storyville,* 35. For a listing of other cities with vice districts in this period, see Mumford, *Interzones,* 189.

8. See, for example, Rose, *Storyville.*

9. Prostitution ordinances that followed the Lorette Ordinance include 3428 O.S., Jun. 4, 1857; 6302 O.S., Jul. 10, 1865; 7141 A.S., Jun. 7, 1881; 7325 A.S., Sept. 6, 1881; 2051 C.S., Dec. 20, 1886; 4101 C.S., Nov. 12, 1889; 4434 C.S., Apr. 21, 1890; 13,032 C.S., Jan. 29, 1897; and 13,485 C.S., Jul. 6, 1897.

10. The wording of ordinance 4434 C.S., Apr. 21, 1890, is curious and convoluted. On the one hand, section four stipulates, "it shall not be lawful for any public prostitutes notoriously abandoned to lewdness to live" within the limits specified between Poydras and St. Louis Streets and Claiborne Street and the river. Yet section five declares that it is unlawful for them to live "outside of the limits specified in section four." Despite the confusing wording, it is clear from testimony given by police officials in *L'Hote v. City of New Orleans* that the limits

specified in section four were the acknowledged limits for the toleration of prostitution until the passage of the Story Ordinances.

11. Brian Gary Ettinger, "John Fitzpatrick and the Limits of Working-Class Politics in New Orleans, 1892–1896," *Louisiana History* 26 (Fall 1985): 341.

12. *Daily Picayune,* Nov. 9, 1895.

13. *The Citizens' League: A History of the Great Reform Movement in New Orleans, April 21st, 1896, with Biographical Sketches of Those Who Took Prominent Part in the Movement* (New Orleans: S. W. Taylor, 1897), 1.

14. Ibid., 25.

15. Ibid., 56.

16. *Times-Picayune,* Jul. 17, 1937; Rose, *Storyville,* 38.

17. For information on medical inspection of prostitutes in European countries see Alain Corbin, *Women for Hire: Prostitution and Sexuality in France after 1850* (Cambridge: Harvard University Press, 1990); Jill Harsin, *Policing Prostitution in Nineteenth-Century Paris* (Princeton: Princeton University Press, 1985); Pivar, *Purity Crusade,* 65–8; Judith Walkowitz, "Male Vice and Female Virtue: Feminism and the Politics of Prostitution in Nineteenth-Century Britain" in Ann Snitow, Christine Stansell, and Sharon Thompson, eds., *Powers of Desire: The Politics of Sexuality* (New York: Monthly Review Press, 1983), 419–38; D'Emilio and Freedman, *Intimate Matters,* 148–9.

18. Walkowitz, "Male Vice and Female Virtue," 421; Pivar, *Purity Crusade,* 52–7; D'Emilio and Freedman, *Intimate Matters,* 148–56.

19. Isadore Dyer, "The Municipal Control of Prostitution in the U.S." (Brussels: H. Lamertin, 1900). PAM HQ 121 N5, Williams Research Center, Historic New Orleans Collection. This is a reprint of an article from the *New Orleans Medical and Surgical Journal* of December 1899.

20. On late-nineteenth-century attitudes about venereal disease as the disease of "the other," see Allen Brandt, *No Magic Bullet: A Social History of Venereal Disease in the United States since 1880* (New York: Oxford University Press, 1987), 10–23.The *Mascot* of Jun. 11, 1892, carries the headline "A Plague of Prostitutes," which is reproduced in Rose, *Storyville,* 35.

21. *L'Hote v. City of New Orleans.*

22. Record Book, Committee on Public Order, May 1, 1896–1897, Louisiana Division, New Orleans Public Library; Pivar, *Purity Crusade,* 222–4.

23. Powell Casey, *Encyclopedia of Forts, Posts, Named Camps, and Other Military Installations in Louisiana, 1700–1981* (Baton Rouge: Citations, 1983), 132.

24. 13,032 C.S., Jan. 29, 1897; 13,485 C.S., Jul. 6, 1897.

25. Ibid.

26. *Daily Picayune,* Jan. 1, 1898.

27. *New Orleans Item,* Feb. 11, 1902; *L'Hote v. City of New Orleans.*

28. 13,032 C.S., Jan. 29, 1897.

29. *L'Hote v. City of New Orleans.*

30. Ibid.; Record Book, Committee on Public Order, May 1, 1896–1897, Louisiana Division, New Orleans Public Library.

31. Ibid.

32. Ibid. Peret noted that "most everybody who owned property there [on Canal]" signed

the petition asking the city to retain the limits "excepting D. H. Holmes and Mercier," two of the city's leading department stores in this period.

33. *Times-Picayune,* Mar. 12, 1920; *L'Hote v. City of New Orleans.*

34. *L'Hote v. City of New Orleans.*

35. Ibid.

36. Ibid.

37. Louis Armstrong recounts his own youth in "The Battlefield" in *Satchmo: My Life in New Orleans* (1954; reprint, New York: Da Capo Press, 1986), 7–22. See also Donald M. Marquis, *In Search of Buddy Bolden: First Man of Jazz* (Baton Rouge: Louisiana State University Press, 1978), 49–59.

38. *L'Hote v. City of New Orleans.*

39. *Biographical and Historical Memoirs of Louisiana: Embracing an Authentic and Comprehensive Account of the Chief Events in the History of the State, a Special Sketch of Every Parish, and a Record of the Lives of Many of the Most Worthy and Illustrious Families and Individuals* (Chicago: Goodspeed, 1892), 547; *City of New Orleans 1894,* 145.

40. Ibid.; *Sunday States,* Aug. 31, 1902.

41. Sanborn Fire Insurance Map, City of New Orleans, 1896.

42. *L'Hote v. City of New Orleans.*

43. Ibid.

44. Ibid.

45. Ibid.

46. Ibid.

47. Ibid.

48. Ibid.

49. Ibid.

50. Ibid.

51. Ibid.

52. Ibid. Both letters are dated Dec. 28, 1897.

53. Ibid.

54. For examples of reformers' critiques of Storyville that focus on race and sexuality rather than prostitution per se, see the *New Orleans Item,* Feb. 2, 5, 10, 22, 1910; Kathy D. Williams, "The 'Painted Inmate' and the 'Aggressive Savage': Sexual and Racial Segregation in Louisville, Kentucky" (paper presented at the fifth Southern Conference on Women's History, Richmond, Va., June 2000), 2.

55. Connelly, *Response to Prostitution in the Progressive Era,* 8.

56. On the connections between race and sexuality see, for example, Clinton, "Bloody Terrain," 313–32; Gilmore, *Gender and Jim Crow;* Jacquelyn Dowd Hall, " 'The Mind That Burns in Each Body': Women, Rape, and Racial Violence" in Snitow et al., eds., *Powers of Desire,* 328–49; Evelyn Brooks Higginbotham, "African American Women's History and the Metalanguage of Race," *Signs* 17 (Winter 1992): 251–74; Evelyn Brooks Higginbotham, *Righteous Discontent: The Women's Movement in the Black Baptist Church* (Cambridge: Harvard University Press, 1993); Hodes, *White Women, Black Men;* Deborah Gray White, "The Cost of Club Work, the Price of Black Feminism" in Nancy A. Hewitt and Suzanne Lebsock, eds., *Visible Women: New Essays on American Activism* (Champaign: University of Illinois Press,

1993), 247–69. For contemporary commentary on the same issue, see the *Southwestern Christian Advocate,* Mar. 10, 1898. On the historical frequency of placing prostitution districts in neighborhoods identified with African Americans and other poor minorities, see Richard Symanski, *The Immoral Landscape: Female Prostitution in Western Societies* (Toronto: Butterworth, 1981).

57. See Peirce Lewis, *New Orleans: The Making of an Urban Landscape* (Cambridge, Mass.: Ballinger, 1976), 61–2.

58. Ibid., 44–7; see also Germaine Reed, "Race Legislation in Louisiana, 1864–1920," *Louisiana History* 6 (Fall 1965): 379–92.

59. *L'Hote v. City of New Orleans.*

60. Ibid.; Sanborn Fire Insurance Map, City of New Orleans, 1896.

61. *Southwestern Christian Advocate,* Mar. 10, 1898.

62. *L'Hote v. City of New Orleans.*

63. Ibid.; *Southwestern Christian Advocate,* Sept. 30, 1897.

64. *L'Hote v. City of New Orleans.* Records from another Louisiana Supreme Court case reveal just how tenuous the Union Chapel's hold on its property had been since its founding in the early 1880s. See *L'Hote and Company v. Church Extension Society of the Methodist Episcopal Church,* Civil District Court, Division C, Docket No. 58734, Feb. 9, 1904. For trial transcript and decision embedded in records from the lower-court hearing, see *L'Hote v. City of New Orleans,* Louisiana Division, New Orleans Public Library. This case was appealed to the Louisiana Supreme Court and was heard under Docket No. 15,549, digested in 115 *Louisiana Reports:* 487, hereafter cited as *L'Hote v. CES MEC.*

65. *L'Hote v. City of New Orleans.*

66. Ibid.

67. Excerpt from brief filed by the City of New Orleans with the United States Supreme Court in the matter of *L'Hote v. City of New Orleans,* reprinted in Rose, *Storyville,* 188.

68. Rev. A. E. P. Albert, D.D., "Methodism in the Life of New Orleans," *Journal of the Louisiana Annual Conference of the Methodist Episcopal Church, 41st Session* (Baton Rouge, Jan. 13–17, 1909): 81–4, Special Collections, Howard-Tilton Library, Tulane University.

69. Ralph Morrow, *Northern Methodism and Reconstruction* (Ann Arbor: Michigan State University Press, 1956), 50. See also Anne Loveland, "The 'Southern Work' of the Reverend Joseph C. Hartzell, Pastor of Ames Church in New Orleans, 1870–1873," *Louisiana History* 16 (Fall 1975): 391–407; Clarence Walker, *A Rock in a Weary Land: The African Methodist Episcopal Church during the Civil War and Reconstruction* (Baton Rouge: Louisiana State University Press, 1982).

70. L. Dale Patterson, archivist, United Methodist Church Archives, Madison, N.J., E-mail to author, August 10, 1999.

71. *Journal of the Louisiana Annual Conference of the Methodist Episcopal Church, 31st Session* (Alexandria, Jan. 25–30, 1899). According to this source, the Union Chapel owed $1,902 on its property, the "probable value" of which was $10,000. This figure is less than the amount calculated by the CES in 1896. Testimony and correspondence embedded in *L'Hote v. CES MEC* reveal that the CES had tried repeatedly to make a financial settlement and transfer of the property to the members of the Union Chapel, but on each occasion the congregation had been unable or unwilling to come up with the settlement sum the CES required. Those

sums ranged from two to three thousand dollars, significantly less than the purchase price and other loan monies the CES had paid for the building and to the congregation. In correspondence to the CES dated Mar. 17, 1896, local MEC leader L. G. Adkinson wrote, "I never saw anything so wonderfully tangled up as that business [at the Union Chapel] is. The congregation is thoroughly disaffected and through the fault of pastors or leaders, in some way, they have been misled until they are afraid to undertake anything. The pastor would be glad to be relieved of the charge. And yet, a large congregation gather Sabbath after Sabbath to hear him preach."

72. *Southwestern Christian Advocate,* Sept. 30, 1897; *L'Hote v. City of New Orleans.*

73. *L'Hote v. City of New Orleans.*

74. Ibid.

75. *Daily Picayune,* Feb. 8, 1898.

76. Ibid.

77. Ibid.

78. Ryan, *Civic Wars,* 220; Mumford, *Interzones.*

79. *L'Hote v. City of New Orleans.*

80. Ibid.

81. Ibid.; *Daily Picayune,* Jun. 19, 1900.

82. *Daily Picayune,* Jun. 19, 28, 1900.

83. Ibid.

84. Ibid.

85. Correspondence of Mayor Paul Capdeville, New Orleans City Archives, Louisiana Division, New Orleans Public Library.

86. Ibid.

87. Ibid.

88. Walter N. Vernon, *Becoming One People: A History of Louisiana Methodism* (Louisiana: United Methodist Church, 1987), 173–4.

89. *Journal of the 9th Session of the North New Orleans District Conference* (Aug. 7–11, 1895); *Journal of the Louisiana Annual Conference of the Methodist Episcopal Church,* 31st Session, Alexandria (Jan. 25–30, 1899); *Journal of the Louisiana Annual Conference of the Methodist Episcopal Church,* 41st Session, Baton Rouge (Jan. 13–17, 1909), all from Special Collections, Howard-Tilton Library, Tulane University; *L'Hote v. CES MEC.*

90. Orleans Parish Conveyance Records.

91. *Sunday States,* Aug. 31, 1902.

92. *Times-Democrat,* May 26, 28, 1899; Orleans Parish Conveyance Records.

93. Orleans Parish Conveyance Records; *Mascot,* Feb. 2, 1884. Ownership of brothel properties by prosperous, upstanding citizens had also been common in the antebellum era. John McDonogh is the best-known example. See Tansey, "Prostitution and Politics in Antebellum New Orleans," 452.

94. *Succession of B. G. Carbajal,* Civil District Court, Parish of Orleans, Division C, Docket No. 130909.

95. *Times-Picayune,* Mar. 12, 13, 1920; *New Orleans States,* Mar. 11, 1920; John Smith Kendall, *History of New Orleans* (New York: Lewis, 1922), 997–9.

CHAPTER 4. "UNUSUAL SITUATIONS AND REMARKABLE PEOPLE":
MARY DEUBLER, RESPECTABILITY, AND THE HISTORY OF STORYVILLE

1. Rose, *Storyville*, 30.

2. See *Succession of Mary A. Deubler*, Docket No. 107603, Civil District Court for the Parish of Orleans, Division C, City Archives, New Orleans Public Library. This case was considered by the Louisiana Supreme Court on two separate occasions; see Docket Nos. 21667 (1915) and 22898 (1917). Although the contents of the lower-court cases and the state supreme court records vary slightly, their substantive content is the same, and the cases will be cited hereafter as *Succession of Deubler*.

3. *Succession of Deubler; Stringer v. Mathis*.

4. *Succession of Deubler*.

5. *Soards' New Orleans City Directory for 1885* (New Orleans: L. Soards & Co., 1885).

6. *Succession of Deubler*.

7. Ibid.

8. On the respectability of working-class women in another context, see Janet F. Davidson, "The Goosing of Violet Nye and Other Tales: White Women and Sexual Respectability on the Pennsylvania Railroad," *Labor History* 41 (November 2000): 437–52.

9. Asbury, *French Quarter*, 449; Rose, *Storyville*, 48.

10. Ibid.; see also the *Daily Picayune*, Jan. 29, 30, 1892.

11. *Mascot*, Dec. 13, 1890.

12. *Succession of Deubler*; Asbury, *French Quarter*, 449.

13. Ray Hanley and Steven G. Hanley, *Images of America: Hot Springs, Arkansas* (Charleston, S.C.: Arcadia, 2000), 20. See also Ray Hanley and Steven G. Hanley, *Hot Springs, Arkansas, in Vintage Postcards* (Charleston, S.C.: Arcadia, 1998).

14. Asbury, *French Quarter*, 450.

15. See, for example, Rose, *Storyville*, 43.

16. On the connections between Storyville and tourism in New Orleans see Long, "'A Notorious Attraction.'"

17. John R. Kemp, ed., *Martin Behrman of New Orleans: Memoirs of a City Boss* (Baton Rouge: Louisiana State University Press, 1977); George Reynolds, *Machine Politics in New Orleans, 1897–1926* (New York: AMS Press, 1936).

18. *L'Hote v. City of New Orleans*; Dyer, "The Municipal Control of Prostitution," 2–3.

19. *Item-Tribune*, Aug. 2, 1931; Rose, *Storyville*, 75.

20. This carriage stone and a variety of other artifacts from Storyville can be seen in the permanent exhibit on New Orleans jazz at the Old U.S. Mint, a property of the Louisiana State Museum in New Orleans.

21. Ord. 1615 N.C.S., Feb. 10, 1903.

22. "Accepted Design, Frisco Depot, Submitted by a Chicago Architect," *Architectural Art and Its Allies*, August 1905.

23. *Times-Democrat*, Jun. 1, 1908.

24. *Blue Book*. Acc. No. 2002.83.3, Louisiana State Museum.

25. Ibid.

26. See, for example, Kristin Hoganson, "Cosmopolitan Domesticity: Importing the American Dream, 1865–1920," *American Historical Review* 107 (February 2002): 55–83.

27. Ibid. See also Jonathan Yardley, *Mrs. Astor's New York: Money and Social Power in a Gilded Age* (New Haven: Yale University Press, 2002); and Jerry E. Patterson, *The First Four Hundred: Mrs. Astor's New York in the Gilded Age* (New York: Rizzoli, 2000).

28. *Blue Book,* Acc. No. 1969.19.6, Williams Research Center, Historic New Orleans Collection. See also Pamela Arceneaux, "Guidebooks to Sin: The Blue Books of Storyville," *Louisiana History* 28 (Fall 1987): 397–405; Rose, *Storyville,* 135–46.

29. Arceneaux, "Guidebooks to Sin," 399; Roach, "Slave Spectacles and Tragic Octoroons," 183.

30. Karen Leathem, "'A Carnival According to Their Own Desires': Gender and Mardi Gras in New Orleans, 1870–1941" (Ph.D. diss., University of North Carolina, 1994), 185–91.

31. Ibid.

32. Ibid.

33. For additional descriptions, drawings, and photographs of the district see the *Blue Books,* Williams Research Center, Historic New Orleans Collection. See also Katy Coyle, "The Intersection of Law and Desire: Sex, Storyville, and Prostitution in Turn-of-the-Century New Orleans" (Ph.D. diss., Tulane University, in progress); Emily Landau, "'Spectacular Wickedness': New Orleans, Prostitution, and the Politics of Sex, 1897–1917" (Ph.D. diss., Yale University, in progress).

34. *L'Hote v. City of New Orleans;* Sanborn Fire Insurance Map, New Orleans, 1896.

35. Handy is cited in Edward Ayers, *The Promise of the New South: Life after Reconstruction* (New York: Oxford University Press, 1992), 388.

36. Reprinted in Rose, *Storyville,* 208.

37. Ibid.; *The Red Book,* Acc. No. 1969.19.5, Williams Research Center, Historic New Orleans Collection; *Wentworth's Souvenir Sporting Guide* (New York, 1885), cited in Williams, "The 'Painted Inmate' and the 'Aggressive Savage'"; Ayers, *Promise of the New South,* 388.

38. For elaboration on the idea of Storyville as an amusement park see Landau, "Spectacular Wickedness." See also *L'Hote v. City of New Orleans* and Dyer, "The Municipal Control of Prostitution," 2, 3, 26.

39. Julian Ralph, "New Orleans, Our Southern Capitol," *Harper's New Monthly Magazine* (February 1899): 365–85.

40. Ownby, *Subduing Satan,* 39, 167. I am indebted to Dr. Ownby for his suggestion that New Orleans was a regional safety valve.

41. Ibid. Also see Mitchell, *All on a Mardi Gras Day,* 2; *Hazelhurst Weekly Copiahan,* Mar. 15, 1884, cited in William Ivy Hair, *Carnival of Fury: Robert Charles and the New Orleans Race Riot of 1900* (Baton Rouge: Louisiana State University Press, 1976), 70, 86. Reverend Hamilton's revival services are described in an undated newspaper article found in the 1909 scrapbook from the Louisiana Society for the Prevention of Cruelty to Children, Records of the Children's Bureau, Acc. No. 2002-1-L, Williams Research Center, Historic New Orleans Collection.

42. *Succession of Deubler.*

43. Ibid.

44. Ibid.

45. Ibid.

46. Ibid.

47. Ibid.

48. Ibid.

49. Ibid.

50. Ibid.

51. Ibid.

52. Ibid.

53. Ibid.

54. Ibid. See also Foster, *Moral Reconstruction.*

55. New Orleans Travelers' Aid Society Papers, 365, Manuscripts Department, Howard-Tilton Library, Tulane University, hereafter cited as Travelers' Aid Society MSS.

56. *Daily-Picayune,* Jan. 18, 1908; Leathem, "A Carnival According to Their Own Desires," 214.

57. Will Irwin, "The American Saloon," excerpted in Rose, *Storyville,* 46.

58. See Foster, *Moral Reconstruction,* 163–220.

59. Ibid. See also Mackey, "Red Lights Out," 2, 15; John Burnham, *Bad Habits: Drinking, Smoking, Taking Drugs, Gambling, Sexual Misbehavior, and Swearing in American History* (New York: New York University Press, 1993).

60. Reynolds, *Machine Politics in New Orleans,* 161.

61. Act. No. 176, *Acts Passed by the General Assembly of the State of Louisiana at the Regular Session* (Baton Rouge, 1908), 238–9. See also Leathem, "A Carnival According to Their Own Desires," 226.

62. *Daily-Picayune,* Jan. 7, 1909, cited in Leathem, "A Carnival According to Their Own Desires," 226.

63. Ibid.

64. *Succession of Deubler.*

65. Ibid.

66. Ibid.

67. Ibid.

68. Ibid.

69. *Item,* Feb. 17, 1914.

70. *Succession of Deubler.*

71. Ibid.

72. Ibid.

73. Ibid.

74. Ibid.

75. Ibid.

76. Ibid.

77. Ibid.

78. Ibid.

79. Ibid.

80. Ibid.

81. *Item,* Feb. 14, 1914; "Segregation versus Morality," Pam HQ 121 N5, Williams Research Center, Historic New Orleans Collection.

CHAPTER 5. "AS RARE AS WHITE BLACKBIRDS": WILLIE PIAZZA,
RACE, AND REFORM IN STORYVILLE

1. For numerous stories and editorials about the "clean up" campaign see the *Times-Picayune* and the *Daily States*, January and February 1917.

2. Ord. 4118 C.C.S., Feb. 7, 1917; *Times-Picayune,* Jan. 24, 1917.

3. *City of New Orleans v. Willie Piazza (1917)*, Supreme Court of Louisiana, Docket No. 22624, digested in 142 *Louisiana Reports:* 167. The lower-court case of the same name was heard in the Recorder's Court of New Orleans with Louis J. Burthe Jr. presiding. Although the content of the two court records varies slightly, their substantive content is the same, and the case will be cited hereafter as *City of New Orleans v. Piazza.*

4. Ord. 4118 C.C.S., Feb. 7, 1917; *City of New Orleans v. Piazza.*

5. Rose, *Storyville,* 39, 193. Many other writers have accepted this claim and uncritically incorporated it into subsequent works. See for example Laurence Bergreen, *Louis Armstrong: An Extravagant Life* (New York: Broadway Books, 1997), 45. For Capdeville's remarks see the *Daily Picayune,* Jun. 19, 28, 1900.

6. Marquis, *In Search of Buddy Bolden,* 50. For a description of Storyville as only the area below Canal Street, see *Blue Book: Tenderloin 400,* Acc. No. 94–092-RL, Williams Research Center, Historic New Orleans Collection.

7. Armstrong, *Satchmo,* 8, 94.

8. Alan Lomax, *Mister Jelly Roll: The Fortunes of Jelly Roll Morton, New Orleans Creole and "Inventor of Jazz"* (New York: Duell, Sloan and Pearce, 1950), 103.

9. Ibid., 127.

10. Ronnie W. Clayton, ed., *Mother Wit: The Ex-Slave Narratives of the Louisiana Writers' Project* (New York: Peter Lang, 1990), 172–5.

11. Ibid.

12. For two explorations of the complex motivations and meanings of sex across the color line in this period, see Landau, "Spectacular Wickedness," and Lott, *Love and Theft.*

13. Hair, *Carnival of Fury,* 70.

14. Higginbotham, *Righteous Discontent,* 189–94.

15. Hair, *Carnival of Fury,* 94; Bureau of the Census, *1880 and 1900 Manuscript Census, Mississippi.*

16. Bureau of the Census, *1880 and 1900 Manuscript Census, Mississippi.*

17. Hair, *Carnival of Fury,* 44; *Soards' New Orleans City Directory for 1898* (New Orleans: L. Soards & Co., 1898).

18. Ibid., 3–5.

19. Ibid., 115–20.

20. Ibid., 121–36.

21. Ibid., 137, 145.

22. Ibid., 152. See also the *Daily Picayune,* Jul. 26, 1900; *Times-Democrat,* Jul. 26, 1900; *Daily Item,* Jul. 26, 1900.

23. Hair, *Carnival of Fury,* 171; *Daily Picayune,* Jul. 26, 1900; *Times-Democrat,* Jul. 26, 1900.

24. Hair, *Carnival of Fury,* 174.

25. On sex across the color line in other cities' vice districts see Mumford, *Interzones;*

Corrales, "Prurience, Prostitution, and Progressive Improvements"; and Gilfoyle, *City of Eros,* 209, 215. For the larger context and social-control aspects of sex across the color line in the postbellum South, see D'Emilio and Freedman, *Intimate Matters,* 104–8.

26. Williams, "The 'Painted Inmate' and the 'Aggressive Savage,'" 2.

27. Warner, "New Orleans," 186–205.

28. Gilmore, *Gender and Jim Crow,* xxi. For earlier works that make similar arguments see Elsa Barkley Brown, "Negotiating and Transforming the Public Sphere: African American Political Life in the Transition from Slavery to Freedom," *Public Culture* 7 (1994): 107–46; Higginbotham, *Righteous Discontent,* especially 185–220; Darlene Clark Hine, "Rape and the Inner Lives of Black Women in the Middle West: Preliminary Thoughts on the Culture of Dissemblance," *Signs* 14 (Summer 1989): 912–20; and Dorothy Salem, *To Better Our World: Black Women in Organized Reform, 1890–1920* (New York: Carlson, 1990).

29. See the *Blue Books,* Williams Research Center, Historic New Orleans Collection.

30. On nineteenth-century sexual ideologies, see Nancy F. Cott, "Passionlessness: An Interpretation of Victorian Sexual Ideology, 1790–1850" in Nancy F. Cott and Elizabeth H. Pleck, eds., *A Heritage of Her Own: Toward a New Social History of American Women* (New York: Simon & Schuster, 1979), 162–81.

31. Rose, *Storyville,* 52–3. According to this source, the titles in Piazza's library included Burton's *The Anatomy of Melancholy* and "several works by Alphonse Daudet, who was said to be her favorite author."

32. *Blue Books,* THNOC 1969.19.3 and 1969.19.8, Williams Research Center, Historic New Orleans Collection.

33. *Blue Book,* THNOC 1969.19.6, Williams Research Center, Historic New Orleans Collection.

34. "New Mahogany Hall," *Blue Book,* THNOC 56–15, Williams Research Center, Historic New Orleans Collection.

35. Ibid. For a general description of Lulu White see Rose, *Storyville,* 40–2.

36. For a thorough examination of these laws, see Virginia Dominguez, *White by Definition: Social Classification in Creole Louisiana* (New Brunswick, N.J.: Rutgers University Press, 1986).

37. Ibid.; *State v. Treadway* (1910), Supreme Court of Louisiana, Docket No. 18149.

38. *Item,* Feb. 2, 15, 1910.

39. Ibid.

40. Ibid.

41. Ibid.; see also Mar. 22, 1910.

42. *Blue Book,* THNOC 1969.19.4, Williams Research Center, Historic New Orleans Collection.

43. See the *Blue Books,* Williams Research Center, Historic New Orleans Collection.

44. *City of New Orleans v. Piazza.*

45. Rose, *Storyville,* 64. See also the *Item,* Feb. 2, 10, 15, 1910.

46. *Daily States,* Jan. 16, 1917.

47. *Times-Picayune,* Jan. 15, 1917. For a history of New York cabarets with many parallels to New Orleans's Tango Belt, see Lewis Erenberg, *Steppin' Out: New York Nightlife and the Transformation of American Culture, 1890–1930* (Westport, Conn.: Greenwood Press, 1981).

48. See, for example, the *Times-Picayune,* Jan. 21, 23, 25, 26, and Feb. 1, 2, 3, 8, 1917.

49. Ibid., Jan. 24, 1917.

50. Ibid.; see also Jan. 29, 1917; and Ord. No. 4118 C.C.S., Feb. 7, 1917. See *City of New Orleans v. Piazza* for a similar summary of events leading up to the adoption of the racial-segregation ordinance.

51. *City of New Orleans v. Piazza.*

52. Ibid.; *Times-Picayune,* Mar. 2, 1917.

53. In addition to White and Piazza, other women of color who filed suit against the city in response to Ordinance 4118 C.C.S. include Goldie Stevens, Celeste Reed, Elizabeth Anderson, Carrie Gross, Jane Churchill, Mattie Mosely, Evelyn Marlen, Hattie Bob, Josephine Evans, Sarah Porter, Myrtle Tobias, Sarah Smith, Mary McDonald, Bertha Willard, Ella Williams, Augusta Grandpre, Agnes Morris, Louisa Lee, Patsy Lee, Juanita Mandez, Jennie Brown, Acey Langs, Mattie Frisbane, Lottie Stanton, and Josephine Evans. A man of color identified only as A. Churchill also filed suit, as did two white property owners, Gertrude Hammel, and Louis Quillon. Details of their cases can be found in the indices and records of New Orleans Civil District Court, City Archives, New Orleans Public Library.

54. *City of New Orleans v. Piazza.*

55. Ibid.

56. Ibid. See also *City of New Orleans v. Miller et al. (1917),* Supreme Court of Louisiana, Docket No. 22625.

57. *City of New Orleans v. Piazza.*

58. Ibid.

59. Ibid.

60. *Bessie Christmas v. City of New Orleans,* Civil District Court Parish of Orleans, Division A, Docket 5, No. 121424, filed Sept. 5, 1917, City Archives, New Orleans Public Library.

61. *Lulu White v. City of New Orleans et al.,* Civil District Court Parish of Orleans, Division E, Docket 5, No. 119511, City Archives, New Orleans Public Library.

62. *City of New Orleans v. Piazza.*

63. See Rose, *Storyville,* 84, and Kay Thompson, "First Lady of Storyville: The Fabulous Countess Willie Piazza," *Record Changer* 10 (February 1951): 5, 14. Also see Piazza's death certificate, Division of Archives, Records Management, and History, Secretary of State's Office, Baton Rouge, Louisiana.

64. *Succession of Willie V. Piazza* (1932), Orleans Parish Civil District Court, Division B, Docket No. 199-705; Orleans Parish Conveyance Records.

EPILOGUE

1. New Orleans Chamber of Commerce Records, RG 66, Special Collections, the Earl K. Long Library, University of New Orleans.

2. Travelers' Aid Society MSS.

3. Records of the War Department General and Special Staffs, War College Division and War Plans Division, Subordinate Offices—Education and Recreation Branch, Commission on Training Camp Activities, Entry 395, Reports Relating to Training Camp Activities, 1917 (National Archives), Record Group 165, Box 8, "Kentucky to Louisiana."

4. Ibid. Being fit to fight meant, of course, being free from venereal disease or contamination. See Brandt, *No Magic Bullet,* 52–95.

5. Joseph Mayer, "The Passing of the Red Light District—Vice Investigations and Results," *Social Hygiene* (1918): 207. For an examination of how similar events unfolded in Chicago, see Joanne J. Meyerowitz, *Women Adrift: Independent Wage Earners in Chicago, 1880–1930* (Chicago: University of Chicago Press, 1988), 120–5.

6. Connelly, *Response to Prostitution in the Progressive Era,* 139.

7. Behrman, *Martin Behrman,* 312.

8. *Times-Picayune,* Feb. 22, 1917.

9. Warner, "New Orleans," 201.

10. *Times-Picayune,* Feb. 22, 1917; Jan. 2, 1920.

11. *Times-Picayune,* Jan. 18, 1920; Jan. 27, 1921.

12. Ibid. See also Sanford Jarrell, *New Orleans—The Civilized and Lively City* (n.p., n.d.), Tourism Miscellany, Rare Vertical File, Louisiana Division, New Orleans Public Library; Christine Wiltz, *The Last Madam: A Life in the New Orleans Underworld* (New York: Faber and Faber, 2000).

13. Edward Anderson, "Uncovering the Vice Cesspool of New Orleans," *Real Detective* (March 1935): 40–3, 66, 68; Marquis W. Childs, "New Orleans Is a Wicked City," *Vanity Fair* (November 1934), 62, 72.

14. "Mardi Gras 2000," *Playboy* (March 2000), 78–85. For reactions to the story, see the *Times-Picayune,* Feb. 24, 27, 29, and Mar. 3, 2000.

15. Ibid.; "Warning: Mardi Gras Visitors/Residents" (broadside printed and distributed by New Orleans Police Department), February 2000.

16. *Times-Picayune,* Dec. 31, 1999.

17. Ibid.; Asbury, *French Quarter,* 455.

Bibliography

COURT CASES

United States Supreme Court
L'Hote v. City of New Orleans, 177 U.S. 587 (1900)

Louisiana Supreme Court (in chronological order)
Viens v. Brickle, 8 Martin's Reports 11 (1820)
Municipality Number One v. Wilson, 5 Louisiana Annual 747 (1850)
Succession of Pereuilhet, 23 Louisiana Annual 294 (1871)
City of New Orleans v. Becker, 31 Louisiana Annual 644 (1879)
Goldsmith v. City of New Orleans, 31 Louisiana Annual 646 (1879)
State v. O'Hara, 36 Louisiana Annual 93 (1884)
State v. Schoenhausen et al., 37 Louisiana Annual 42 (1885)
Stringer v. Mathis, 41 Louisiana Annual 985 (1889)
State v. Wenger, 42 Louisiana Annual 556 (1890)
Koehl et al. v. Schoenhausen, 47 Louisiana Annual 1316 (1895)
L'Hote v. City of New Orleans, 51 Louisiana Annual 93 (1898)
L'Hote and Company v. Church Extension Society of the Methodist Episcopal Church,
    115 Louisiana Reports 487 (1905)
Succession of Jahraus, 114 Louisiana Reports 456 (1905)
State v. Treadway, 126 Louisiana Reports 300 (1910)
Succession of Deubler, 139 Louisiana Reports 551 (1916)
City of New Orleans v. Miller et al., 142 Louisiana Reports 163 (1917)
City of New Orleans v. Piazza, 142 Louisiana Reports 167 (1917)
Succession of Deubler, 144 Louisiana Reports 322 (1918)

New Orleans First District Court
State v. Schoenhausen and Duffy, Docket Nos. 5439–5441 (1873)

New Orleans Civil District Court (in chronological order)
Succession of Mathis, Division B, Docket No. 20866 (1887)
Stringer v. Mathis, Division E, Docket No. 217888 (1888)

Koehl et al. v. Schoenhausen, Division B, Docket No. 40999 (1893)

L'Hote v. City of New Orleans et al., Division B, Docket No. 54533 (1897)

L'Hote and Company v. Church Extension Society of the Methodist Episcopal Church, Division C, Docket No. 58734 (1904)

Succession of Deubler, Division C, Docket No. 107603 (1914)

White v. City of New Orleans, Division E, Docket 5, No. 119511 (1917)

Christmas v. City of New Orleans, Division A, Docket 5, No. 121424 (1917)

Succession of Carbajal, Division C, Docket No. 130909 (1920)

Succession of Piazza, Division B, Docket No. 199-705 (1932)

GOVERNMENT DOCUMENTS AND OFFICIAL RECORDS

Archives of the City of New Orleans, New Orleans Public Library
City Council ordinances related to prostitution include:
Ordinance 3267 O.S., Mar. 10, 1857.
Ordinance 3428 O.S., Jun. 4, 1857.
Ordinance 6302 O.S., Jul. 10, 1865.
Ordinance 7141 A.S., Jun. 7, 1881.
Ordinance 7325 A.S., Sept. 6, 1881.
Ordinance 2051 C.S., Dec. 20, 1886.
Ordinance 4101 C.S., Nov. 12, 1889.
Ordinance 4434 C.S., Apr. 21, 1890.
Ordinance 13,032 C.S., Jan. 29, 1897.
Ordinance 13,485 C.S., Jul. 6, 1897.
Ordinance 1615 N.C.S., Feb. 10, 1903.
Ordinance 4118 C.C.S., Feb. 7, 1917.
Coroner's Office, Record of Inquests and Views. 19 (1868–1870), 20 (1868–1870).
Correspondence of Mayor Paul Capdeville.
Record Book, Committee on Public Order, May 1, 1896–1897.
Tax Assessments, City of New Orleans, 1903–1904.

Federal Records
U.S. Bureau of the Census, Records for Alabama, 1900.
U.S. Bureau of the Census, Records for Louisiana, 1870, 1880, 1900.
U.S. Bureau of the Census, Records for Mississippi, 1860, 1870, 1880.

Louisiana State Archives, Baton Rouge
Death certificate for Mary Deubler (issued Feb. 15, 1914).
Death certificate for Willie V. Piazza (issued Nov. 3, 1932).

Orleans Parish Conveyance Office and Notarial Archives
All notices of the sale or transfer of personal and real property, including from wills
and successions, are indexed in the Orleans Parish Conveyance office in the Civil
Court Building, 421 Loyola Avenue, New Orleans. Complete copies of those nota-
rized acts can be found in the Orleans Parish Notarial Archives, also at 421 Loyola
Avenue, or at the Archives Research Center, 1340 Poydras Street, Suite 360.

United States Official Papers, National Archives
Records of the War Department General and Special Staffs, War College Division and
War Plans Division, Subordinate Offices—Education and Recreation Branch, Com-
mission on Training Camp Activities, Entry 395, Reports Relating to Training Camp
Activities, 1917. RG 165, Box 8, "Kentucky to Louisiana."

MANUSCRIPT SOURCES

Louisiana and Special Collections, Earl K. Long Library, University of New Orleans
New Orleans Chamber of Commerce Records, MSS 66.
Josie Arlington Collection, MSS 270.

Louisiana and Special Collections, Howard-Tilton Library, Tulane University
Master Rolls, Battalion Washington Artillery: 1861–1865.
New Orleans Travelers' Aid Society Papers, RG 365.
Al Rose Collection, RG 606.

Louisiana Division and Special Collections, New Orleans Public Library
Jarrell, Sanford. *New Orleans—The Civilized and Lively City.* N.p., n.d., Rare Vertical
    File, Tourism Miscellany.

Williams Research Center, Historic New Orleans Collection
Blue Books. The Williams Research Center's collection, probably the largest extant, is
    available on microfilm for research. See Acc. Nos. 56-15; 1969.19.1–1969.19.12; 77-
    370-RL; 77-2346-RL; 85-517-RL; 86-165-RL; and 94-092-RL.
*Committee of 15 for the Suppression of Commercial Vice in Louisiana: An Appeal to the
    People of Louisiana.* New Orleans: Hauser Printing Co., 1913.
Committee on Social Hygiene. "Segregation versus Morality." New Orleans City Fed-
    eration of Clubs, ca. 1909. PAM HQ 121 N5.
Dyer, Isadore. "The Municipal Control of Prostitution in the United States." Brus-
    sels: H. Lamertin, 1900. PAM HQ 121 N5. Reprint of an article from the *New Or-
    leans Medical and Surgical Journal* (December 1899).
Records of the Children's Bureau, 1892–1999. Acc. No. 2002-1-L.

Tulane University. *Vieux Carre Survey of 108 Municipal Squares.* New Orleans: unpublished, 1961–1966.

CONTEMPORARY PERIODICALS AND PUBLISHED PRIMARY SOURCES

"Accepted Design, Frisco Depot, Submitted by a Chicago Architect." *Architecture and Allied Arts* (August 1905): 4, 5, 11.

Acts Passed by the General Assembly of the State of Louisiana at the Regular Session. Baton Rouge: 1908.

Albert, Rev. A. E. P. "Methodism in the Life of New Orleans." *Journal of the Louisiana Annual Conference of the Methodist Episcopal Church,* 41st Session, Baton Rouge (Jan. 13–17, 1909): 81–184.

Anderson, Edward. "Uncovering the Vice Cesspool of New Orleans." *Real Detective* (March 1935): 40–68.

Bernhard, Karl, Duke of Saxe-Weimar Eisenach. *Travels through North America, during the Years 1825 and 1826.* Vol. 2. Philadelphia: Carey, Lea & Carey, 1828.

Biographical and Historical Memoirs of Louisiana: Embracing an Authentic and Comprehensive Account of the Chief Events in the History of the State, a Special Sketch of Every Parish, and a Record of the Lives of Many of the Most Worthy and Illustrious Families and Individuals. Chicago: Goodspeed, 1892.

Childs, Marquis W. "New Orleans Is a Wicked City." *Vanity Fair* (November 1934): 62–72.

The Citizens' League: A History of the Great Reform Movement in New Orleans, April 21st, 1896, with Biographical Sketches of Those Who Took Prominent Part in the Movement. New Orleans: S. W. Taylor, 1897.

The City of New Orleans: The Book of the Chamber of Commerce and Industry of Louisiana and Other Public Bodies of the "Crescent City." New Orleans: George W. Engelbardt, 1894.

"City Taxes on Trades, Professions, &c." *Cohen's New Orleans and Southern Directory for 1856.* New Orleans: Daily Delta Print, 1856.

Clayton, Ronnie W., ed. *Mother Wit: The Ex-Slave Narratives of the Louisiana Writers' Project.* New York: Pete Lang, 1990.

"A Colored Woman, However Respectable, Is Lower than the White Prostitute." *The Independent* (Sept. 18, 1902). Reprinted in *Black Women in White America: A Documentary History.* New York: Pantheon Books, 1972.

Compiled Edition of the Civil Codes of Louisiana: Louisiana Legal Archives. Baton Rouge: Louisiana State Law Institute, 1940.

Davidson, James. "A Journey through the South in 1836: Diary of James D. Davidson," ed. Herbert A. Kellar, *Journal of Southern History* 1 (August 1935): 357–62.

Jackson, Marion M. "The Atlanta Campaign against Commercialized Vice." *Social Hygiene* 3 (1916–1917): 177–84.

Journal of the Louisiana Annual Conference of the Methodist Episcopal Church, 31st Session, Alexandria, Louisiana (Jan. 25–30, 1899).

Journal of the 9th Session of the North New Orleans District Conference of the Methodist Episcopal Church (Aug. 7–11, 1895).

Kemp, John R., ed. *Martin Behrman of New Orleans: Memoirs of a City Boss.* Baton Rouge: Louisiana State University Press, 1977.

Latrobe, Benjamin. "Congo Square" (1819). In *Louisiana Sojourns: Travelers' Tales and Literary Journeys,* Frank De Caro, ed. Baton Rouge: Louisiana State University Press, 1998: 78–9.

"Mardi Gras 2000." *Playboy* (Mar. 2000): 78–85.

Martineau, Harriet. *Society in America,* Seymour Martin Lipset, ed. 1828. Reprint, New Brunswick, New Jersey: Transaction Books, 1981.

Mayer, Joseph. "The Passing of the Red-Light District—Vice Investigations and Results." *Social Hygiene* (1918): 197–209.

New Orleans Police Department. "Warning: Mardi Gras Visitors/Residents," broadside. (February 2000).

Olmsted, Frederick Law. *The Cotton Kingdom: A Traveller's Observations on Cotton and Slavery in the American Slave States,* Arthur M. Schlesinger Sr., ed. 1861. Reprint, New York: Modern Library, 1984.

Ralph, Julian. "New Orleans, Our Southern Capitol." *Harper's New Monthly Magazine* (February 1899): 365–85.

"A Resident." *New Orleans As It Is.* Utica, N. Y.: DeWitt C. Grove, Printer, 1849.

"Resume of Legislation upon Matters Relating to Social Hygiene Considered by the Various States during 1914." *Social Hygiene* (Dec. 1914): 93–107.

Tasistro, Louis F. *Random Shots and Southern Breezes Containing Critical Remarks on the Southern States and Southern Institutions, with Semi-Serious Observation on Men and Manners.* Vol. 2. New York: Harper & Brothers, 1842.

Trollope, Frances. *Domestic Manners of the Americans.* 1832. Reprint, New York: Dodd, Mead, 1894.

Warner, Charles Dudley. "New Orleans." *Harper's New Monthly Magazine* (January 1887): 186–205.

Watson, John Fanning. "Notitia of Incidents at New Orleans in 1804 and 1805." *American Pioneer* (May 1843): 233–6.

NEWSPAPERS

New Orleans Bee (1869)

New Orleans Daily Delta (1855)

New Orleans Daily Item (1900)

New Orleans Daily Picayune (1864–1908)

New Orleans Daily States (1891–1917)

New Orleans Item (1902–1910)
New Orleans Mascot (1886–1892)
New Orleans Republican (1873)
New Orleans Southwestern Christian Advocate (1896–1898)
New Orleans States (1920)
New Orleans Sunday States (1902)
New Orleans Times (1869–1874)
New Orleans Times-Democrat (1890–1908)
New Orleans Times-Picayune (1917–2000)

DIRECTORIES AND GUIDEBOOKS

Cohen's New Orleans Directory. New Orleans: n.p., 1854–1857.

Edwards's Annual Directory to the Inhabitants, Institutions, Incorporated Companies, Manufacturers, Establishments, Etc. in the City of New Orleans. New Orleans: Southern Publishing Co., 1871, 1872.

Gardner's New Orleans Directory for 1859. New Orleans: n.p., 1858.

Graham's Crescent City Directory for 1867. New Orleans: L. Graham, 1866.

Historical Sketch Book and Guide to New Orleans and Environs, 3rd Issue with Map. Edited and compiled by "Several Leading Writers of the New Orleans Press." New York: Will H. Coleman, 1885.

New Orleans: What to See and How to See It: A Standard Guide to the City of New Orleans. New Orleans: New Orleans Progressive Union Press, 1910.

Sanborn Fire Insurance Map, City of New Orleans, 1896. Teaneck, N.J.: Chadwick-Healey, 1896.

Soards' New Orleans City Directory for 1880. New Orleans: L. Soards & Co., 1880.

Soards' New Orleans City Directory for 1898. New Orleans: L. Soards & Co., 1898.

Wentworth's Souvenir Sporting Guide to Louisville, Kentucky. New York: 1885.

SECONDARY SOURCES

Books

Allen, Robert C. *Horrible Prettiness: Burlesque and American Culture.* Chapel Hill: University of North Carolina Press, 1991.

Armstrong, Louis. *Satchmo: My Life in New Orleans.* 1954. Reprint, New York: Da Capo Press, 1986.

Arnesen, Eric. *Waterfront Workers of New Orleans: Race, Class, and Politics, 1863–1923.* New York: Oxford University Press, 1991.

Asbury, Herbert. *The French Quarter: An Informal History of the New Orleans Underworld.* Garden City, New York: Garden City Publishing, 1938.

Ayers, Edward. *The Promise of the New South: Life after Reconstruction.* New York: Oxford University Press, 1992.

Bederman, Gail. *Manliness and Civilization: A Cultural History of Gender and Race in the United States, 1880–1917.* Chicago: University of Chicago Press, 1995.

Bergreen, Laurence. *Louis Armstrong: An Extravagant Life.* New York: Broadway Books, 1997.

Blassingame, John. *Black New Orleans, 1860–1880.* Chicago: University of Chicago Press, 1973.

Brandt, Allen. *No Magic Bullet: A Social History of Venereal Disease in the United States since 1880.* New York: Oxford University Press, 1987.

Burnham, John C. *Bad Habits: Drinking, Smoking, Taking Drugs, Gambling, Sexual Misbehavior, and Swearing in American History.* New York: New York University Press, 1993.

Cangelosi, Robert J. Jr., and Dorothy G. Schlesinger, eds. *New Orleans Architecture.* Vol. 8, *The University Section.* Gretna, La.: Pelican Publishing Co., 1997.

Carrigan, Jo Ann. *The Saffron Scourge: A History of Yellow Fever in Louisiana, 1796–1905.* Lafayette: University of Southwestern Louisiana, 1994.

Casey, Powell. *Encyclopedia of Forts, Posts, Named Camps, and Other Military Installations in Louisiana, 1700–1981.* Baton Rouge: Citations, 1983.

———. *An Outline of the Civil War Campaigns and Engagements of the Washington Artillery of New Orleans.* Baton Rouge: Claitor's, 1986.

Chase, John. *Frenchmen, Desire, Good Children, and Other Streets of New Orleans.* 2nd ed. New Orleans: Robert L. Crager, 1960.

Chauncey, George. *Gay New York: Gender, Urban Culture, and the Making of the Gay Male World, 1890–1940.* New York: Basic Books, 1994.

Clinton, Catherine. *Public Women and the Confederacy.* Milwaukee: Marquette University Press, 1999.

Clinton, Catherine, and Michele Gillespie, eds. *The Devil's Lane: Sex and Race in the Early South.* New York: Oxford University Press, 1997.

Cohen, Patricia Cline. *The Murder of Helen Jewett: The Life and Death of a Prostitute in Nineteenth-Century New York.* New York: Alfred A. Knopf, 1998.

Connelly, Mark Thomas. *The Response to Prostitution in the Progressive Era.* Chapel Hill: University of North Carolina Press, 1980.

Conrad, Glenn, ed. *Dictionary of Louisiana Biography.* Lafayette: Center for Louisiana Studies, 1988.

Corbin, Alain. *Women for Hire: Prostitution and Sexuality in France after 1850.* Cambridge: Harvard University Press, 1990.

Cott, Nancy. *Public Vows: A History of Marriage and the Nation.* Cambridge: Harvard University Press, 2001.

D'Emilio, John, and Estelle Freedman. *Intimate Matters: A History of Sexuality in America.* New York: Harper & Row, 1988.

Dominguez, Virginia. *White by Definition: Social Classification in Creole Louisiana.* New Brunswick, N.J.: Rutgers University Press, 1986.

Edwards, Laura. *Gendered Strife and Confusion: The Political Culture of Reconstruction.* Champaign: University of Illinois Press, 1997.

Erenberg, Lewis. *Steppin' Out: New York Nightlife and the Transformation of American Culture, 1890–1930.* Westport, Conn.: Greenwood Press, 1981.

Foner, Eric. *Reconstruction: America's Unfinished Revolution, 1863–1877.* New York: Harper & Row, 1988.

Fontenot, Kevin. *A History of Lafayette Insurance Co.* New Orleans: Lafayette Insurance Co., 1994.

Foster, Gaines. *Moral Reconstruction: Christian Lobbyists and the Federal Legislation of Morality, 1865–1920.* Chapel Hill: University of North Carolina Press, 2002.

Fout, John, and Maura Shaw Tantillo, eds. *American Sexual Politics: Sex, Gender, and Race since the Civil War.* Chicago: University of Chicago Press, 1993.

Genovese, Eugene. *Roll, Jordan, Roll: The World the Slaves Made.* New York: Pantheon Books, 1974.

Gilfoyle, Timothy. *City of Eros: New York City, Prostitution, and the Commercialization of Sex, 1790–1920.* New York: W. W. Norton, 1992.

Gilmore, Glenda. *Gender and Jim Crow: Women and the Politics of White Supremacy in North Carolina, 1896–1920.* Chapel Hill: University of North Carolina Press, 1996.

Hair, William Ivy. *Carnival of Fury: Robert Charles and the New Orleans Race Riot of 1900.* Baton Rouge: Louisiana State University Press, 1976.

Hale, Grace. *Making Whiteness: The Culture of Segregation in the South, 1890–1940.* New York: Pantheon, 1998.

Hall, Gwendolyn Midlo. *Africans in Colonial Louisiana: The Development of Afro-Creole Culture in the Eighteenth Century.* Baton Rouge: Louisiana State University Press, 1992.

Halttunen, Karen. *Confidence Men and Painted Women: A Study of Middle-Class Culture in America, 1830–1870.* New Haven: Yale University Press, 1982.

Hanchett, Thomas. *Sorting Out the New South City: Race, Class, and Urban Development in Charlotte, 1875–1975.* Chapel Hill: University of North Carolina Press, 1998.

Hanger, Kimberly S. *Bounded Lives, Bounded Places: Free Black Society in Colonial New Orleans, 1769–1803.* Durham: Duke University Press, 1997.

———. *A Medley of Cultures: Louisiana History at the Cabildo.* New Orleans: Louisiana Museum Foundation, 1996.

Hanley, Ray, and Steven G. Hanley. *Images of America: Hot Springs, Arkansas.* Charleston, S.C.: Arcadia Publishing, 2000.

———. *Hot Springs, Arkansas, in Vintage Postcards.* Charleston, S.C.: Arcadia Publishing, 1998.

Harsin, Jill. *Policing Prostitution in Nineteenth-Century Paris.* Princeton: Princeton University Press, 1985.

Hartog, Hendrik. *Man and Wife in America: A History.* Cambridge: Harvard University Press, 2000.

Hearn, Lafcadio. *Lafcadio Hearn's America: Ethnographic Sketches and Editorials,* Simon Bronner, ed. Lexington: University of Kentucky Press, 2002.

Higginbotham, Evelyn Brooks. *Righteous Discontent: The Women's Movement in the Black Baptist Church.* Cambridge: Harvard University Press, 1993.

Hobson, Barbara Meil. *Uneasy Virtue: The Politics of Prostitution and the American Reform Tradition.* New York: Basic Books, 1987.

Hodes, Martha. *White Women, Black Men: Illicit Sex in the Nineteenth-Century South.* New Haven: Yale University Press, 1997.

Hollandsworth, James. *An Absolute Massacre: The New Orleans Race Riot of July 30, 1866.* Baton Rouge: Louisiana State University Press, 2001.

Hunter, Tera. *To 'Joy My Freedom: Southern Black Women's Lives and Labors after the Civil War.* Cambridge: Harvard University Press, 1997.

Ingersoll, Thomas. *Mammon and Manon in Early New Orleans: The First Slave Society in the Deep South, 1718–1819.* Knoxville: University of Tennessee Press, 1999.

Jackson, Joy. *New Orleans in the Gilded Age: Politics and Urban Progress, 1880–1896.* Baton Rouge: Louisiana State University Press, 1969.

Jacobson, Matthew. *Whiteness of a Different Color: European Immigrants and the Alchemy of Race.* Cambridge: Harvard University Press, 1998.

Johnson, Walter. *Soul by Soul: Life inside the Antebellum Slave Market.* Cambridge: Harvard University Press, 2000.

Kasson, John. *Rudeness and Civility: Manners in Nineteenth-Century Urban America.* New York: Hill and Wang, 1990.

Kendall, John. *The Golden Age of the New Orleans Theater.* Baton Rouge: Louisiana State University Press, 1952.

———. *History of New Orleans.* New York: Lewis Publishing Co., 1922.

Lewis, Peirce. *New Orleans: The Making of an Urban Landscape.* Cambridge, Mass.: Ballinger, 1976.

Lomax, Alan. *Mister Jelly Roll: The Fortunes of Jelly Roll Morton, New Orleans Creole and "Inventor of Jazz."* New York: Duell, Sloan and Pearce, 1950.

Lott, Eric. *Love and Theft: Blackface Minstrelsy and the American Working Class.* New York: Oxford University Press, 1993.

Marquis, Donald M. *In Search of Buddy Bolden: First Man of Jazz.* Baton Rouge: Louisiana State University Press, 1978.

Meyerowitz, Joanne J. *Women Adrift: Independent Wage Earners in Chicago, 1880–1930.* Chicago: University of Chicago Press, 1988.

Mitchell, Reid. *All on a Mardi Gras Day: Episodes in the History of New Orleans Carnival.* Cambridge: Harvard University Press, 1995.

Morrow, Ralph. *Northern Methodism and Reconstruction.* Ann Arbor: Michigan State University Press, 1956.

Mumford, Kevin J. *Interzones: Black and White Sex Districts in Chicago and New York in the Early Twentieth Century.* New York: Columbia University Press, 1997.

Nau, John Frederick. *The German People of New Orleans, 1850–1900.* Leiden, The Netherlands: E. J. Brill, 1958.

Ownby, Ted. *Subduing Satan: Religion, Recreation, and Manhood in the Rural South.* Chapel Hill: University of North Carolina Press, 1990.

Patterson, Jerry. *The First Four-Hundred: Mrs. Astor's New York in the Gilded Age.* New York: Rizzoli, 2000.

Peiss, Kathy. *Cheap Amusements: Working Women and Leisure in Turn-of-the-Century New York.* Philadelphia: Temple University Press, 1986.

Peiss, Kathy, and Helen Lefkowitz Horowitz, eds. *Love across the Color Line: The Letters of Alice Hanley to Channing Lewis.* Amherst: University of Massachusetts Press, 1996.

Pivar, David. *Purity Crusade: Sexual Morality and Social Control, 1868–1900.* Westport, Conn.: Greenwood Press, 1973.

Rabinowitz, Howard. *Race Relations in the Urban South: 1865–1890.* New York: Oxford University Press, 1978.

Remini, Robert. *The Battle of New Orleans.* New York: Viking Press, 1999.

Reynolds, George. *Machine Politics in New Orleans, 1897–1926.* New York: AMS Press, 1936.

Rose, Al. *Storyville, New Orleans: Being an Authentic, Illustrated Account of the Notorious Red-Light District.* Tuscaloosa: University of Alabama Press, 1974.

Rosen, Ruth. *The Lost Sisterhood: Prostitution and the Progressive Era.* Chicago: University of Chicago Press, 1982.

———. *The Maimie Papers.* 1977. Reprint, Bloomington: Indiana University Press; Old Westbury, N.Y.: Feminist Press, 1985.

Rowland, Dunbar, and A. G. Sanders, eds. *Mississippi Provincial Archives: French Dominion.* 3 vols. Jackson: Press of the Mississippi Department of Archives and History, 1927–1932.

Ryan, Mary. *Civic Wars: Democracy and Public Life in the American City in the Nineteenth Century.* Berkeley: University of California Press, 1997.

———. *Women in Public: Between Banners and Ballots.* Baltimore: Johns Hopkins University Press, 1990.

Salem, Dorothy. *To Better Our World: Black Women in Organized Reform, 1890–1920.* New York: Carlson, 1990.

Saxon, Lyle. *Gumbo Ya-Ya: A Collection of Louisiana Tales.* Boston: Houghton Mifflin, 1945.

Schlesinger, Dorothy G., Robert J. Cangelosi Jr., and Sally Kittredge Reeves, eds. *New Orleans Architecture.* Vol. 7, *Jefferson City.* Gretna, La.: Pelican Publishing Co., 1989.

Stansell, Christine. *City of Women: Sex and Class in New York, 1789–1860.* Champaign: University of Illinois Press, 1987.

Symanski, Richard. *The Immoral Landscape: Female Prostitution in Western Societies.* Toronto: Butterworth, 1981.

Taylor, Joe Gray. *Louisiana Reconstructed, 1863–1877.* Baton Rouge: Louisiana State University Press, 1974.

Toll, Robert. *Blacking Up: The Minstrel Show in Nineteenth-Century America.* New York: Oxford University Press, 1974.

Vernon, Walter. *Becoming One People: A History of Louisiana Methodism.* Louisiana: United Methodist Church, 1987.

Walker, Clarence. *A Rock in a Weary Land: The African Methodist Episcopal Church during the Civil War and Reconstruction.* Baton Rouge: Louisiana State University Press, 1982.

Walkowitz, Judith. *Prostitution in Victorian Society: Women, Class and State.* New York: Cambridge University Press, 1980.

Walters, Ronald G. *The Antislavery Appeal: American Abolitionism after 1830.* Baltimore: Johns Hopkins University Press, 1976.

Wiltz, Christine. *The Last Madam: A Life in the New Orleans Underworld.* New York: Faber and Faber, 2000.

Woodward, C. Vann. *The Strange Career of Jim Crow.* 3rd ed. New York: Oxford University Press, 1974.

Yardley, Jonathan. *Mrs. Astor's New York: Money and Social Power in a Gilded Age.* New Haven: Yale University Pres, 2002.

Articles

Arceneaux, Pamela. "Guidebooks to Sin: The Blue Books of Storyville." *Louisiana History* 28 (Fall 1987): 397–405.

Baade, Hans. "The Law of Slavery in Spanish Louisiana, 1769–1803." In *Louisiana's Legal Heritage,* Edward Haas, ed. Pensacola: Perdido Bay Press for the Louisiana State Museum, 1983.

Baptist, Edward. " 'Cuffy,' 'Fancy Maids,' and 'One-Eyed Men': Rape, Commodification, and the Domestic Slave Trade in the United States." *American Historical Review* 106 (December 2001): 1619–1650.

Best, Joel. "Careers in Brothel Prostitution: St. Paul, 1865–1883." *Journal of Interdisciplinary History* 12 (Spring 1982): 597–619.

Brasseaux, Carl. "The Moral Climate of French Colonial Louisiana, 1699–1763." *Louisiana History* 27 (1986): 27–41.

Brock, Eric, and Jim Montgomery. "Shreveport's Legalized Red-Light District." *Louisiana Cultural Vistas* 8 (Spring 1997): 50–1.

Brown, Elsa Barkley. "Negotiating and Transforming the Public Sphere: African

American Political Life in the Transition from Slavery to Freedom." *Public Culture* 7 (1994): 107–46.

Clark, Emily. "'By All the Conduct of Their Lives': A Laywomen's Confraternity in New Orleans, 1730–1744." *William and Mary Quarterly* 24 (October 1997): 769–94.

Clinton, Catherine. "Bloody Terrain: Freedwomen, Sexuality, and Violence During Reconstruction." *Georgia Historical Quarterly* 76 (Summer 1992): 313–32.

"A Colored Woman, However Respectable, Is Lower than the White Prostitute." *The Independent* (Sept. 18, 1902). In *Black Women in White America: A Documentary History*, Gerda Lerner, ed. New York: Pantheon Books, 1972.

Cott, Nancy. "Passionlessness: An Interpretation of Victorian Sexual Ideology, 1790–1850." In *A Heritage of Her Own: Toward a New Social History of American Women*, Nancy F. Cott and Elizabeth H. Pleck, eds. New York: Simon & Schuster, 1979.

Davidson, Janet. "The Goosing of Violet Nye and Other Tales: White Women and Sexual Respectability on the Pennsylvania Railroad." *Labor History* 41 (November 2000): 437–52.

Ettinger, Brian Gary. "John Fitzpatrick and the Limits of Working-Class Politics in New Orleans, 1892–1896." *Louisiana History* 26 (Fall 1985): 341–67.

Fischer, Roger. "Racial Segregation in Antebellum New Orleans." *American Historical Review* 74 (February 1969): 926–37.

Gehman, Mary. "Toward an Understanding of the Quadroon Society in New Orleans." In *Southern Women*, Caroline Dillman, ed. New York: Hemisphere Publishing, 1988.

Hall, Jacquelyn Dowd. "'The Mind That Burns in Each Body': Women, Rape, and Racial Violence." In *Powers of Desire: The Politics of Sexuality*, Ann Snitow, Christine Stansell, and Sharon Thompson, eds. New York: Monthly Review Press, 1983.

Higginbotham, Evelyn Brooks. "African American Women's History and the Metalanguage of Race." *Signs* 17 (Winter 1992): 251–74.

Hine, Darlene Clark. "Rape and the Inner Lives of Black Women in the Middle West: Preliminary Thoughts on the Culture of Dissemblance." *Signs* 14 (Summer 1989): 912–20.

Hoganson, Kristin. "Cosmopolitan Domesticity: Importing the American Dream, 1865–1920." *American Historical Review* 107 (February 2002): 55–83.

Holmes, Jack. "Do It! Don't Do It!: Spanish Laws on Sex and Marriage." In *Louisiana's Legal Heritage*, Edward Haas, ed. Pensacola: Perdido Bay Press for the Louisiana State Museum, 1983.

Johnson, Jerah. "New Orleans' Congo Square: An Urban Setting for Early Afro-American Culture Formation." *Louisiana History* 23 (Spring 1992): 117–57.

Johnson, Walter. "The Slave Trader, the White Slave, and the Politics of Racial Determination in the 1850s." *Journal of American History* 87 (June 2000): 13–38.

Long, Alecia. "A Notorious Attraction: Sex and Tourism in New Orleans, 1897–1917."

In *Southern Journeys: Tourism, History, and Culture in the Modern South,* Richard Starnes, ed. Tuscaloosa: University of Alabama Press, 2003.

Loveland, Anne. "The 'Southern Work' of the Reverend Joseph C. Hartzell, Pastor of Ames Church in New Orleans, 1870–1873." *Louisiana History* 16 (Fall 1975): 391–407.

Magill, John. "That Disgraceful French Dance—Cancan in the Crescent City." *The Historic New Orleans Collection Quarterly* 18 (Autumn 1998): 8–9.

Reckless, Walter. "Indices of Commercialized Vice Areas." *Journal of Applied Sociology* 10 (1926): 249–57.

Reed, Germaine. "Race Legislation in Louisiana, 1864–1920," *Louisiana History* 6 (Fall 1965): 379–92.

Roach, Joseph. "Slave Spectacles and Tragic Octoroons: A Cultural Genealogy of Antebellum Performance." *Theatre Survey* 33 (November 1992): 175–82.

Schafer, Judith K. "'Open and Notorious Concubinage': The Emancipation of Slave Mistresses by Will and the Supreme Court in Antebellum Louisiana." *Louisiana History* 28 (Spring 1987): 165–82.

Spear, Jennifer. "'They Need Wives': Metissage and the Regulation of Sexuality in French Louisiana." In *Sex, Race, Love: Crossing Boundaries in North American History,* Martha Hodes, ed. New York: New York University Press, 1999.

Tandberg, Gerilyn. "Sinning for Silk: Dress-for-Success Fashions of the New Orleans Storyville Prostitute." *Women's Studies International Forum* 13 (1990): 229–48.

Tansey, Richard. "Prostitution and Politics in Antebellum New Orleans." *Southern Studies* 20 (Winter 1980): 455–70.

Taylor, Robert. "Crime and Race Relations in Jacksonville, 1884–1892." *Southern Studies* 2 (Spring 1991): 17–37.

Thompson, Kay. "First Lady of Storyville, The Fabulous Countess Willie Piazza." *Record Changer* 10 (February 1951): 5–14.

Walkowitz, Judith. "Male Vice and Female Virtue: Feminism and the Politics of Prostitution in Nineteenth-Century Britain." In *Powers of Desire: The Politics of Sexuality,* Ann Snitow, Christine Stansell, and Sharon Thompson, eds. New York: Monthly Review Press, 1983.

Wetta, Frank J. "Bloody Monday: The Louisiana Scalawags and the New Orleans Riot of 1866." *Southern Studies* 2 (Spring 1991): 5–16.

White, Deborah Gray. "The Cost of Club Work, the Price of Black Feminism." In *Visible Women: New Essays on American Activism,* Nancy Hewitt and Suzanne Lebsock, eds. Champaign: University of Illinois Press, 1993.

Zanger, Jules. "'The Tragic Octoroon' in Pre–Civil War Fiction." *American Quarterly* 18 (Spring 1966): 63–70.

Dissertations, Theses, and Unpublished Papers

Duchein, Mary Scott. "Research on Charles Etienne Arthur Gayerré." Master's thesis, Louisiana State University, 1934.

Corrales, Barbara Smith. "Prurience, Prostitution, and Progressive Improvements: The Crowley Connection, 1909–1918." Paper presented at the annual meeting of the Louisiana Historical Association, 2001.

Coyle, Katy. "The Intersection of Law and Desire: Sex, Storyville, and Prostitution in Turn-of-the-Century New Orleans." Ph.D. dissertation, Tulane University, in progress.

Gould, Virginia Meachem. "In Full Enjoyment of Their Liberty: The Free Women of Color of the Gulf Ports of New Orleans, Mobile, and Pensacola, 1769–1860." Ph.D. dissertation, Emory University, 1991.

Guillory, Monique. "Some Enchanted Evening on the Auction Block: The Cultural Legacy of the New Orleans Quadroon Balls." Ph.D. dissertation, New York University, 1999.

Landau, Emily. "'Spectacular Wickedness': New Orleans, Prostitution, and the Politics of Sex, 1897–1917." Ph.D. dissertation, Yale University, in progress.

Leathem, Karen. "'A Carnival According to Their Own Desires': Gender and Mardi Gras in New Orleans, 1870–1941." Ph.D. dissertation, University of North Carolina, Chapel Hill, 1994.

Mackey, Thomas. "Red Lights Out: A Legal History of Prostitution, Disorderly Houses, and Vice Districts, 1870–1971." Ph.D. dissertation, Rice University, 1984.

Politzer, Marie. "Federal Laws, Regulations and Programs Dealing with Prostitution and Venereal Diseases." Master's thesis, Tulane University, 1943.

Spear, Jennifer. "'Whiteness and Purity of Blood': Race, Sexuality, and Cultural Identity in Colonial Louisiana, 1699–1795." Ph.D. dissertation, University of Minnesota, 1999.

Williams, Kathy D. "The 'Painted Inmate' and the 'Aggressive Savage': Sexual and Racial Segregation in Louisville, Kentucky." Paper presented at the fifth Southern Conference on Women's History, 2000.

Index

Page numbers in italics refer to illustrations and maps.